QUESTIONING VYGOTSKY'S LEGACY

This accessible collection of essays critically examines Vygotsky's scientific legacy. The book is solidly grounded in the "revisionist revolution" context and encourages constructive questioning of Vygotsky's theory of human development. It tackles thought-provoking issues such as the true value of his scholarship, the possible falsification of his scientific legacy, and the role of political factors and the Communist parties in the worldwide dissemination of his work. It is essential reading on Vygotskian psychology and of interest to students and researchers in developmental psychology, history of psychology, history of science, Soviet/Russian history, philosophical science and education.

Anton Yasnitsky, Ph.D., is an independent researcher who specializes in the Vygotsky-Luria Circle. He is the author of *Vygotsky: An Intellectual Biography* (2018) and has co-edited (with René van der Veer and others) *The Cambridge Handbook of Cultural-Historical Psychology* (2014), *Revisionist Revolution in Vygotsky Studies* (2015), and *Vygotski revisitado: una historia crítica de su contexto y legado* (2016).

QUESTIONING VYGOTSKY'S LEGACY

Scientific Psychology or Heroic Cult

Edited by Anton Yasnitsky

Routledge
Taylor & Francis Group

LONDON AND NEW YORK

First published 2019
by Routledge
2 Park Square, Milton Park, Abingdon, Oxon OX14 4RN

and by Routledge
711 Third Avenue, New York, NY 10017

Routledge is an imprint of the Taylor & Francis Group, an informa business

British Library Cataloguing in Publication Data
A catalogue record for this book is available from the British Library

Library of Congress Cataloging in Publication Data
Names: Yasnitsky, Anton, 1972- editor.
Title: Questioning Vygotsky's legacy : scientific psychology or heroic cult / edited by Anton Yasnitsky.
Description: Abingdon, Oxon ; New York, NY : Routledge, 2019. | Includes bibliographical references and index.
Identifiers: LCCN 2018013971| ISBN 9781138481268 (hbk : alk. paper) | ISBN 9781138481275 (pbk : alk. paper) | ISBN 9781351060639 (ebk)
Subjects: LCSH: Vygotskiæi, L. S. (Lev Semenovich), 1896-1934. | Psychologists--Soviet Union. | Psychology.
Classification: LCC BF109.V95 Q44 2019 | DDC 150.92--dc23
LC record available at https://lccn.loc.gov/2018013971

ISBN: 978-1-138-48126-8 (hbk)
ISBN: 978-1-138-48127-5 (pbk)
ISBN: 978-1-351-06063-9 (ebk)

Typeset in Bembo
by Taylor & Francis Books

CONTENTS

ILLUSTRATIONS

Figures

Tables

1

VYGOTSKY'S SCIENCE OF SUPERMAN

From Utopia to concrete psychology

Anton Yasnitsky

Lev Vygotsky and "Vygotskian" buzzwords

Lev Vygotsky (1896–1934) is definitely the most well-known Russian psychologist worldwide, who is considered among the most prominent thinkers and pioneers in education and developmental psychology these days. Yet, fame does not necessarily go hand in hand with knowledge and understanding. As it was noted twenty years ago, Vygotsky's fame is in reverse relation to the knowledge of his legacy: the more often his name is invoked, the less people seem to understand what the person did as a thinker and practitioner and what exactly his legacy is (Valsiner, 1988). The chief proponents and ardent advocates of his work virtually uniformly refer to him as a genius, almost immediately adding the attribute of "elusive" (or its equivalents) to this "genius" (Bruner, 1985). Then, almost universally they claim the need for "understanding Vygotsky" (van der Veer & Valsiner, 1991). Commonly shared opinion of Vygotsky's genius and consensus on his importance and relevance today appears the main reason for his name's appearance on top-100 list of the most prominent psychologists of the 20th century (Haggbloom et al., 2002).

No Vygotsky theory was fully accomplished and published during his lifetime (Yasnitsky & van der Veer, 2016a). Yet, apparently the field of knowledge exists under the name of "cultural-historical psychology" (Yasnitsky, van der Veer, & Ferrari, 2014) and is directly associated with Lev Vygotsky, his closest collaborator, Alexander Luria (1902–1977) and their legacy. Not only is Vygotsky well known, but also – for a number of reasons – he is very much adored and admired by his self-appointed followers and advocates worldwide. Others just do not know him and his work. This situation has been variably described as the "cult of Vygotsky", "Vygotsky cult", or even Vygotsky's "cult of personality" (Yasnitsky, 2012). The origin of this cult dates back to the period of early Stalinism in the 1930s with its cultist atmosphere, the *Zeitgeist*, in the Soviet Union. This was the time when the god-like status of Vygotsky the "genius" prevailed among a few of his students, as evident from their memoirs of several decades after his death in 1934 (Yasnitsky, 2018). In the post-WWII period the image of Vygotsky the genius was exported from behind the Iron Curtain and gradually spread widely, primarily in the United States, but also in a few other – Anglophone, Francophone, Lusophone and Spanish-speaking – regions of the world. Recent publications provide considerable critical discussion of the cult and its history, the most important of these are the twin volumes in English and Spanish titled "Revisionist Revolution in Vygotsky Studies" (Yasnitsky & van der Veer, 2016a) and "Vygotski revisitado: Una historia crítica de su contexto y legado" (Yasnitsky, van der Veer, Aguilar, & García, 2016), respectively.

In the absence of a clearly defined theory as such, Vygotsky's followers have at their disposal a few "Vygotskian" buzzwords, the most popular of which being the so-called "*zone of proximal development*", the phrase that is alternatively translated from the original Russian "*zona blizhaishego razvitiia*" as the "*zone of potential development*" (Simon, 1987). This way, it is certainly much clearer, but not necessarily to the benefit of the Vygotsky's fans, who sometimes seem to have preferred the appearance of "scientificity" and obscurity to clarity. This phenomenon is not new in the history of humanity and has been recently described and discussed in the beautiful book of Michael Billig, titled "Learn to write badly: How to succeed in the Social Sciences" (Billig, 2013). Yet, the notion of the "*ZPD*" – as it is known in its abbreviated form – has for a while guided educationists, who put it on their banners in the struggle for their independence and their original status as the leading force in the classroom that for a while considerably shrank under the influence of various so-called "constructivist" (or "child-centered") educational theories of the preceding period. These were typically associated with the name of the Swiss scholar and high-ranking practitioner in psychology and education, Jean Piaget (1896–1980), very popular in North America in the 1960s and 1970s and whose influence had started to decrease by the end of his life. Vygotsky's "zone of proximal development" (with all the associated exotic connotations of a relatively obscure Russian name, the "scientificity" of the phrase and the authority of Vygotsky's leading advocates in North America, such as Jerome Bruner, 1915–2016) became a helpful metaphor for a new movement in education. The new trend manifested itself in educational theories of "social constructivism" (as opposed to Piaget-associated "constructivism", or "cognitive constructivism", of the preceding period of "child-centered" educational theories) and has been somewhat critically and controversially described as a behaviorist restoration in mainstream educational thinking in North America (Yasnitsky, 2014a).

The "ZPD" – although definitely the most popular – is not the only buzzword that is associated with Vygotsky and his alleged legacy. Another buzzword that is often presented in the "Vygotskian" vocabulary is *mediation* (the common English translation of *oposredovanie* or *oposredstvovanie* in Russian) and its derivatives such as *mediate* or *mediated*. Yet, there is nothing distinctly linked to Vygotsky in this word that on number of occasions occurs in the writings of behaviorist writers such as

Vygotsky's and Luria's slightly younger contemporary Burrhus Frederic Skinner (1904–1990), a renowned psychologist and social utopian thinker, in his exciting post-war novel "Walden Two" (Skinner, 1948); Skinner was well-known for his operant conditioning research, applied behavior analysis, and "radical behaviorism" theories. It was in the 1930s that Skinner finished and defended his doctoral study (in 1931) and, somewhat later, published his first book that summarized a decade of his research, in which he used a notion of "verbal field," which he defined as "that part of behavior which is reinforced only through the mediation of another organism" (Skinner, 1938, p. 116). His later programmatic book of 1957 "Verbal behavior," published five years before the first major Vygotsky publication appeared in English (Vygotsky, 1962), is often positioned as a manifesto, in effect, of Skinnerian "radical behaviorist" thinking that apparently bears no influences of Vygotsky whatsoever, but still profusely used the term "mediation" in the meaning very close to its use in traditional "Vygotskian" parlance and thought style with its emphasis on the ideas of 1) the subject's personal agency and activity, and 2) voluntary improvement and advancement of psychological performance, supported and facilitated by a peer, or, more generally, "knowledgeable other" and the "social situation of development."

Skinner defined "verbal behavior as behavior reinforced through the mediation of other persons" (Skinner, 1957, p. 2) and, somewhat in the spirit of "Vygotskian" tradition, repeatedly returned to this idea throughout this book. Furthermore, the phrases "social reinforcement" and even "socially mediated reinforcement" are used in educational literature these days in a manner highly reminiscent of the "zone of proximal development" and "social situation of development" of Vygotsky and, at the same time, of Skinner's "operant conditioning" and "reinforcement". This choice of vocabulary certainly blurs the lines between the two theoretical systems and makes one wonder about the deeper reasons behind the popularity of Vygotsky's phraseology among educators in North America, who are hitherto apparently still very much under the considerable influence of Skinnerian tradition and, broader, somewhat simplistic and mechanistic behaviorist philosophy (Bandura, 1963; Bandura, 1977). This is why, one might argue, both the Skinnerian and the "Vygotskain" traditions in educational thinking, especially in North America, can be grouped together and thought of as belonging equally to the "social behaviorism" trend and intellectual movement.

There is another reason why *mediation* does not qualify as a notion distinctly originating with Vygotsky. There are contexts in which the word is used in contemporary literature in a fashion that appears quite similar to Vygotsky's discourse. These are typically focused on the mass media, social and cultural issues and their interrelations with psychological performance of people in the contemporary, 21st century world. As an example, consider a book titled "Mediated Memories in the Digital Age" (van Dijck, 2007). What is interesting in this particular case is that such a seemingly pure instance of a "Vygotskian" term – introduced in the early 1930s in perhaps the only really and fully Vygotskian book ever written and published (Leontiev, 1931) and widely popularized since then – the phrase "mediated memory" is used here without any relation to Vygotsky's or his associates' work whatsoever. Indeed, the author is doing pretty well without invocation of any long dead Russian scholar of the 20th century, focuses on the realities of our days, and successfully deals with the issues of media, culture, psychology, and mind in the 21st century, instead. The contexts seem similar, though, and the media that mediate our psychological performance are treated as some kind of "psychological instruments," but the meaning of the phrase and the direction of discussion is very different, if not opposite to that of Vygotsky. For Vygotsky, these cultural tools are merely relatively insignificant "signs" devoid of their own meaning or importance of their own that are only instrumental in advancing our psychological performance, like in mnemonic experiments on "mediated memory" and its ontogenetic development of Vygotsky and his close associate Aleksei N. Leontiev (1902–1979). For cultural studies like that of José van Dijck, "mediated memory" belongs to a larger topic of "cultural memory" that is supported and preserved by technologies in the Digital Age, but, unlike for Vygotsky, quite to the detriment of individual psychological abilities to memorize, remember, and recall. Simply put, now we do not need to remember as much as before when we did not have the ubiquitous gadgets with easy access to the world wide web as the resource and storage of information of virtually any kind. This naturally brings us to yet another still popular allegedly "Vygotskian" notion.

It is common to attribute the origin of the idea of *the social origin of mind and psychological processes* (also known as *sociogenesis*) to Vygotsky, which seems to compete for the second position on the list of "Vygotskian" ideas, key words, and expressions. This view dates back to the end of the 1970s when a relatively small book came out under the title "Mind in society", which had been, by admission of its four editors, "constructed" from bits and pieces of the texts of Vygotsky and his associates. Yet, the book was published under Vygotsky's name and despite an editor's expectation of an imminent "fiscal disaster, not to say personal embarrassment" (Cole, 2004, p. xi), it became the most well-known "Vygotsky" book and the main source of Vygotsky's citations in literature, way ahead of all others, until now.

Yet, the idea is absolutely trivial as such, and this is obvious to any loving and caring parent, at least. Mowgli can speak and reasonably think only in a work of fiction – a book or a movie – but in the real life a child born to human parents and raised by wolves or monkeys will develop into a wild "feral child", and nothing else. The saddest critical cases of socially neglected, abused and abandoned children only prove the rule. Then, the theories based on the idea of sociogenesis – the *sociogenetic theories* – are numerous and proliferated well before Vygotsky. In their excellent book "The Social Mind", Valsiner and van der Veer (2000) provide a convincing discussion of the "construction of the idea" and related theories by Vygotsky's predecessors and contemporaries. The earliest known efforts of the kind that are documented by these two authors date back to the time when Lev Vygotsky was not yet born. Apparently, Vygotsky might be considered a pioneer and an innovator, by some, but definitely not along this line of sociogenetic thinking. We largely owe this understanding to Valsiner and van der Veer and their splendid work. Besides, the idea of social origin of the human psyche is particularly self-evident nowadays, in the era of the absolute dominance of pervasive social media and social networks, so that a reference to any author – especially one who lived more than a century ago and died before the first electronic computer was produced – is hardly needed now, in the 21st century in order to support any sociogenetic claim.

This might be the reason for what appears as the beginning of the decline of Vygotsky's fame and the popularity of Vygotsky's writings on the "mind and society" as measured by Google Scholar citation rate. Indeed, over the last four decades Vygotsky's citation rate has continuously grown from the 1970s and 1980s (Valsiner, 1988) well into the 21st century. This process continued until roughly 2015–2016 when the trend changed for the first time, and started to decline. This process is highly reminiscent of a similar one, a few decades ago, when Jean Piaget's prominence in North America started shrinking. Nonetheless, Piaget has remained a scholarly celebrity and the classic of developmental psychology. What a few decades ago looked like – in stock market parlance – a "Piaget citation bubble" seems to repeat these days as the "Vygotsky bubble" that started shrinking most recently, to the yet unknown end (Yasnitsky & van der Veer, 2016b).[1]

Science of Superman: Vygotsky's utopia

As it is already perfectly clear from considerable research and publications (Chaiklin, 2003; Valsiner & van der Veer, 1993), "Vygotskian ZPD" is neither original, nor the most essential of Vygotsky's contributions to the social and human sciences. First, the notion of "zone" migrated into Vygotsky's work from his contemporary German American scholar Kurt Lewin (1890–1947), the founder of the so-called "topological and vector psychology" and, allegedly, "field theory" in psychology. The analogy between the "zone" and "field" is quite clear, and Lewin's considerable influence on Vygotsky of the last two or three years of the latter's life is well documented and discussed at length (Yasnitsky, 2018; Yasnitsky & van der Veer 2016a). On the other hand, the idea of measuring the difference between an individual's actual performance and the potential performance of this individual in the situation of facilitated, peer-assisted problem-solving, first appeared in the work of Vygotsky's American contemporary Dorothea McCarthy, and Vygotsky did duly acknowledge the original authorship of this borrowing. Second, the "ZPD" does not appear in Vygotsky thinking and writing until 1933, and figures on the margins of his work at the time (Chaiklin, 2003).

In contrast, there is one idea that apparently passed through Vygotsky's entire academic career in the last decade of his life, and in different shapes, forms, phrasings and formulations resurfaced and re-emerged in his thought. The idea is old and dates back to the period of European Renaissance or even earlier, but in Vygotsky's case, he borrowed it from inflammatory writings and oral speeches of one of the most prominent leaders of the Russian Communist Party, Lev Trotskii (1879–1940), or Leon Trotsky, which is the traditional spelling of his name in

English. In his newspaper article (later included in his book of 1924, republished in 1925), Trotsky proclaimed the distant goal of a "new man" that would eventually come about after Russian Revolution as a result of a deliberate effort at beautification and perfection of human soul and nature. This would be the Superman of the Communist future, and the average person of the future would reach the peaks of the human genius of the pre-Revolutionary period, the greatest artists and thinkers like Aristotle, Johann Wolfgang von Goethe, and Karl Marx, whereas the peaks of the "new man" of the future would far surpass what we have known about human being. Trotsky never bothered even to hint how exactly this would happen, and this was not a goal of his – a poet and prophet of Russian Revolution as he was. Yet, to Vygotsky, who exactly at that time was entering the field of academic research, the timing was perfect, and the call for the Superman fell into the well-prepared soil of Vygotsky's own youthful prophetic stance and eager post-Revolutionary zeal of the self-identified creator of the "new world". This call for the "new man" first appeared and was publicly presented in his discourse as early as his presentation at the Psychoneurological Congress in Petrograd (immediately thereafter renamed Leningrad) in January 1924, and continuously reappeared in Vygotsky's proclamations of the forthcoming "new psychology", "new man", "socialist alteration of the man", and the "peak psychology" that would explore the heights (as opposed to the depths, like in the Freudian "depth psychology") of human performance and existence (Yasnitsky, 2014b).

This was definitely a utopia. There was no clear understanding how this Superman of Communism would appear, or, more precisely, how this new human type would be constructed, raised, educated, remolded, not to mention how this new human being would look like. Yet, Vygotsky seemed to have firmly believed that this was his own, original, and the only possible pathway in science: the "new psychology" of and for the "new man". The image of the Superman was too strong and too compelling to resist the temptation of its promise. To relate the story of Vygotsky's struggle for the "new psychology" would equate to the task of narrating the story of his life and writing down a fundamentally novel intellectual biography of Vygotsky. Luckily, such a 21st century account of Vygotsky's life and legacy has just been published (Yasnitsky, 2018). Thus, let us just focus on some highlights – and related buzzwords – of Vygotsky's transition from his Superman utopia to concrete psychology and how these relate to this very book the reader is now holding in her or his hands.

From utopia to philosophy: Marxism

Vygotsky lived in a time and place that was very different from that of where and when most readers of this book live. Specifically, his scholarly career spanned the post-Revolutionary period of the Soviet Russia, which imposed a few idiosyncratic limitations on him. One needs to understand that Soviet Russia was a new state in the process of its development, and this formation of the new state took place under the more or less strict control of the one-party political system, which, in turn, was established with respect to the precepts of a specific philosophical system. This philosophy had been introduced by the great German thinker and political activist Karl Marx (1818–1883) and his long-time friend and collaborator Friedrich Engels (1820–1895). This was the official ideology of the state and all its social institutions. Science and academic research was among them (Joravsky, 1961).

Thus, Vygotsky was compelled to be a Marxist of some kind, by the nature of his vocation. Yet, unlike a great many of his peers, Vygotsky was apparently quite enthusiastic about the post-Revolutionary social project and the promise of the controlled evolution of the human being of the Communist kind, therefore, the call for a new, Marxist psychology came as quite natural and desired for him. In other words, Vygotsky was a social and socialist activist of the post-Revolutionary type, and a great sympathizer of the Communist (also referred to as the "Bolshevik") government. He even participated in its work at different periods of his life as a mid-level bureaucrat in the administrative structures of *Narkompros* (roughly, equivalent to a Ministry of Science, Culture and Education) and the local organs of the people's councils, the *Soviet* of one of Moscow's inner-city regions. Vygotsky's philosophical sympathies and inclinations, thus, were reflected in his empirical scientific studies and theoretical interpretations, and vice versa.

Yet, this is where further questions arise. Vygotsky was a university-educated intellectual, but not a philosopher by training. He never wrote a considerable scholarly work of his own, a thesis or dissertation in philosophy proper, like his slightly older contemporaries and the most renowned peer psychologists in Russia such as Sergei Rubinstein (1889–1960) or Dimitri Uznadze (1887–1950). Furthermore, Vygotsky did not participate in philosophical debates of his time, never published a work in a philosophical journal, and was not read by Soviet Marxist philosophers (at least not during his lifetime). Besides, even for an avid reader self-educated in the field of Marxist philosophy, the task of deliberately creating a psychological theory (and related experimental and social practice) on the basis of a philosophical system is a huge enterprise. It is highly questionable if such an undertaking is in principle achievable for a thinker self-taught in psychology and philosophy (such as Vygotsky), even the brightest and the smartest one.

Vygotsky appears to have been fully aware of the magnitude and the complexity of the task. In his unfinished manuscript of the mid-1920s he pointed out that "dialectical method is far from universally applicable to biology, history, and psychology". A "system of intermediate, concrete, applied to specific discipline concepts" was needed in addition. Such "system of concepts", according to Vygotsky, is the "methodology" of specific scientific discipline. Furthermore, Vygotsky drew the parallel between the Marxist philosophical system and *dialectical materialism* and between its specific implementation in a scientific discipline and *historical materialism*:

> The *direct* application of the theory of *dialectical materialism* to the problems of natural science and in particular to the group of biological sciences or psychology is *impossible,* just as *it is impossible* to apply it *directly* to history and

sociology. It is thought that the problem of "psychology and Marxism" can be reduced to creating a psychology which is up to Marxism, but in reality it is far more complex. Like history, sociology is in need of the intermediate *special theory* of historical materialism which explains the *concrete* meaning, for the given group of phenomena, of the abstract laws of dialectical materialism. In exactly the same way we are in need of an as yet undeveloped but inevitable theory of biological materialism and psychological materialism as an intermediate science which explains the concrete application of the abstract theses of dialectical materialism to the given field of phenomena.

Vygotsky, 1997b, p. 330

In the late 1980s a Russian author reflected on the path of development of Russian and Soviet psychology as a discipline and commented on the task of creating a Marxist psychology that was put forward and briefly outlined in the 1920s and 1930s. Yet, the goal remained unfulfilled in the period from the 1940s through to the 1970s and, in the late 1980s, was still an unsolved problem as much as it was during Vygotsky's lifetime (Radzikhovskii, 1988). This conclusion still holds true now, at the end of the second decade of the 21st century.

Therefore, the questions of interest on the topic of Vygotsky's Marxism are related to the depth and intellectual integrity of his philosophical preparation and performance in application to psychology as theoretical and empirical science. Thus, for instance, there are publications that tend to present Vygotsky as a Marxist thinker of enormous magnitude and importance (Ratner & Silva, 2017). On the other hand, this view is indirectly contested by some publications that present Vygotsky's attempts of Marxist psychology as quintessentially shallow and "vulgar Marxist" instances of the so-called "economic reductionism" (Lamdan & Yasnitsky, 2016).

The problem of understanding Vygotsky's Marxism remains underdeveloped both in Russia and the rest of the world. Given the interest in this theme among the left-leaning intellectuals around the world, perhaps, primarily those in Spanish- and Portuguese-speaking South and Central America, the Marxist foundations of psychology (and, specifically, of Vygotsky-influenced psychology) will predictably remain an important and highly debatable issue for years to come. For a discussion of the topic of Vygotsky's Marxism see Chapter 2, "Vygotsky and Marx – resetting the relationship", authored by Peter E. Jones.

From philosophy to a theory and concrete psychology

By Vygotsky's own admission, the science of Superman must be inspired by Marxist philosophy, but in order to become a concrete psychology it requires an intermediate layer of scientific vocabulary characteristic of and applied to this specific scientific discipline. Such vocabulary is the conceptual apparatus of the potential Marxist psychology, which makes the use of words and phraseology particularly important. This explains our interest in the words that are used in discussions of the "Vygotskian" psychology as we typically know it nowadays. The complete analysis of the entire network of special words and phrases is an enormous task beyond the scope of this paper. Yet, it seems worthwhile to focus on just a few of these such as "internalization", "higher psychical (mental, cognitive, psychological) functions" and "cultural-historical" theory in psychology.

"Internalization"

There is a range of other buzzwords that are commonly associated with Vygotsky as his alleged innovations in science. One of these is the so-called "*internalization*", the word that Vygotsky used in a few works, perhaps, most notably in his untitled, unfinished and abandoned manuscript that was later published under the totally ridiculous and falsified title "The history of the development of higher psychic functions". What makes this title ridiculous is the fact that the text has virtually nothing to do with any "history" whatsoever, and the phrase ascribed to him as the key term and the foundation of the whole theory runs contrary to what Vygotsky strongly and openly objected. Not only did Vygotsky use the word *internalization* (and its derivatives) in a few works, but also − when he did − he did so very rarely, from purely quantitative standpoint. Table 1.1 presents the data.

TABLE 1.1 The frequency of use of the word "internalization" (and its derivatives) in the six-volume *Collected Works of L. S. Vygotsky* (Plenum/Kluwer Press, 1987, 1993, & 1997–1999)

	Vol. 1	Vol. 2	Vol. 3	Vol. 4	Vol. 5	Vol. 6	Total
Vygotsky's own text	−	2	−	6	3	−	11
Not Vygotsky's text (comments, introductions, indexes, etc.)	2	7	14	3	4	2	32
Total	2	9	14	9	7	2	43

The "original" Russian word is "interiorizatsiia". In his publications Vygotsky used the word in quotation marks in order to underline its foreign, borrowed, alien nature. (These quotation marks were later removed in his posthumous publications and republications.) Yet, in English, the word has yet another translation that should certainly be taken into consideration, especially since it also occurs in the Collected Works, translated by a few different individuals. The alternative English translation is "interiorization". It is even more illustrative to have a look at how often Vygotsky − as opposed to his followers, opponents, editors, publishers, and censors (quite often the very same individuals) − used it in his collected works (see Table 1.2).

TABLE 1.2 The frequency of use of the word "interiorization" (and its derivatives) in the six-volume *Collected Works of L. S. Vygotsky* (Plenum/Kluwer Press, 1987, 1993, & 1997–1999)

	Vol. 1	Vol. 2	Vol. 3	Vol. 4	Vol. 5	Vol. 6	Total
Vygotsky's own text	–	–	–	1	1	3	5
Not Vygotsky's text (comments, introductions, indexes, etc.)	2	2	–	3	–	15	22
Total	2	2	–	4	1	18	27

Finally, the cumulative data for both "internalization" and "interiorization" (and their derivatives and cognate words) are presented in Table 1.3.

TABLE 1.3 The frequency of cumulative use of the words "internalization" and "interiorization" (and their derivatives) in the six-volume *Collected Works of L. S. Vygotsky* (Plenum/Kluwer Press, 1987, 1993, & 1997–1999)

	Vol. 1	Vol. 2	Vol. 3	Vol. 4	Vol. 5	Vol. 6	Total
Vygotsky's own text	–	2	–	7	4	3	16
Not Vygotsky's text (comments, introductions, indexes, etc.)	4	9	14	6	4	17	54
Total	4	11	14	13	8	20	70

For a better illustration, all these statistics have been summarized in a simple pie diagram in Figure 1.1.

Let us pause for a moment to think about what these data show and what this possibly means. It is perfectly clear that a collection of works of an author must consist mostly of this author's texts. Exceptions are not unthinkable, but this is definitely the case with this particular edition: despite a "layer" – or, more precisely, two layers – of quite lengthy additional materials added to this collection by the original Russian and, then, Anglophone editors and commentators, their cumulative text within the Collected Works slightly exceeds twenty percent in the most generous assessment (see Figure 1.2). Given that "interiorizatsiia" is commonly believed to be one of Vygotsky's fundamental ideas, one would expect it to be a very frequent term that would occur in his texts at least as often as in the texts of others. Yet, what we observe is dramatically different from expectations based on such an assumption. First, Vygotsky used the word 16 times within a 1,695-page corpus of his writings and transcribed oral presentations included into the six volumes of his Collected Works. This means slightly less than 2.7 instances on

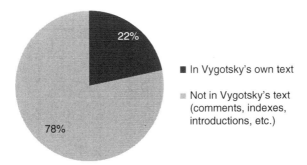

FIGURE 1.1 The ratio of the occurrence of the words "internalization" and "interiorization" (*interiorizatsiia*) and their derivatives in the six-volume *Collected Works of L. S. Vygotsky* (Plenum/Kluwer Press, 1987, 1993, & 1997–1999)

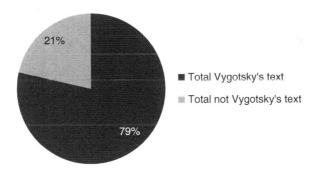

FIGURE 1.2 The ratio between Vygotsky's and not Vygotsky's text in the six-volume *Collected Works of L. S. Vygotsky* (Plenum/Kluwer Press, 1987, 1993, & 1997–1999)

average per volume. Second, other authors' use of the word in their discussion of Vygotsky and his legacy considerably exceeds the use of the word by the author and the alleged proponent and advocate of the "term": roughly, the word occurs well over 15 times more often in supplementary "Vygotskiana" than in Vygotsky!

Volume 3 (of the English edition, which corresponds to volume one of the Russian edition) is particularly illustrative in this respect and provides a hint at understanding what stands behind this highly strange and most curious phenomenon. Indeed, in the texts that are presented here, Vygotsky never used the word "interiorizatsiia". In sharp contrast, in Alexei N. Leontiev's introduction to the whole six-volume collection (originally published in volume 1 of the Russian edition and translated here), the word is used 13 times, and another time it occurs in the index of the book. Something is definitely and fundamentally wrong here, and it is obvious that the terminological system of those who talk and write about Vygotsky is utterly different from either Vygotsky's own conceptual apparatus or the use of this very term in theoretical psychological systems that are considerably different from that of Vygotsky. For a discussion of the independent use of "internalization" in other psychological systems see Schafer, 1968. How exactly this situation developed is beyond the scope of this chapter, but it is clear that considerable research is needed in order to get a better understanding of this huge gap between Vygotsky and the self-proclaimed "Vygotskians", Russian and Western alike. Luckily, some important work has already been done in this area. A good example of this work is presented in the direct predecessor of this volume – a recent book titled "Revisionist revolution in Vygotsky studies" (Yasnitsky & van der Veer, 2016a).

In sum, Vygotsky's brief and episodic flirtation in 1930–1931 with an awkward metaphor of "internalization" (or "interiorization") was overinflated and exaggerated beyond any reasonable measure in the writings of the "Vygotskians", who did exactly what he objected to: substantializing – presenting something as existing as such independently and separately – the individual human "psyche" ("mind", "cognition") and making it the main object of their research. Instead, those willing to remain true to the spirit of Vygotsky's proposal would need to reconsider the vague metaphor of the "internalization" and substitute it with a more elaborate and refined conceptual apparatus, for instance, based on the notions of dialogue and the like (Bertau & Karsten, 2018). On the other hand, this case is also interesting from the perspective of the research on the social construction and global dissemination of "Vygotskiana". Good examples of such research can be found in this very book: in Chapter 5 by Peter Keiler that discusses the situation in the Soviet Union and Chapter 6 and Chapter 7 by Clay Spinuzzi and Luciano Nicolás García, respectively, who focus on the affairs outside the USSR.

"Higher" (psychological): functions, systems, processes and behavior

So, there is a notable gap between the considerable popularity of "internalization" among the so-called "Vygotskians" and its use in Vygotsky's own texts, used rarely and *ad hoc*, i.e. on just a few special occasions: virtually half of all noticed instances belong to volume 4 of the English edition of the Collected Works, where the word appears in the text of an unfinished manuscript from around 1930. Unlike "internalization", Vygotsky frequently talked and wrote about a wide range of "the higher" functions, phenomena and processes in psychological research and practice. Vygotsky typically experimented with his scientific terminology and did not leave a rigorous and consistent system of scientific notions. His terminology and word use are constantly in flux, like in this specific case, and he used the attribute "the higher" in very different phrases and word combinations. Two remarks are in place, though.

First, the meaning of the word as Vygotsky uses it in his texts is far from clear. He never gave a precise definition of "higher" in his works, but made it clear that its opposite is "lower", which he also never rigorously defined. The original Russian adjective "vysshii" ("vysshie" in plural) allows for two distinct interpretations of the word: the comparative "higher" and the superlative "highest". Vygotsky's original proposal of the Science of Superman suggests the reading in favor of the superlative "highest". Yet, the usual opposition of the "higher"

(Russian: "vysshie") and the "lower" (Russian: "nizshie") in Vygotsky's text suggests the alternative interpretation in favor of the comparative "higher". This is the ambiguity of Vygotsky's use of the word we have to live with, and this is no doubt an alarming issue for a good scientific theory as far as its most basic terminology is concerned. Furthermore, the metaphor of the opposing "higher" and "lower" functions eventually lost its intellectual force for Vygotsky when, in his public presentation made for a relatively limited circle of his associates on 4 December 1932, he admitted:

> The higher and lower functions are not built in two floors: their number and names do not coincide. But neither our previous conception [is correct]: the higher function is the mastery of the lower one (voluntary attention is the subordination of involuntary attention), for this also implies two floors.
>
> *Zavershneva & van der Veer, 2018, p. 275*

Second, in one respect Vygotsky is unusually – and very uncharacteristically for him – consistent in word use. He very explicitly and vehemently attacked the idea of pure "psychical (mental, cognitive) functions" and strongly insisted on the "psychological functions" instead. Vygotsky quoted the passage from Max Wertheimer, a strong advocate of the unified, holistic approach: "Think of someone dancing. In his dance there is joy and grace. How is that? Does it represent on the one hand a display of muscles and movement of the limbs, and on the other hand psychic consciousness? No" (Wertheimer, 1944, p. 96). In the spirit of this quote and related vantage point, Vygotsky stated in his Russian publication of 1930:

> Dialectical psychology [...] does not mix up the psychic(al) [i.e., the mental, cognitive, etc.] and physiological processes. It accepts the non-reducible qualitatively unique nature of the psyche [i.e., the mind]. But it does claim that psychological processes are unitary. We thus arrive at the recognition of unique psycho-physiological unitary processes. These represent the higher forms of human behavior, which we suggest calling psychological processes, in contradistinction to psychic(al) [i.e., mental, cognitive, etc.] processes and in analogy with what are called physiological processes.
>
> *Vygotsky, 1997a, p. 113*

Apparently, this distinction between the "psychological" and the "psychic" was very important for Vygotsky, who was often careless about the precision of formulations. Indeed, he preserved his methodological stance on the unitary notion of the "psychological" throughout the 1930s, and reiterated the importance of this distinction in one of his last notes (on the psychology of thinking) that he scribbled roughly a month before his death in 1934. This quote might also give an idea as to why this distinction was so important from Vygotsky's viewpoint.

As soon as we separated thinking from life (from the dynamics), we viewed it as a concept of the psychic and not as a concept of the psychological. We blocked all roads to the clarification and explanation of its most important property: to determine the lifestyle and behavior, to act, to influence.

Zavershneva & van der Veer, 2018, p. 487

Therefore, the idea of Vygotsky dealing with anything "higher psychic(al)" appears impossible, given Vygotsky's theoretical standpoint. Yet, there is a phrase, which is commonly attributed to Vygotsky and is very popular, especially among Russian psychologists of the last half century or so, starting with the first post-WWII generation. The phrase is: the *"higher psychic(al) functions"* (alternatively, "higher mental, intellectual or cognitive functions"; *"vysshie psikhicheskie funktsii"* in original Russian, which is often commonly abbreviated as "VPF"). There is a definite contradiction here. In order to resolve it, the phrase was put on a serious textological and historiographic trial. The main conclusion of this research is the finding that the phrase in question appears to be yet another fabrication and falsification of Vygotsky's legacy and texts in the posthumous publications. The phrase never occurs in Vygotsky's writings, either published during his lifetime or in his archival documents. For a detailed and in-depth discussion of this discovery see Chapter 5, authored by Peter Keiler, who presents his meticulously researched "history of the social construction" of "Vygotskian" tradition and related terminology. This discovery was further corroborated by a newly published volume with the archival materials that comprise an impressive selection of Vygotsky's notebooks and notes that Vygotsky wrote in order to keep important ideas for himself or for private use, his future works plans and drafts, or some other documents created for a wide range of occasionally personal, but mainly public scientific events. The twin volumes are available in Russian and English, both under the editorship of Ekaterina Zavershneva and René van der Veer (Zavershneva & van der Veer, 2017; Zavershneva & van der Veer 2018)

From the studies of Vygotsky's works finished and published during his lifetime (Yasnitsky & van der Veer, 2016a), we see that Vygotsky's ambitious project of the Science of Superman in its various guises was never accomplished as such, especially at the theoretical, conceptual level. Perhaps, the most important and significant of Vygotsky's contributions to psychological science is his work associated with a number of themes and topics covered in his posthumously published collection of essays published under the title "Thinking and speech" in late 1934 in Russian, then partially – the last chapter only – translated into English and published in 1939 (Vygotsky, 1939). Then, the work first appeared in English in a very abbreviated translation, yet included all seven chapters of the book, in 1962 (Vygotsky, 1962). The most important of Vygotsky's innovations presented in this book concerns his work on what he believed to be a study on conceptual development in children and his speculations on the presumably multidirectional transitions between the observable "external" speech, so-called "internal speech", and non-verbal thinking. These topics truly constitute Vygotsky's original empirical and theoretical research and have long been believed to be his claim for fame in psychology as his investigation of the concrete "higher psychological" processes in their dynamics and historical development, although notably influenced by German philological tradition (Bertau, 2014; Werani, 2014).

However, this research on language and thinking appears problematic and underwent considerable scrutiny lately. It seems vulnerable to criticisms of various sorts, especially from contemporary linguists and psycholinguists, who question a number of Vygotsky's basic assumptions as well as the design and execution of his studies. Thus, a particular example of a critique of Vygotsky's theorizing about conceptual development, language, speech, and thinking was put on trial in a recent important and audacious study (Zhang, 2013), which is presented in this very book in Chapter 3 titled "Rethinking Vygotsky: A critical reading of the semiotics in Vygotsky's Cultural-Historical Theory", authored by Ruihan Zhang.

"Cultural-historical" theory as concrete psychology that was not

Vygotsky's utopian Science of Superman of the Communist future, his unconditional belief in the plasticity and mutability of the human mind and body, the idiosyncratically interpreted Marxist philosophy, the ever evolving "higher psychological" processes, and, finally, the striving towards the concrete psychology – all these merged into a particularly interesting blend in a Vygotsky-Luria research project that they jointly carried out in the naturalistic settings of the rapid forceful collectivization of Uzbek peasants in Central Asia in 1931–1932. This project has for a long time been interpreted as one of the greatest success stories of the so-called "cultural-historical" psychology, but – as recent studies convincingly demonstrate – it was in fact probably the worst ever failure of Vygotsky and Luria in their way of creating a Marxist concrete psychology outside the psychological laboratory. This case study has already been sufficiently discussed elsewhere (Allik, 2013; Goncharov, 2013; Lamdan, 2013; Lamdan & Yasnitsky, 2016; Proctor, 2013; Yasnitsky, 2013a; Yasnitsky, 2013b), but it has also been revisited in this book in Chapter 4, written by Eli Lamdan, that focuses on Vygotsky's "significant other" – Alexander Luria – and deals with his contribution to and influence upon Vygotsky's legacy in the making.

However, the case of this phrase, the "cultural-historical" psychology (or theory) is of particular interest not only because of this. "Cultural-historical psychology" seems to be the terminological label reserved for Vygotsky's (or, in more recent accounts, Vygotsky's and Luria's) brand of psychological theory. A handbook of "cultural-historical psychology" published by Cambridge University Press under the editorship of Anton Yasnitsky, René van der Veer and Michel Ferrari in 2014 demonstrates the wide range of theoretical tenets, methodological principles, and a variety of applications, both within and outside psychology proper (Yasnitsky et al.,

2014). The last chapter of the book, contributed by the late medical doctor, visionary neuroscientist and best-selling author Oliver Sacks (1933–2015), quite correctly characterizes this intellectual legacy as a "Romantic Science" (Sacks, 2014), widely known under the label of "cultural-historical psychology". Yet, there is one main problem here: neither Vygotsky nor Luria would ever call it by this name. Indeed, in his discussion of his theory that has been found among Vygotsky's archival notes the statement is perfectly clear.

> NB! The name, the designation that we lack. […] *Not* instrumental, *not* cultural, *not* signifying, *not* constructive, etc. Not just because of the mixing up with other theories, but also because of its intrinsic obscurity: For example, the idea of the analogy with an instrument = just scaffolding, more essential is the *dissimilarity*. Culture: But where does culture itself come from? (It is not primary, but this is hidden.)
>
> *Zavershneva & van der Veer, 2018, p. 121*

True, a Marxist psychological theory must take into consideration culture, but cannot be "cultural" and exactly for the reason that Vygotsky provides that culture, according to the Marxist worldview, belongs to the "superstructure" and as such is a derivative of the economic "base" of society and the concrete historical "mode of production". The "base", in turn, is constituted by the complex interplay of the "productive forces" and the "relations of production". In this sense, Vygotsky is perfectly right: "culture is not primary", and something else – some other, deeper processes and forces – stand behind it, and "this is hidden", therefore, culture cannot serve as an explanatory principle. This is a theoretical rationale behind the reasoning why Vygotsky's Marxist psychology and his Science of Superman – both in the making – could not and cannot be named "cultural". There is another reason: a historical one.

Peter Keiler did a meticulous study of the terminology that Vygotsky, Luria, their supporters, opponents, and associates used for several decades. This study is presented in much detail in Keiler's Chapter 5, titled "A history of the social construction of the 'Cultural-Historical'". In brief the study came to a surprising conclusion that Vygotsky, Luria and their associates never used the phraseology of "cultural-historical" theory, school, or psychological tradition in order to describe their research. However, curiously enough, Keiler argues that "cultural-historical" phraseology originally was introduced in the mid-1930s by critics of these scholars with defamatory aims and was later appropriated by a larger psychological community of scholars – including those that identified themselves as Vygotsky's followers. Keiler provides an explanation of this rather strange situation and proposes that this is an instance of a psychological defense mechanism that, in the terminology of the post-Freudian psychological tradition, he refers to as "identification with the aggressor".

In the aftermath of the period of the "Thaw" in the Soviet Union (roughly a decade after the death of Joseph Stalin in 1953) the Soviet "Vygotskians" such as

Leontiev, Luria and their supporters had established, in sociological terminology, strong patron-client relations by that time and, thus, constituted the primary members of the Leontiev-Luria clan in the Soviet psychological community. This clan worked with gears of power in Soviet and even international psychology: both Leontiev and Luria were top-level administrators not only in Soviet institutions (e.g. Leontiev became the founding dean of the one of the first two Departments of Psychology in the USSR, in 1966), but also in major international psychological organizations, such as International Union of Psychological Science (Leontiev served the member of the Executive Committee of this organization in 1960–1966 and 1969–1976, its Vice-President in 1966–1969, and Luria also being a Committee member in 1948–1951, the Executive Committee member in 1966–1969 and Vice-President in 1969–1972) (Rosenzweig et al., 2000). This was the time when the term "cultural-historical" became generally accepted among Soviet scholars as a quintessentially "Vygotskian" label.

"Vygotskian" concrete psychology against the challenges of the 21st century

As we see it was not until the 1960s and 1970s that "Vygotskian" psychology spread widely outside the walls of Moscow State University that harbored the majority of Soviet "Vygotskians". Interestingly, this process developed at virtually the same time and in parallel courses in both the Soviet Union and abroad. In the East, the "Vygotskian" label was used mainly as a "lowest common denominator" and the legitimization of the alleged theoretical unity of several disparate, virtually unrelated psychological theories such as Leontiev's quasi-Marxist theoretical speculations and Luria's psychoneurological clinical research and practice, and a few loosely interrelated developmental psychological theories of Lidiia Bozhovich, Piotr Gal'perin, Daniil El'konin and his closest collaborator (and Gal'perin's former student) Vasilii Davydov – all but Davydov former associates of Vygotsky. All these psychological studies were often portrayed as growing from common a "Vygotskian" root, but allegedly belonging to the same theoretical stem, Leontiev's so-called "activity theory".

In the West, "Vygotskiana" advanced in a number of different ways depending on time and place, but in North America – perhaps the main "importer" and, then, global "distributor" of non-Soviet "Vygotskian" science – it was assimilated under the somewhat curious blended phraseology of the so-called "cultural-historical activity theory", also known under its abbreviation as CHAT. Not only have Western scholars *appropriated* some "Vygotskian" ideas, but they have also *adapted* them in accordance with their needs and local goals in the social contexts of their lives, work, and research. Thus, quite naturally, these "Vygotskian" ideas, isolated from their original context and deprived of the minds of their originators and earliest advocates, would get "alienated" and stride quite far away from what they originally might have meant. The story of these ideas' reception, social construction and reconstruction, and, in a few instances, transnational circulation

constitutes a truly exciting field of recent (Yasnitsky & van der Veer, 2016a; Yasnitsky et al., 2016) and future research, the first good examples of which can be
found in the last two chapters of this very book, authored by Clay Spinuzzi and
Luciano Nicolás García. All interested readers are invited to enjoy the logic and
beauty of their analysis and presentation.

Yet, the question remains: now that Vygotsky's citation rates have started gradually decreasing and his popularity as a proponent of a "social constructivism" is
apparently declining, what is the future of "Vygotskiana" in the 21st century? For
some, Vygotsky is and will remain an undisputable authority and a thinker far
"ahead of his time", whose relevance in the contemporary context is beyond any
doubt. This is worldview and attitude to Vygotsky that was born in the period of
early Stalinism in the Soviet Union that one of his former students thus described
as late as the end of the 1980s:

> Even if there was anything funny about him, we never took it as funny,
> because nothing related to him could have been funny. We never judged him
> by human standards. He was a genuine spiritual father to us. We trusted him
> in everything without any limit. We related to him as disciples to Christ.
>
> *Vygodskaya & Lifanova, 1996, p. 256*

This position can perhaps be best described as the "heroic cult" of Vygotsky the
genius. This standpoint is the extreme that identifies the frontier of the tradition-
alist, conservative and "archaic" strand in global "Vygotskiana". The alternative,
"futuristic" worldview and assessment of Vygotsky's legacy in psychology can be
found in the memoirs of another of Vygotsky's somewhat more distant associates,
Piotr Gal'perin, who did acknowledge Vygotsky's genius in his interview of the
same period in the late 1980s, but then presented a more critical stance towards his
scientific legacy and gave quite a pessimistic assessment of its future.

> In my view, he was the only real man of genius in the history of Russian and
> Soviet psychology. He was also a child of his time. To those in the West who
> are so enthusiastic now about Vygotsky I want to say that they are con-
> siderably delayed in turning to him. In the meantime, we have made some
> progress, not so much from a theoretical point of view, but, I should rather
> say, from a historical one. In the West this process must, apparently, still be
> experienced; but eventually, they will also become disappointed in Vygotsky.
>
> *Haenen & Galperin, 1989, p. 15*

Regardless of whether Gal'perin's pessimistic prediction proves correct or not
quite, it is already at this point clear that the archaic cultist standpoint is hardly
productive. It is critical attitudes to Vygotsky's legacy – like that of the contributors
to this book – that might bring us some understanding of its potential for contemporary practice and research in "scientific psychology" as a concrete, empirical
science of the 21st century.

Questioning Vygotsky's Legacy (this very book) is a collection of papers, in which every chapter is unique and expresses the uniquely distinct and dissimilar voice of its authors united in a polyphonic dialogue about Vygotsky, his life and work. And still, the dialogue between the "archaists" and the "futurists" is not over yet. The future will show the outcome.

Note

1 For links to the data and discussion of the materials of the longitudinal study in progress see the sources online: https://psyanimajournal.livejournal.com/16165.html.

References

Allik, J. (2013). Do primitive people have illusions? *PsyAnima, Dubna Psychological Journal*, 6 (3), pp. 40–42.

Bandura, A. (1963). *Social learning and personality development*. New York: Holt, Rinehart and Winston.

Bandura, A. (1977). *Social Learning Theory*. Oxford: Prentice-Hall.

Bertau, M.-C. (2014). Inner form as a notion migrating from West to East: Acknowledging the Humboldtian tradition in cultural-historical psychology. In A. Yasnitsky, R. van der Veer, & M. Ferrari (Eds.), *The Cambridge Handbook of Cultural-Historical Psychology* (pp. 247–271). Cambridge: Cambridge University Press.

Bertau, M.-C., & Karsten, A. (2018). Reconsidering interiorization: Self moving across language spacetimes. *New Ideas in Psychology*, 49, pp. 7–17.

Billig, M. (2013). *Learn to write badly: How to succeed in the social sciences*. New York: Cambridge University Press.

Bruner, J. (1985). Vygotsky: a historical and conceptual perspective. In J. Wertsch (Ed.), *Culture, communication, and cognition: Vygotskian perspectives* (pp. 21–34). Cambridge: Cambridge University Press.

Chaiklin, S. (2003). The zone of proximal development in Vygotsky's analysis of learning and instruction. In A. Kozulin, V. S. Ageyev, S. M. Miller, & B. Gindis (Eds.), *Vygotsky's educational theory in cultural context* (pp. 39–64). Cambridge: Cambridge University Press.

Cole, M. (2004). Prologue: Reading Vygotsky. In R. W. Rieber & D. K. Robinson (Eds.), *The essential Vygotsky* (pp. vii–xii). New York: Kluwer Academic/Plenum Publishers.

Goncharov, O. A. (2013). Commentary on A. Yasnitsky's article "Kurt Koffka: 'Uzbeks DO HAVE illusions!' The Luria-Koffka controversy". *PsyAnima, Dubna Psychological Journal*, 6(3), pp. 34–36.

Haenen, J., & Galperin, P. I. (1989). An interview with P. Ya. Gal'perin. *Soviet Psychology*, 27(3), pp. 7–23.

Haggbloom, S. J., Warnick, R., Warnick, J. E., Jones, V. K., Yarbrough, G. L., Russell, T. M., Borecky, C. M., McGahhey, R., Powell, J. L., Beavers, J. and Monte, E. (2002). The 100 most eminent psychologists of the 20th century. *Review of General Psychology*, 6(2), pp. 139–152.

Joravsky, D. (1961). *Soviet Marxism and Natural Science: 1917–1932*. London: Routledge & Kegan Paul.

Lamdan, E. (2013). Who had illusions? Alexander R. Luria's Central Asian experiments on optical illusions. *PsyAnima, Dubna Psychological Journal*, 6(3), pp. 66–76.

Lamdan, E., & Yasnitsky, A. (2016). Did Uzbeks have illusions? The Luria – Koffka controversy of 1932. In A. Yasnitsky & R. van der Veer (Eds.), *Revisionist Revolution in Vygotsky Studies* (pp. 175–200). London & New York: Routledge.

Leontiev, A. N. (1931). *Razvitie pamiati. Eksperimental'noe issledovanie vysshikh psikhologicheskikh funktsii* [Development of memory. Experimental research on higher psychological functions]. Moscow: Uchpedgiz.

Proctor, H. (2013). Kurt Koffka and the Expedition to Central Asia. *PsyAnima, Dubna Psychological Journal*, 6(3), pp. 43–52.

Radzikhovskii, L. A. (1988). Diskussionnye problemy marksistskoi teorii v sovetskoi psikhologicheskoi nauke [The acute problems for discussion on the Marxist theory in Soviet psychological science]. *Voprosy Psikhologii*, 6, pp. 124–131.

Ratner, C., & Silva, D. N. H. (Eds.) (2017). *Vygotsky and Marx: Toward a Marxist Psychology.* London & New York: Routledge.

Rosenzweig, M. R., Holtzman, W., Sabourin, M., & Bélanger, D. (2000). *History of the International Union of Psychological Science (IUPsyS).* Hove: Psychology Press.

Sacks, O. (2014). Luria and 'Romantic Science'. In A. Yasnitsky, R. van der Veer, & M. Ferrari (Eds.), *The Cambridge Handbook of Cultural-Historical Psychology* (pp. 517–528). Cambridge: Cambridge University Press.

Schafer, R. (1968). *Aspects of Internalization.* Madison, CT: International Universities Press.

Simon, J. (1987). Vygotsky and the Vygotskians. *American Journal of Education*, 95(4), pp. 609–613.

Skinner, B. F. (1938). *The Behavior of Organism.* New York: Appleton-Century-Crofts.

Skinner, B. F. (1948). *Walden Two.* New York: Macmillan.

Skinner, B. F. (1957). *Verbal Behavior.* New York: Appleton-Century-Crofts.

Valsiner, J. (1988). *Developmental psychology in the Soviet Union.* Brighton: Harvester Press.

Valsiner, J., & van der Veer, R. (1993). The encoding of distance: The concept of the zone of proximal development and its interpretations. In R. R. Cocking & K. A. Renninger (Eds.), *The development and meaning of psychological distance* (pp. 35–62). Hillsdale, NJ: Lawrence Erlbaum.

Valsiner, J., & van der Veer, R. (2000). *The social mind: Construction of the idea.* Cambridge: Cambridge University Press.

Van der Veer, R., & Valsiner, J. (1991). *Understanding Vygotsky: A quest for synthesis.* Oxford: Blackwell.

van Dijck, J. (2007). *Mediated Memories in the Digital Age.* Stanford, CA: Stanford University Press.

Vygodskaya, G. L., & Lifanova, T. M. (1996). *Lev Semenovich Vygotskii. Zhizn'. Deiatel'nost'. Shtrikhi k portretu* [Lev Semenovich Vygotsky: Life, Career, Brushstrokes of a Portrait]. Moscow: Smysl.

Vygotsky, L. S. (1939). Thought and speech. *Psychiatry*, 2, pp. 29–54.

Vygotsky, L. S. (1962). *Thought and language.* Cambridge: M.I.T. Press.

Vygotsky, L. S. (1997a). Mind, Consciousness, the Unconscious. In R. W. Rieber & J. Wollock (Eds.), *The collected works of L. S. Vygotsky* (Vol. 3. Problems of the Theory and History of Psychology, pp. 109–121). New York: Plenum Press.

Vygotsky, L. S. (1997b). The historical meaning of the crisis in psychology: A methodological investigation. In R. W. Rieber & J. Wollock (Eds.), *The collected works of L. S. Vygotsky* (Vol. 3. Problems of the History and Theory of Psychology, pp. 233–344). New York: Plenum Press.

Werani, A. (2014). A review of inner speech in cultural-historical tradition. In A. Yasnitsky, R. van der Veer, & M. Ferrari (Eds.), *The Cambridge Handbook of Cultural-Historical Psychology* (pp. 272–294). Cambridge: Cambridge University Press.

Wertheimer, M. (1944). Gestalt Theory. *Social Research*, 11(1), pp. 78–99.

Yasnitsky, A. (2012). Revisionist revolution in Vygotskian science: Toward cultural-historical Gestalt psychology. Guest editor's introduction. *Journal of Russian and East European Psychology*, 50(4), pp. 3–15.

Yasnitsky, A. (2013a). Bibliografiia osnovnykh sovetskikh rabot po kross-kul'turnoi psikhonevrologii i psikhologii natsional'nykh men'shinstv perioda kollejktivizatsii, industrializatsii i kul'turnoi revoliutsii (1928–1932) [Bibliography of main Soviet publications on cross-cultural psychoneurology and psychology of national minorities during the period of collectivization, industrialization, and Cultural Revolution (1928–1932)]. *PsyAnima, Dubna Psychological Journal*, 6(3), pp. 97–113.

Yasnitsky, A. (2013b). Psychological expeditions of 1931–1932 to Central Asia. Chronicle of events in letters and documents. *PsyAnima, Dubna Psychological Journal*, 6(3), pp. 114–166.

Yasnitsky, A. (2014a). Vygotsky, Lev. In D. Phillips (Ed.), *Encyclopedia of educational theory and philosophy* (Vol. 2, pp. 844–846). Thousand Oaks, CA: Sage Publications.

Yasnitsky, A. (2014b, August). Higher functions & "Height" Psychology: Vygotsky (Ab) Uses Leon Trotsky and Friedrich Nietzsche. Presented at the 2nd Congresso Internacional sobre a Teoria Histórico-Cultural and at the 13th Jornada do Núcleo de Ensino de Marília, Marília, Brasil. Online: http://individual.utoronto.ca/yasnitsky/texts/Yasnitsky%20(2014).%20Nietzsche-Trotsky-Vygotsky.pdf.

Yasnitsky, A. (2018). *Vygotsky: An Intellectual Biography*. London & New York: Routledge.

Yasnitsky, A. & van der Veer, R. (Eds.) (2016a). *Revisionist Revolution in Vygotsky Studies*. London & New York: Routledge.

Yasnitsky, A. & van der Veer, R. (2016b). Revisionist Revolution in Vygotsky Studies: The State of the Art & New Perspectives. Presented at the Joint Meeting of the European Society for the History of the Human Sciences (ESHHS) & International Society for the History of Behavioural and Social Sciences (CHEIRON), Barcelona, Spain. Online: http://individual.utoronto.ca/yasnitsky/texts/presentationBarcelona-2016 pdf.

Yasnitsky, A., van der Veer, R., Aguilar, E., & García, L. N. (Eds.) (2016). *Vygotski revisitado: una historia crítica de su contexto y legado*. Buenos Aires: Miño y Dávila Editores.

Yasnitsky, A., van der Veer, R., & Ferrari, M. (Eds.). (2014). *The Cambridge Handbook of Cultural-Historical Psychology*. New York: Cambridge University Press.

Zavershneva, E., & van der Veer, R. (Eds.) (2017). *Zapisnye knizhki L.S. Vygotskogo. Izbrannoe* [L.S. Vygotsky's Notebooks. A Selection]. Moscow: Kanon+.

Zavershneva, E., & van der Veer, R. (Eds.) (2018). *Vygotsky's Notebooks. A Selection*. New York: Springer.

Zhang, R. (2013). *Rethinking Vygotsky: A Critical Reading of Vygotsky's Cultural-Historical Theory and Its Appropriation in Contemporary Scholarship*. Pokfulam: University of Hong Kong. Online: http://dx.doi.org/10.5353/th_b5194765.

2

VYGOTSKY AND MARX – RESETTING THE RELATIONSHIP

Peter E. Jones

Introduction: Vygotsky as Marxist

As[1] a student and then as a professional psychologist, Vygotsky presented himself, and undoubtedly thought of himself, as a committed Marxist. A young man of 21 when the October Revolution took place, he was one of a new generation of intellectuals who embraced the aims of the revolution as well as its formidable challenges. His contribution to the forging of a new psychological paradigm was at once of a piece with the visionary aspirations of the Socialist Revolution and at the same time grounded in the daunting practical tasks of education and rehabilitation of child and adult casualties of the volcanic social upheaval that the revolution brought.

Vygotsky was also a literate Marxist, familiar with those classic texts of Marx and Engels then available, with key works of the Russian Marxist tradition (in particular those of Plekhanov), and with the contemporary writings of Bolshevik leaders, notably Lenin, Trotsky and Bukharin. In that respect, like S. L. Rubinstein, Vygotsky stood out in the crowd of wannabe Marxist psychologists of the day, his own close associates and collaborators included, whose personal engagement with Marxist thinking was patchy and superficial at best.

Vygotsky also distinguished himself by the relative circumspection which he displayed in approaching the task of creating a Marxist psychology and in reflecting on his own claims to fame in that department. He acknowledged the dangers of bending the process of open-minded intellectual exploration to fit passages from the classic Marxist texts plucked out of context. Vygotsky believed that significant theoretical advances would only come through creative assimilation of the distinctive analytical method of Marx's *Capital*; a Marxist psychology was a dream of the future rather than an existing paradigm. Nevertheless, Vygotsky explicitly appealed to Marxist writings in developing his new psychology and it is his reading of these texts which is of primary interest here.

For scholars sympathetic to Marxist views, including this author, the link between Vygotsky and Marx is more than a topic in the history of ideas. Marx was one of the most powerful voices for freedom in the whole history of humanity. His life's work was dedicated to helping the international working-class movement clarify the nature of their struggle against capitalist exploitation and assisting their self-organization in and for that struggle. For this task, Marx and Engels developed a revolutionary new outlook on humanity and human potential which informed and inspired struggles for socialism and national liberation throughout the world, including the cataclysmic social overturn of October 1917. At stake, then, is the place of Vygotsky's own perspective on human-ness and human potential within the liberatory socialist project, the contribution his psychology offers to the demystification of the mind's workings in the service of social transformation and renewal.

We may be satisfied that Vygotsky was a 'Marxist psychologist' on the basis of his own self-avowal and openly stated aims, but that would leave open the question of the precise quality of the continuity, or compatibility, of Vygotsky's innovations with their Marxian inspiration.[2] And this takes us into much more difficult territory, not least because of a lack of agreement about what it is to be 'Marxist' in the first place. The history of Marxism itself is one of splits and violent conflicts over fundamental philosophical, theoretical and political tenets, with live disputes still ongoing (Jones, 2016; Ratner, 2016). Despite a fair degree of consensus among contemporary scholars over Vygotsky's Marxist credentials, the situation clouds when we ask them what Vygotsky took from Marx: compare, for example, Newman and Holzman (1993), Packer (2008), Ratner (2017), Stetsenko (2016), Veresov (1999), Wertsch (1985). In some discussions, the presence of Marxian influence is often handled in terms of abstract notions like 'materialism', 'monism', 'historicity', 'dialectics', 'germ cell methodology', etc., as if Marx was advancing a general philosophy or metaphysics or a 'framework' for sociological analysis (see Jones, 2009b). By contrast, there is a marked absence of critical discussion of Vygotsky's work in relation to the *findings* of Marx and Engels in their concrete examination of socio-historical development and their attempts to summarize the *methodological implications* of this work. At the same time, of course, there have always been 'Marxist' objections to Vygotsky's work, from the Rubinsteinian psychological camp, for instance (Brushlinsky, 1968), but also from closer to home in the circle of cultural-historical/Activity Theory psychologists (Kozulin, 1984; Yasnitsky and van der Veer, 2016).

Secondly, we should bear in mind that the 'Marxism' with which Vygotsky was directly acquainted was a set of doctrines or positions uniquely tied up with the history of the Russian revolutionary movement and, more to the point, in the evolving realpolitik of the Soviet state itself, its policies and pronouncements, its institutions and, not least, the commitments, ambitions, struggles and personal fate of the Communist rulers and theoreticians themselves. Nothing succeeds like success and the October earthquake gave the architects of 'Soviet Marxism' unprecedented (if fragile) authority over questions of Marxist doctrine. For a flavour of this ideological influence, it is instructive to look at the Marxist work most cited by

Vygotsky in his early writing on the psychology of art: Nikolai Bukharin's popular Soviet-era theoretical textbook, *Historical Materialism: a System of Sociology*, first published in 1921 and going through several editions (Bukharin, 1926). The text dogmatically sets out an assemblage of supposedly Marxist positions which were clearly common currency among the communist intellectuals of the day.

i   A rigid, mechanistic social determinism with the individual as the point of absorption or intersection of outside social pressures or influence:

> if we examine each individual in his development, we shall find that at bottom he is filled with the influences of his environment, as the skin of a sausage is filled with sausage-meat. ... Like a sponge he constantly absorbs new impressions. And thus he is "formed" as an individual. Each individual at bottom is filled with a social content. The individual himself is a collection of concentrated social influences, united in a small unit.
>
> *Bukharin, 1926: p. 98*

ii   A philosophy of language based on an epistemology of 'correspondence' or 'reflection theory' with language and linguistic meaning reflecting or representing actions and things in the real world.

iii   A psychology of language consisting of various ingredients:
– an age-old equation of thinking with speaking combined with Pavlov's reflexology[3]: 'Thought always operates with the aid of words, even when the latter are not spoken; thought is speech minus sound' (Bukharin, 1926: p. 204);
– a view of concepts as abstract generalizations which can only be conveyed in words;
– a view of cognitive history in terms of the degree of 'abstractness' which verbal concepts have attained; following Lévy-Brühl, whose 1910 book, *Les fonctions mentales dans les sociétés inférieures* (*How Natives Think* in English), was a major influence on Vygotsky himself; Bukharin argues that 'primitive mentality' is 'pre-logical', i.e. incapable of generalization or abstraction.[4]

Thirdly, neither in Marx nor in Vygotsky do we find a finished body of work but passing products of thinkers engaged in restless revision of their own assumptions and conclusions. Moreover, and perhaps most importantly, Vygotsky was breaking new ground. In constructing his unique, always evolving, perspective on human psychological capacities, Vygotsky was weaving together a novel system of *semiological* constructs that had no parallel in Marx and Engels and it is in this creative legacy that the formidable challenge of evaluating Vygotsky's relation to Marx ultimately lies. If Vygotsky departed significantly from Marx, that may mean that Marx himself, a child of the 19th century, was 'wrong' against Vygotsky's 20th century scholarship and insights. If we found Vygotsky 'wrong' against Marx, the 'error' may be more useful and important in the history of the endeavour overall, in opening up the subject matter to broader consideration and contextualization, than dogged consistency.

If such considerations (amongst others) make assessment of the Vygotsky-Marx relation very difficult to say the least, that does not mean that is a pointless exercise, given the issues at stake. The way forward, I believe, is in taking bearings from our current standpoint of knowledge and experience on the overall 'arc' of Vygotsky's contribution – its fundamental assumptions, positions, orientation, practical application and potential – in relation to the 'arc' of Marx's own work, itself viewed critically in the light of 21st century knowledge and events. This is a task demanding considerable collaborative effort and debate and while consensus will not be reached, the process of clarification of the fault lines of intellectual (and political) difference will be revealing and productive in itself. A powerful opening bid in this collective endeavour is Anna Stetsenko's magisterial overview of the cultural-historical field from a 'transformative activist stance' (Stetsenko, 2016). Stetsenko argues persuasively for Vygotsky as contributor and innovator in the Marxist tradition of struggle for intellectual and social liberation. In terms of the 'big picture', I cannot disagree. But we may need to qualify that assessment when we look in detail at the conceptual fabric of Vygotskian principles.

In this chapter, I zoom in, tentatively, on one strand of the overarching task in a critical reading of Vygotsky's own reading of Marx and Engels in constructing his psychological theory. I will begin by stating in general terms how I think Vygotsky's overall contribution was informed by, and creatively extended, Marx's view of human potential. I will end with some reflections on the significance and implications of this reading of readings.

Marx and psychology

There are some basic things one could draw from Marx about the human mind and how to study it. Firstly, human mental powers are neither innately given, nor are they immutable across time and circumstance: they are the powers of real individuals living their lives under particular conditions. Secondly, human beings are naturally *social* creatures whose mental capacities arise as forms and means of living in cooperation and association with others. Thirdly, social life is above all *practical*, an ever-renewed process of creation and transformation of the life world in the production of the material and spiritual means of existence and, in that process, a making and re-making of people themselves, with all their powers and potential. Understanding how people see the world and themselves, how they think and reason and how they communicate with one another means, therefore, understanding the qualitative texture of their lives – how they act, how they produce, how they organize and reorganize their activities and social relations. Finally, such enquiry is no mere intellectual exercise but part of humanity's struggle – *our* struggle – for a communal life free from want and exploitation within which the full flowering of our creative powers can be enabled and enjoyed.

Aligning himself with this Marxian vision, Vygotsky's sought to liberate psychological science from the prejudices, preconceptions and fantasies of idealistic and mechanistic views of the human mind. He took it that human mental powers are neither biologically given nor the expression of some other-worldly 'spiritual' force; rather, they are *created by us*: they are a purely human accomplishment, forged in a historical process of self-development and self-knowledge. More specifically, these powers are formed in a social life built around the making and use of tools for productive activity. Indeed, human mental functioning *included* within it these extra-corporeal instruments which were themselves subject to historical change and re-design. Such producing and self-producing beings were *conscious* beings, their consciousness a function of this communal productive life which gave a distinctive 'free' and purposeful character to their collective and individual behaviour. The clear goal of Vygotsky's research, therefore, was to account for conscious action and to develop and apply, in the course of engagement with the problem, a methodology adequate to the subject matter. This is a perspective which, in outline, follows and enriches the main contours of the intellectual revolution that Marx and Engels inaugurated.

In pursuing his goal, Vygotsky chose to foreground the function of signs, and notably linguistic signs, in the development of distinctively human thought and action, attributing to them a singular and pivotal role in the organization and control of social activity and, on that basis, in the conscious, voluntary action of the individual. Signs were 'psychological tools' due to the influence on the mind (and behaviour) that they could effect. These 'psychological tools', both the product and the vehicle of *historically* developing *culture*, now properly became part of the study of the human mind itself which was, accordingly, now also a *historical* study of essentially *cultural* psychological functions. This was Vygotsky's original vision and the heart of his contribution as a psychologist. The theory is 'sign-centric', as Vygotsky's Rubinsteinian critics emphasised (Brushlinsky & Polikarpov, 1990), sign-centrism being, in their view, its main weakness and the clearest point of its divergence from Marxism. In forging a 'sign-centric', or, perhaps more accurately, *logocentric* approach, Vygotsky drew liberally on well-established traditions of linguistic thought and the cutting edge developments of his day. Ultimately, then, a judgement on Vygotsky's relationship to Marx hinges on our view of these ideas and Vygotsky's own use of them (Jones, 2007; Jones, 2016; Jones, in press; Jones, in preparation). Furthermore, while the semiological infrastructure of cultural-historical psychology represents a novel departure from the ideas of Marx and Engels, all such communicationally related concepts nevertheless embody deeper assumptions about mental life and social relations which may be examinable, and criticisable, from a Marxian perspective (Jones, 2007).[5]

Vygotsky reading Marx

The role of consciousness in human behaviour

In Vygotsky's writings of the mid-1920s (e.g. 'Consciousness as a problem for the psychology of behaviour, 1925, in Vygotsky, 1997a: pp. 63–79), he cites Marx's familiar description of labour in *Capital* to warrant the pivotal status he wishes to accord to consciousness in the study of human behaviour. Marx begins: 'We pre-suppose labour in a form in which it is an exclusively human characteristic' (Marx, 1976: pp. 283–284). He then elaborates:

> A spider conducts operations which resemble those of the weaver, and a bee would put many a human architect to shame by the construction of its hon-eycomb cells. But what distinguishes the worst architect from the best of bees is that the architect builds the cell in his mind before he constructs it in wax. At the end of every labour process, a result emerges which had already been conceived by the worker at the beginning, hence already existed ideally. Man not only effects a change of form in the materials of nature; he also realizes [*verwirklicht*] his own purpose in those materials. And this is a purpose he is conscious of, it determines the mode of his activity with the rigidity of a law, and he must subordinate his will to it. This subordination is no mere momentary act. Apart from the exertion of the working organs, a purposeful will is required for the entire duration of the work. This means close attention. The less he is attracted by the nature of the work, and the way in which it has to be accomplished, and the less, therefore, he enjoys it as the free play of his own physical and mental powers, the closer his attention is forced to be.
>
> *Marx, 1976: p. 284*

Vygotsky's reading of Marx is instructive. At the time, he considered consciousness as 'an interaction, reflection, and mutual excitation of different systems of reflexes' (Vygotsky, 1925, in Veresov, 1999: p. 269). 'Consciousness', as he put it, 'is wholly reduced to the transmitting mechanisms of reflexes operating according to general laws' (Vygotsky, 1925, in Veresov, 1999: p. 271). The distinctive character of human labour, as described by Marx, was therefore to be explained in terms of the causal action of sequences of reflexes following from an initial impulse or stimulus. At this stage, Vygotsky 'felt the need to reconcile Marx's idea with the general reflexological approach and sought for a reflexological basis of planning activities and free will' (van der Veer & Valsiner, 1991: 52). In plainer terms, Vygotsky tried to reconcile the irreconcilable, flattening Marx's 'free play of physical and mental powers' under the mechanical tread of Pavlov's physiological reductionism. If, for Marx, purpose may operate during (unenjoyable) work 'with the rigidity of a law', the point he is making is that *it is not a law*; the law-like appearance that the course of the labour process may present (in some circumstances) is the *result* of constant, conscious and selectively (voluntarily) focussed application to the task. The 'will' in Marx – or the 'ideal' as here in his description of labour – is not an initial winding of the clock followed by automatic movement of the hands but a power constantly exercised in scrutinizing (and adjusting) the progress of the activity under way in relation to the planned outcome. Furthermore, what in Marx is clearly to be taken as an observation about *social activity,* and implicitly the social division of labour between architects and builders is translated by Vygotsky into an inner *psychological* process working on reflexological lines *within the individual*. Indeed, it is perhaps worth emphasising that *there is no attempt to analyse the social labour process at all in Vygotsky* (or in Leont'ev for that matter).[6]

The reflex model was one half (the mechanistic half, as it were) of Descartes' dualistic conception of human action and thinking (Yaroshevsky, 1985). Reflexologically minded researchers (including Vygotsky) uncritically assumed that this model captured what human behaviour had in common with animal behaviour and that any theory of distinctively human psychology must, therefore, begin to build up from this common ground. This is the rationale for the 'instrumental' semiology of 'mediation' (Vygotsky, 1981) which Vygotsky begins to apply to such 'higher mental functions' as voluntary attention, voluntary memory and 'cultural will' (Vygotsky, 1997b). Vygotsky's key innovation consisted in a view of signs as affording control of one's own psychological reactions ('autostimulation'). As his succinct definition states: 'We call artificial stimuli-devices introduced by man into a psychological situation where they fulfill the function of autostimulation "signs"' (Vygotsky, 1997b: p. 54).

If there is no direct criticism of reflexology itself in Marx or Engels, there can be no doubt of their distance from the mechanical materialism of the 18th century which reflexology represented and continued. As Engels puts it: 'What the animal was to Descartes, man was to the materialists of the eighteenth century – a machine'. And, while acknowledging the progressive sides of this 18th century materialism, Engels derides 'the shallow, vulgarised form in which the materialism of the eighteenth century continues to exist today in the heads of naturalists and physicians, the form which was preached on their tours in the fifties by Büchner, Vogt and Moleschott' (Marx and Engels, 1970: p. 349).

The rise and rise of 'reflex' physiological reductionism, through Sechenov to Pavlov, had begun in the mid-1800s as a scientific working out of 18th century materialist thinking. Due to the challenge it represented to the idealistic psychology of the establishment old-guard, this scientific ideology was also embraced by politically radical currents which would attain their ascendancy, and sharpest edge, in the Russian Revolution, as we see in Bukharin.[7] Sensualism and physiological mechanism seeped into the general outlook of the militant materialists and Marxists of the day, including Plekhanov and Lenin himself, in whose *Empirio-Criticism* Marx's philosophy glows but faintly beside a militant naturalistic materialism based on a picture theory of sensation. In the same way, and for similar reasons, that the 'materialism' advocated by Lenin, via Plekhanov, owed more to 18th century materialism and sensualism than it did to Marx, so the currents of 'Marxist psychology' developing under the Revolution took their cue from the pre-Marxist 'vulgar materialism' of 'the naturalists and physicians'.

Sociality and the individual

In various places, Vygotsky appeals to Marx's sixth thesis on Feuerbach to ground his conception of the role of semiotic and linguistic processes in social life and individual behaviour. Marx's thesis reads:

the human essence is no abstraction inherent in each single individual. In its reality it is the ensemble of the social relations.

Marx and Engels, 1969: p. 14

Vygotsky's reading, again, is instructive:

Changing the well-known thesis of Marx, we could say that the mental nature of man represents the totality of social relations internalized and made into functions of the individual and forms of his structure. We do not want to say that this is specifically the meaning of the thesis of Marx, but we see in this thesis the most complete expression of everything to which our history of cultural development leads.

Vygotsky, 1997b: p. 106

This passage requires cautious reflection given Vygotsky's own caveat. Nevertheless, it is difficult to see what warrant Vygotsky finds in Marx for his own reading. Marx is not talking about 'the mental nature of man' at all (a problematic proposition in the first place). More to the point, he is clearly not describing *individual people* as 'aggregates of social relations', as constructed on a social model (by internalization of social influences). By 'man', Marx means the human *community* or *collectivity*; it is this community which is constituted as an 'ensemble of social relations', a system of different individuals in their concrete interconnections. Vygotsky's reading arguably chimes more comfortably with the relationship between individual and social as painted by Bukharin above.

In the reflexological tradition, as in Western behaviourism, there was no way of thinking about the behaviour and thinking of the individual person other than as *determined* or *controlled* from the outside by the action of external 'stimuli'. Reflexology, then, was not simply a part of a psychological or physiological model, but allowed the all-important hook-up between individual psychology and sociology as Vygotsky stressed from his earliest psychological writings (e.g. Vygotsky, 1997c). Human behaviour, as opposed to animal behaviour, thus represented 'a new type of behavior', namely 'the social determination of behavior carried out with the aid of signs' (Vygotsky, 1997b: p. 56). As Vygotsky put it:

Social life creates the need to subject the behavior of the individual to social requirements and together with this, creates complex signalization systems, means of communication that guide and regulate the development of conditioned connections in the brain of each person.

Vygotsky, 1997b: p. 56

On this basis, the individual's mental life was formed as 'a copy from the social' (Vygotsky, 1997b: p. 106). As Vygotsky put it: 'All higher psychological functions are the essence of internalized relations of a social order, a basis for the social structure of the individual' (Vygotsky, 1997b: p. 106).[8]

And while we find no concrete study of the sphere of social activity or social production at all in Vygotsky, as noted above, we do find the mythology of social evolution that Vygotsky took lock, stock and barrel from Pierre Janet (cf. van der Veer & Valsiner, 1988), built around the causal communicative power of the 'command' in social regulation and, subsequently, 'self-regulation': 'According to Janet, the word was initially a command for others... the word is always a command because it is a basic means of controlling behaviour' (Vygotsky, 1997b: p. 103).

Janet's view was that 'the power of the word over mental functions is based on the real power of the superior over the subordinate' (in Vygotsky, 1997b: p. 104) – a sourly dissonant proposition in itself from any Marxist perspective. This verbalized form of the boss-subordinate relationship in Vygotsky (as in Janet) becomes the means of individual self-control: 'Regulating another's behavior by means of the word leads gradually to the development of verbalized behavior of the individual himself' (Vygotsky, 1997b: p. 104). In the following passage we see clearly how Vygotsky's reflexologically derived conception of the command provides the link between social organization and the conscious or voluntary action of the individual:

> If we consider the initial forms of work activity, then we see that the function of fulfilling and the function of directing are separated there. An important step in the evolution of work is the following: what the supervisor does and what the underling does is united in one person. This, as we shall see below, is the basic mechanism of voluntary attention and work.
>
> *Vygotsky, 1997b: p. 104*

Mediation

Vygotsky sees 'the basis for the analogy between sign and tool' in 'the mediating function of the one and the other'. 'From the psychological aspect', he argues, 'they may, for this reason, be classified in the same category', namely that of 'mediating activity' (Vygotsky, 1997b: p. 61). Vygotsky's position is underscored with references to Marx's use of Hegel's conception of mediation in his account of tool use in *Capital*:

> Marx refers to this definition when speaking about the tools of work and indicates that man "makes use of mechanical, physical, chemical properties of things in order to change them into tools to act on other things according to his purpose".
>
> *Vygotsky, 1997b: p. 62*

Vygotsky's semiological notion of mediation is constructed via an analogy between Marx's 'tools of work' and signs:

> It seems to us that on this basis, the use of signs should be classified as a mediating activity since the essence of this is that man acts on behavior through signs, that is, *stimuli*, letting them *act according to their psychological nature*.
>
> *Vygotsky, 1997b: p. 62, my emphasis*

The analogy, then, is as follows: just as physical objects may serve as tools due to *their chemical or mechanical nature*, some objects may serve as signs due to *their 'psychological nature'*. But how, one might ask, do objects come to possess a 'psychological nature' as a precondition for their use in behavioural influence? Clearly, here, the answer is: by being *stimuli* in the reflexological sense. That is, the semiotic use of objects as a means of behavioural influence presupposes their accession to the status of Pavlovian stimuli in accordance with the laws of the conditioned reflex. Possessed of such a 'psychological nature' – a stimulating power acquired through reflex mechanisms – a semiotic object can be deployed deliberately to elicit the relevant reaction. The assumption, then, is that there is something fundamental in common between using a hammer to alter the behaviour of the nail and using a sign to alter the behaviour of a person: in both cases, there is a causal process at work through which a particular outcome is achieved.

However, Vygotsky's extension of Marx here is highly questionable. Marx's description of the mediating role of 'tools of work' belongs to his discussion of the active relationship between 'man', understood as the human community, and the natural world. Accordingly: 'We did not, therefore, have to present the worker in his relationship with other workers; it was enough to present man and his labour on one side, nature and its materials on the other' (Marx, 1976: p. 290).

In other words, Marx's notion of 'mediation' applies to the social use of natural properties of things for human ends and *not* to the sphere of social intercourse – 'the worker in his relationship with other workers' – itself. Instead, Marx takes the forms of social organization and interaction, including communication, as a necessary presupposition of such instrumental mediation. Thus, for Marx, people's relations to one another (including their communicative activities) do not 'come between' them (as individuals) in the way that labour tools 'come between' them (collectively) and the natural world. Vygotsky's analogy, on the other hand, projects precisely such a parallel between people's use of (natural) properties of objects for causally influencing nature and people's use of ('psychological') properties of objects for causally influencing their own 'nature', between acting on Nature with material tools and acting on Human Nature with psychological tools. The scope of causal-mechanical mediation is thereby extended, on reflexological premises, from the relationship 'people-nature' to the relationship 'person-person'.

For Marx, I suggest, the analogy is inconceivable since a human relationship – an ethically charged relating of *people as people* – does not involve, and cannot be equated with, the control of a *natural* (i.e. physical) process. Marx's whole philosophical and ethical position is based on a refusal to conceive of the relationship between people as a *relationship between things or between a person and a thing*. The reader may object that this criticism of Vygotsky is unconvincing without an account of how Marx might have addressed the communicative and interactional dimensions of social labour. Is it not likely, or even inevitable, that some notion of 'symbolic mediation' would be on the cards? Indeed so, as in Marx's treatment of money in commodity exchange and capitalist production. The issue, then, is not about a notion of communicational mediation as such, but to Vygotsky's reflexologically inspired extension of the reach of mechanical causation to the sphere of interpersonal relations.

Self-mastery/self-control

Studies in the History of Behavior: Ape, Primitive, Child (Vygotsky & Luria, 1993)[9] provides the most substantial account of the philosophical rationale and scientific orientation of cultural-historical psychology in explicit dialogue with passages from Marx and Engels. The authors pay particular attention to Engels' distinction between human and animal activity in terms of the concept of *labour* (or *work*):

> Put briefly, an animal uses only external nature and causes changes in it merely by virtue of its presence. Man, on the other hand, through the changes he makes, compels nature to serve his purposes, he dominates it, and this latter fact is an important distinction between man and the other animals – a distinction which is also due to man's work.
>
> *Engels, in Vygotsky & Luria, 1993: p. 34*

This ability to 'dominate nature' is taken by the authors to be fundamental to the historical problem of human freedom, again appealing to Engels:

> freedom is control over oneself and external nature, based on an understanding of natural necessity, and for that reason it is necessarily the product of historical development. The first people to break away from the animal kingdom were as lacking in freedom as the animals themselves; but the gradual progress of culture took them forward, step by step, towards freedom.
>
> *Engels, in Vygotsky & Luria, 1993: p. 35*

The authors argue that 'something similar' to this historical process of self-control or self-mastery also occurs in 'the sphere of human psychological development':

> Here again, we may say that animals merely use their own nature, whereas man compels nature to serve his own purposes and dominates it. For this, too, he is indebted to work. The process of work requires man *to exercise a certain degree of control over his own behaviour. This self-control, in essence, is based on the same principle as our dominion over nature.*
>
> *Vygotsky & Luria, 1993: p. 34, my emphasis*

Picking up Marx's point that the production of tools allows for the artificial 'augmentation' of the 'body's natural dimensions', they argue for a second parallel 'in man's psychological development':

> Once *symbols enabling man to control his own behavioural processes* had been invented and were in use, the history of the development of behaviour

became transformed, to a large extent, into *the history of the development of those auxiliary artificial "means of behaviour", and the history of man's control over his own behaviour.*

Vygotsky & Luria, 1993: p. 35; my emphasis

In similar vein, they argue:

> The enhancement of the "means of work" and the "means of behaviour", *in the form of language and other systems of symbols*, serve [sic] as auxiliaries in the process of the control of behaviour, *now becomes pre-eminent*, supplanting the development of the "bare hand and the intellect left to itself".

Vygotsky & Luria, 1993: p. 36, my emphasis

Here we see how the problematic analogy embodied in the Vygotskian conception of 'mediation' has been amplified and extended onto a more detailed theoretical landscape. In effect, the picture of the cultural development of the human mind presented by Vygotsky and Luria is a *psychological* analogue of the *socio-historical* process of 'self-mastery' presented by Marx and Engels. The 'materialist conception of history' gives way to a picture in which 'the history of the development of behaviour' is transformed into the history of 'language and other systems of symbols'.

As a perspective on human history, the authors' position entails a back-projection of 'natural psychological functions' working on reflex lines as the raw material for subsequent control by cultural symbols. Compare, then, Engels, for whom '[a]ctive social forces work exactly like natural forces: blindly, forcibly, destructively, so long as we do not understand, and reckon with them' (Marx and Engels, 1970: p. 146), with Vygotsky and Luria, for whom it is the memory of 'primitive man' which 'functions spontaneously, like a natural force' (Vygotsky & Luria, 1993: p. 61). Similarly, the authors paint the 'remarkable story of writing' as a story of 'man's efforts to control his memory' marking the transition from 'the biological or internal form of its development' to 'the historical or external form' (Vygotsky & Luria, 1993: p. 61). This conception of psychological control and self-mastery is better described as a historicized Pavlovianism rather than a Marxian view. In psychologizing symbol systems in this way, all communicational processes and their products – whether speech, writing, the casting of lots, or the infamous knots for memory – are abstracted from their role in social activity and, thereby, stripped of their social meaning and function. It is as if we tried to explain the development and use of money as an 'auxiliary means' of controlling individuals' natural impulse to steal their neighbours' goods.

This 'self-control' perspective is also the heart of their view of child development. The child, they tell us, 'is born in a ready cultural and productive environment; and therein lies the decisive, radical difference between him and the primitive' though, 'when born, the child is not in contact with that environment, and *is incorporated into it only gradually*' (Vygotsky & Luria, 1993: p. 113, original emphasis). At first the child is in a 'primitive phase, or one characterized by *natural forms of behavior*' in which the child is incapable of 'functionally using stimuli as symbols' (Vygotsky & Luria, 1993: p. 140). At this 'primitive phase' children are pre-social, organic and animal beings and it is only in 'the second phase of cultural development' that 'intermediate processes make their appearance in the child's behavior, altering that behavior through the use of stimulus-symbols' (Vygotsky & Luria, 1993: p. 117).[10]

In sum, what, in Marx, is presented as a socio-historical process in which *communities may come to critically confront and collectively exert control over their own previously developed practices and social relations* becomes, in Vygotsky and Luria, a psychological process in which individual behaviour is subject to social control via the power of symbols. This conceptual swerve from the Marxian view towards the symbolic is pivotal as it licences all the fundamental principles of cultural-historical psychology at all stages of its evolution, principally, of course, the basic distinction between 'natural' and 'cultural' (or 'lower' and 'higher') psychological functions. Thus, the Vygotsky-Luria picture assumes that the 'behavioural processes' to be controlled by symbols are 'natural psychological operations' (Vygotsky & Luria, 1993: p. 80), or 'natural forms of behaviour' (Vygotsky & Luria, 1993: p. 140) resulting from conditioned reflex processes, in contrast with the stages of 'cultural development' which 'artificial' symbols embody and enable. In this way, Marxism is made to sound like the vision of human malleability offered by the various schools of reflexological and behaviourist thought in Soviet Russia and the West at that time and since.

For Marx, by contrast, intelligent, conscious social practices (individual or collective) constitute the historic presupposition of the process of collective self-development, as opposed to putative 'psychological functions' in the raw. In consequence, Marx's view would require us to examine communicational activity of whatever kind as an integrated dimension of the *historically* given *socially organized life activity* of a particular community of which the individual is already a member. From this perspective, communicational practices (including spoken language, reading and writing) can then be studied in terms of their specific social functions and values and the forms of social organization and alignments which they presuppose and afford rather than being reduced a priori to the function of 'controlling' *naturally* given psychological capacities.

If Marx's vision of historical development is couched in a discourse that appears to chime with Vygotsky's own – self-control, self-mastery, voluntary/involuntary, spontaneous/conscious, and, perhaps crucially, natural/social – the subtleties of Marxian terminology demand a deeper appreciation of the fundamental philosophical and scientific commitments of Marx and Engels. Marx certainly talks about the historical growth of human freedom as a progressive extension of conscious control over 'natural' productive activity and social organization. But by 'natural' he does not mean a primitive, pre-social psychological zero point from which cultural history will take off, but to forms of social organization prior to that state of 'socialized humanity' which Marx referred to as communism, as for example:

Labour begins with a certain foundation – *naturally arisen, spontaneous*, at first – then historic presupposition. Then, however, this foundation or presupposition is itself suspended, or posited as a vanishing presupposition which has become too confining for the unfolding of the progressing human pack.

Marx, 1973: 497, my emphasis

By 'naturally arisen' or 'spontaneous' Marx does not imply 'animal-like' behaviours governed by 'natural' psychological functions in Vygotsky's sense. As Ollman puts it:

'Spontaneity', for Marx, is just the response that man, being who he is, must offer – he has no real choice – inside his circumstances, being what they are. Its opposite is 'voluntary action' where the individual is in control of his circumstances or in control of what controls him … Activity only becomes fully voluntary in communism where people subordinate the whole of nature to a common plan. Consequently, Marx refers to communism as a time when man's 'natural limitations' are cast off.

Ollman, 1976: p. 293, footnote 21

Thus, 'natural' for Marx, in this context, relates to practices and forms of social organization which are already distinctively human but have developed in circumstances when 'needs must', when the exigencies of daily coping, giving little scope for leisurely exercise of creative capacities, lead the collective to improvise and cling to forms of practice (and social organization) based on what their biological endowments easily afford, what is to hand, what is given, what they have already got, what they are not in a position to change through lack of resources, poor technology, ignorance or social taboo or constraint. Consider the following passage in which the term 'natural society' is used to mean any form of society whose organization is beyond collective control:

And finally, the division of labour offers us the first example of how, *as long as man exists in natural society*, that is, as long as a cleavage exists between the particular and the common interest, as long, therefore, as activity is *not voluntarily, but naturally divided*, man's own deed becomes an alien power opposed to him, which enslaves him instead of being controlled by him.

Marx & Engels, 1969: p. 35, my emphasis

By 'natural society' Marx here means human communities past and present, including our own! Slave societies or other exploitative forms of society were – are – forms of *human* existence, subordinated to the power of *social* forces (along with their symbolic means such as money), but which were 'natural' in being socially untameable. It is the social power of the human community itself in its forms of organization and practice, whatever degree of symbolic control (or 'symbolic violence') may be exercised, which Marx describes as 'natural' in this sense. This 'natural society' was not a herd of animal-like creatures waiting to be 'civilized' or 'socialized' by education and the cultural trappings of polite society. It was the unavoidably immature state of people who were nevertheless living together by labour 'in a form in which it is an exclusively human characteristic'. It was the collective social power – the 'ensemble of social relations' – which was out of control and it would take more than words or other signs to bring it to heel. Progress towards freedom, towards a society where people were fully in control of their lives, was therefore dependent on developing sufficient productive power to create an effortless abundance of material resources via intelligent application and mastery of the powers of nature as well as by the rational distribution of social effort, itself a productive force. 'Liberation', as Marx and Engels put it, 'is a historical and not a mental act, and it is brought about by historical conditions, the [development] of industry, commerce, [agri]culture, the [conditions of intercourse]' (Marx & Engels, 1969, p. 27), a function of all-round development of practical, intellectual, and social powers. Consequently, Marx's conception of historically developing 'self-control' or 'self-mastery' had to do with a social, collective process in which people became aware of and set out to consciously change the ways they – *as people* – had been doing things up to that point:

> Freedom in this sphere can consist only in this, that socialised man, the associated producers, govern the human metabolism with nature in a rational way, bringing it under their collective control, instead of being dominated by it as a blind power; and accomplishing it with the least expenditure of energy and in conditions worthy and appropriate for their human nature.
>
> *Marx, 1981*

Human cultural progress was, therefore, not about people mastering their 'animal' psychological nature by subordinating it to social influence (through symbolic means), but about mastering their *human* nature – their potential as a *social collectivity* to live humanly. It appears that Vygotsky and Luria have converted Marx's vision of the ultimate supercession of 'natural society' by 'socialized humanity' under communism into a psychological theory of control of 'natural psychological functions' by social symbols.

Verbal thinking

In *Thinking and Speech*, Vygotsky argues that:

> Verbal thought is not an innate, natural form of behavior, but is determined by a historical-cultural process and has specific properties and laws that cannot be found in the natural forms of thought and speech. Once we acknowledge the historical character of verbal thought, we must consider it subject to *all the premises of historical materialism, which are valid for any historical phenomenon in human society.*
>
> *Vygotsky, 1986: pp. 94–95, my emphasis*

Setting aside the question of whether 'verbal thought' refers to a possible object of historical exploration in this way, let us examine what Vygotsky had in mind by this statement. In their early attempts to formulate their 'materialist conception of history', Marx and Engels announced: 'Its premises are men, not in any fantastic isolation and rigidity, but in their actual, empirically perceptible process of development under definite conditions' (Marx & Engels, 1969: p. 25).

In methodological terms:

> we do not set out from what men say, imagine, conceive, nor from men as narrated, thought of, imagined, conceived, in order to arrive at men in the flesh. We set out from real, active men and on the basis of their real-life process we demonstrate the development of the ideological reflexes and echoes of this life process ... Where speculation ends – in real life – there real, positive science begins: the representation of the practical activity, of the practical process of development of men. Empty talk about consciousness ceases, and real knowledge has to take its place.
>
> *Marx & Engels, 1969: pp. 25–26*

If we were to be blunt, we might simply note that Vygotsky did not set out in this way in his treatment of 'verbal thinking'. The divergence is perhaps most evident in two key areas of cultural-historical research: a) the thinking of 'primitive' people, and b) the 'cross-cultural' research in Central Asia which Luria carried out in 1931–1932 (Luria, 1976).

As for the first, we noted Bukharin's uncritical acceptance of the conclusions of Lévy-Brühl's decidedly *un-Marxist* book. While not in complete agreement with Lévy-Brühl, Vygotsky did not object to the approach. And so, when we turn to '[t]hinking in connection with the development of language in primitive society' (Vygotsky & Luria, 1993: p. 108), we discover that the language of 'primitive man' 'turns out to be more meagre in means, cruder, and less developed than the language of a cultural man' (Vygotsky & Luria, 1993: p. 108). More specifically:

> The wealth of vocabulary is directly dependent on the concrete and precise nature of primitive man's language. In the same way that he photographs and reproduces all his experience, he also recalls it, just as precisely. He does not know how to express himself abstractly and conditionally, as the cultural man does.
>
> *Vygotsky & Luria, 1993: p. 110*

The point here is not just that Vygotsky and Luria bought into this perspective (for reasons explored in Jones, in press) but that they did not object to what Marx and Engels called 'speculation', that is an approach to language as a separate and self-contained mental realm independently of the 'real-life process' of language-makers.

As for the second, the glaring divorce of communicational and cognitive activity from the 'real-life process' in this research has attracted critical commentary from scholars from diverse ideological backgrounds (e.g. Cole, 1999, Harris, 2009). For Lamdan and Yasnitsky, for example, the whole research programme 'was ahistorical and non sensitive to the cultural specificity of the local population', due, at least in part, to 'the vulgar Marxist economic determinism in their interpretation of the data' (Lamdan & Yasnitsky, 2016: p. 200). Whatever we might make of the aims and rationale for this project, Luria's execution involved a stark and simplistic decontextualization of communicational practices and, with it, the denigration of 'concrete' classifications, calculations and judgements imbued with the wisdom of experience in contrast with so-called 'abstract' (or 'conceptual') thinking in which objects were categorized by scholastic methods (notably the traditional syllogism) independently of their real-life practical utility or connections.

Reflections and conclusion

If Vygotsky's psychological theory, viewed from a suitable distance, is clearly influenced by Marxian thinking in general terms, his readings of Marx in connection with theoretical specifics are questionable at best or, at worst, implausible. This does not mean that Marx was 'right' against Vygotsky but shows how Marx's original vision was read and refracted through a hotchpotch 'Marxist' optic which had grown up in the pre-revolutionary years to become uncritically absorbed in the thinking and public discourse of influential Bolshevik leaders. The *philosophical* hallmarks of 'Soviet Marxism' – as distinct from the views of Marx – were a) a grinding social determinism, with the biological human specimen subject to influence by the social environment, and b) an epistemology grounded in a naturalistic sensualism upon which a 'reflection' or 'representational' view of language (and thinking) was erected. In this way, the intellectual revolution represented by Marx's 'materialist conception of history' was wound back towards the socially naïve and mechanistic materialism of the 18th century.

In Vygotsky's case, these two ingredients intersected via an initial extension of Pavlovian reflexology to human sociality and culture in the shape of a theory of symbolic control of 'natural' psychological functions working on reflex lines. Vygotsky did not, therefore, adopt an approach which began from the 'real-life process', i.e. from the study of social activity as such in its intellectual, practical, ethical and communicational complexity. Instead, on the reflexologically inspired assumption that causally-acting *signs* were key to understanding behaviour, Vygotsky sought a psychological *mechanism* responsible for distinctively human thought and action in the shape of the semiological principle of mediation.

The general orientation towards the conceptual and semantic dimensions of language in Vygotsky's later work arguably follow a parallel line of this symbolic control perspective. So, in research on word meaning, the initial 'natural'-'cultural' dichotomy was re-contextualized, in line with a representational view of thinking, as a distinction between the 'concrete' image of particular objects tied to immediate circumstances and the 'abstract' conceptual content of linguistically-enabled thinking.[11] If Vygotsky's views and priorities certainly undergo often radical revision over the course of his career, the basic rationale for cultural-historical psychology remains a commitment to an explanation of human mental capacities in semiotic terms, and, more specifically in terms of symbolic control or regulation. The turn towards meaning and sense in his later work did not, therefore, signify a departure from this agenda. Indeed, the previously developed conceptions of word meaning and internalization remained presuppositions. Similarly, while Vygotsky's introduction of the concept of 'perezhivanie' (van der Veer, 2001) challenged mechanistic conceptions of the relationship between acting subject and social 'environment', that perspective, and its implications for Vygotsky's project as a whole, remained, for obvious reasons, substantially undeveloped.

This rather stark assessment of Vygotsky's relation to Marx, however, clearly ignores the complexities of the historical context, in particular the significance of the Russian Revolution itself, and, more to the point, the hugely positive, and radical, intellectual contribution that Vygotsky made in that context to our understanding of the human condition, however we might evaluate his reading of Marx. The alignment between Vygotsky's work and the progressive power of October is evident, for example, in the way he concretized his general guiding principles – the limitlessness of human potential, the historical transformability of social practice, the mutability of human nature – in methods and concepts, including 'mediation', which informed and served the practical tasks of special needs education and rehabilitation. Through mediation *as a practice*, Vygotsky demonstrated that human psychological capacities were culturally *constructed* since they could be *reconstructed* by 'roundabout means', through the active incorporation of 'cultural' aids into the relevant activity (of reading, walking, etc.). Vygotsky thereby proved that the poverty and partiality of cultural and social history had blinded us to the different routes that individuals could take into the life of the mind, a partiality based on fetishizing signs in particular sensory modes (spoken language versus sign language) or by confusing the constraints on individual development imposed by the social environment with inborn limits to intellectual potential. Even the fundamental distinction Vygotsky drew between 'natural' and 'cultural', one he would later regret but could not shake off, was, in context, a way of foregrounding the transformative role of the social and cultural spheres over against the supposedly 'natural' foundation, taking the latter as a precondition for human development rather than as pre-determining its course and limits. If the interpretative stick was bent too far in the direction of materialist mechanism, via the then insurgent reflexologically informed discourse, it was being bent away from the influence of the 'idealistic' psychology of pre-revolutionary times.

To approach Vygotsky in this way, therefore, is to approach the Russian Revolution itself from a particular angle – to feel its daring and iconoclasm, its blinding insights, its colossal achievements, its promise and, at the same time, its haste, its contradictions, its difficulties, mistakes and failures. We should be able to learn from both. I hope the provocative discussion of Vygotsky's reading of Marx which I have offered here will meet with robust response and challenge and that, in such a debate, we may understand more clearly what we ourselves have invested in Vygotsky's 'Marxism' and what that investment implies for present and future endeavours, both theoretical and practical.

Notes

1 This chapter builds on my presentation, 'Vygotsky's legacy in prospect: to build on or build around?', to the symposium 'Continuities and disruptions in renegotiating Vygotsky's legacy: a four-cornered debate' at the International Society for Cultural and Activity Research (ISCAR) World Congress in Quebec, Canada, August–September 2017. I would like to thank the symposium audience for their responses and my fellow and sister presenters, Ines Langemeyer, Fernando González Rey and Anna Stetsenko, for valuable criticisms.

2 A similar question hangs over 'Activity Theory', though I think it is clear how this tradition departs from Marx, for better or for worse (Jones, 2009b; Jones 2011b; Jones & Collins, 2016).

3 In his response to Pavlov's 1924 diatribe against the Bolsheviks, Bukharin argued that 'whether Pavlov realized it or not, his [reflex] doctrine was "a weapon from the iron arsenal of materialism"' (Joravsky, 1989: p. 213).

4 As Buhkarin explains, Lévy-Brühl considered 'the mode of thought of savages' as 'pre-logical' (Bukharin, 1926: p. 204): 'In savage thought, details and specific things are often not distinguished from the general or even the whole; one thing is confused with another'.

5 This problem is recognized but skated over in Ratner (2017). Arguing for the continuity of Marxist thinking in Vygotsky's psychological work, Ratner claims that 'Vygotsky drew upon historical materialism as his guiding social theory' (Ratner, 2017: p. 7). At the same time, he appears to draw a pointed contrast between Vygotsky and Marx with respect to their approach to language. Vygotsky, Ratner argues, 'emphasized language *as the basis of thought*' (my emphasis) while 'Marx and Engels cautioned that language is grounded in social life and reflects its features; it is not an independent realm' (Ratner, 2017: p. 27). Consequently: 'Advancing Vygotsky's Marxism must utilize Marx and Engels' criticism of philosophical idealism to develop a historical-materialist conception of language as the basis of psychology' (Ratner, 2017: p. 28). Ratner appears to imply here that Vygotsky does not have 'a historical-materialist conception of language' at the basis of his psychology. Given the fundamental role of language in Vygotsky, it is hard then to see the continuity Ratner claims.

6 Why that is the case is an interesting question. The short answer – as peculiar as it may sound – is that labour activity was not considered a matter of particular psychological significance for Vygotsky's developing project, given the then current reflexological assumptions about practical activity. As Vygotsky states: 'Every type of labor is formed out of particular combinations of reactions which are inherent to it … It is for this reason an extraordinarily simple matter to decompose every form of occupational labor into several primitive constituent elements, i.e., to reduce all of labor activity to a series of known types of reactions and to combinations of these reactions' (Vygotsky, 1997c: p. 307).

7 As Steila (1991: 108) argues, 18th century 'sensualism' had really come to fruition in the physiological materialism of Moleschott and Vogt and was 'turned' into 'a real experimental science' in Russia: 'Russian revolutionary-democrats and nihilists found therein solid ground for their own theories'.

8 For a semiological approach (an 'activity semiotic') which rejects the 'internalization' principle in toto see Jones (2011a) and Jones (2009a).

9 The very title of the book announces a telling absence, namely *adult* human psychology (and the productive social activities of the adult community). The reasons for this peculiar absence, and for Vygotsky's psychology being essentially a psychology of *child* development, are again rooted in reflexological assumptions (Vygotsky, 1997c).

10 Implicit in this discussion is the rationale set out originally in Vygotsky (1997c) for approaching human psychology as a theory of *child development*, rather than, say, an approach to social activity *per se*.
11 For an opposing, and much more positive view of Vygotsky's approach to meaning and concepts see the interesting discussion in Derry (2013).

References

Brushlinsky, A. V. (1968). *Kul'turno-istoricheskaia teoriia myshleniia* [The Cultural-Historical Theory of Thinking]. Moscow: Vysha Shkola.

Brushlinsky, A. V. & Polikarpov, V. A. (1990). *Myshlenie i Obshchenie* [Thinking and Communicating]. Minsk: Universitetskoe.

Bukharin, N. (1926). *Historical Materialism: a System of Sociology*. London: Allen & Unwin.

Cole, M. (1999). 'Cross-cultural research in the sociohistorical tradition', in P. Lloyd & C. Fernyhough (Eds.). *Lev Vygotsky: Critical Assessments*. London: Routledge.

Derry, J. (2013). *Vygotsky: Philosophy and Education*. Malden, MA: Wiley Blackwell.

Harris, R. (2009). *Rationality and the Literate Mind*. New York: Routledge.

Jones, P. E. (2007). 'Language as problem and problematic in the cultural-historical and activity theory tradition', in R. Alanen and S. Pöyhönen (Eds.). *Language in Action: Vygotsky and Leontievan Legacy Today* (pp. 57–78). Newcastle: Cambridge Scholars Publishing.

Jones, P. E. (2009a). 'From "external speech" to "inner speech" in Vygotsky: a critical appraisal and fresh perspectives'. *Language and Communication*, 29(2): pp. 166–181.

Jones, P. E. (2009b). 'Breaking away from Capital? Theorising activity in the shadow of Marx'. *Outlines: Critical Practice*, 1: pp. 45–58.

Jones, P. E. (2011a). 'Signs of activity: integrating language and practical action', *Language Sciences* 33(1): pp. 11–19.

Jones, P. E. (2011b). 'Activity, Activity Theory and the Marxian Legacy', in Jones (Ed.). *Marxism and Education: Renewing the Dialogue. Pedagogy and Culture* (pp. 193–214). New York: Palgrave Macmillan.

Jones, P. E. (2016). 'Language and social determinism in the Vygotskian tradition: A response to Ratner (2015)', *Language and Sociocultural Theory*, 3(1): pp. 3–10.

Jones, P. E. (2017a). 'Language – The transparent tool: Reflections on reflexivity and instrumentality'. *Language Sciences*, 61, pp. 5–16.

Jones, P. E. (2017b). 'Language and Freedom Vol. 1: the Abstract and the Concrete', in A. Pablé (Ed.). *Critical Humanist Perspectives: The integrational turn in philosophy of language and communication*. Abingdon: Routledge.

Jones, P. E. (forthcoming). 'Vygotsky, signs and language: critical observations', to appear in A. T. Neto (Ed.). *Vygotsky – Key Concepts*.

Jones, P. E. (in preparation). *Language and human potential in Vygotsky's Cultural-Historical Psychology*. New York: Cambridge University Press.

Jones, P. and Collins, C. (2016). "Activity Theory" meets austerity – or does it? The challenge of relevance in a world of violent contradiction and crisis. *Theory and Struggle*, 117, pp. 93–99.

Joravsky, D. (1989). *Russian Psychology. A Critical Analysis*. Oxford: Basil Blackwell.

Kozulin, A. (1984). *Psychology in Utopia. Toward a Social History of Soviet Psychology*. Cambridge, MA: MIT Press.

Lamdan, E. & Yasnitsky, A. (2016). 'Did Uzbeks have illusions? The Luria-Koffka controversy of 1932', in A. Yasnitsky & R. van der Veer (Eds.). *Revisionist Revolution in Vygotsky Studies* (pp. 175–200). London: Routledge.

Luria, A. R. (1976). *Cognitive Development: its Cultural and Social Foundations.* Cambridge, MA: Harvard University Press.

Marx, K. (1973). *Grundrisse.* Harmondsworth: Penguin.

Marx, K. (1976). *Capital.* Vol. 1. Harmondsworth: Penguin.

Marx, K. (1981). *Capital.* Vol. 3. New York: Vintage.

Marx, K. & Engels, F. (1969). *Selected Works in Three Volumes.* Vol. 1. Moscow: Progress.

Marx, K. & Engels, F. (1970). *Selected Works in Three Volumes.* Vol. 3. Moscow: Progress.

Newman, F. & Holzman, L. (1993). *Lev Vygotsky: Revolutionary Scientist.* London: Routledge.

Ollman, B. (1976). *Alienation. Marx's Conception of Man in Capitalist Society.* 2nd edn. Cambridge: Cambridge University Press.

Packer, M. (2008). 'Is Vygotsky Relevant? Vygotsky's Marxist Psychology'. *Mind, Culture, and Activity,* 15(1): pp. 8–31.

Ratner, C. (2016). 'Culture-centric versus person-centered cultural psychology and political philosophy'. *Language and Sociocultural Theory,* 2(1): pp. 51–83.

Ratner, C. (2017). 'Marxist psychology, Vygotsky's cultural psychology, and psychoanalysis: the double helix of science and politics', in Ratner, C. & Silva, D. N. H. (Eds.). *Vygotsky and Marx. Toward a Marxist Psychology.* London: Routledge.

Steila, D. (1991). *Genesis and Development of Plekhanov's Theory of Knowledge: A Marxist between Anthropological Materialism and Physiology.* Kluwer Academic Publishers: Dordrecht.

Stetsenko, A. P. (2016). *The transformative mind. Expanding Vygotsky's approach to development and education.* Cambridge: Cambridge University Press.

van der Veer, R. (2001). 'The idea of units of analysis: Vygotsky's contribution', in S. Chaiklin (Ed.). *The Theory and Practice of Cultural-Historical Psychology.* Aarhus: Aarhus University Press.

van der Veer, R. & Valsiner, J. (1988). 'Lev Vygotsky and Pierre Janet. On the origin of the concept of sociogenesis'. *Developmental Review,* 8, pp. 52–65.

van der Veer, R. & Valsiner, J. (1991). *Understanding Vygotsky. A Quest for Synthesis.* Oxford: Blackwell.

Veresov, N. (1999). *Undiscovered Vygotsky. Etudes on the Pre-history of Cultural-Historical Psychology.* Frankfurt: Peter Lang.

Vygotsky, L. S. (1981). 'The instrumental method in psychology', in J. V. Wertsch (Ed.). *The Concept of Activity in Soviet Psychology.* New York: Sharpe.

Vygotsky, L. S. (1986). *Thought and Language.* A. Kozulin (Ed.). Cambridge, MA: MIT Press

Vygotsky, L. S. (1987). *The Collected Works of L. S. Vygotsky.* Vol. 1. New York: Plenum.

Vygotsky, L. S. (1997a). *The Collected Works of L. S. Vygotsky.* Vol. 3. New York: Plenum.

Vygotsky, L. S. (1997b). *The Collected Works of L. S. Vygotsky.* Vol. 4. New York: Plenum.

Vygotsky, L. S. (1997c). *Educational Psychology.* Boca Raton, FL: St. Lucie Press.

Vygotsky, L. S. & Luria, A. R. (1993). *Studies on the History of Behavior: Ape, Primitive, and Child.* Hillsdale, NJ: Lawrence Erlbaum.

Wertsch, J. V. (1985). *Vygotsky and the social formation of mind.* Cambridge, MA: Harvard University Press.

Yaroshevsky, M. G. (1985). *The History of Psychology.* 3rd edn. Moscow: Mysl' (in Russian).

Yasnitsky, A. & van der Veer, R. (Eds.). (2016) *Revisionist Revolution in Vygotsky Studies.* London: Routledge.

3

RETHINKING VYGOTSKY

A Critical reading of the semiotics in Vygotsky's cultural-historical theory

Ruihan Zhang

This paper is part of a larger project which was originally inspired by the surge of intellectual interest, starting from the late 1980s and early 1990s in western academia, in the former Soviet psychologist Lev S. Vygotsky's cultural-historical theory of psychology. Vygotsky's approach to the development of the psychological functions of man places much emphasis on the transformative roles played by social and cultural tools such as language, and thus distinguishes itself from other popular methodologies, such as behaviorism and Chomskyan generative grammar, which study human thinking and its relationships with language by cutting off the connections between the inner mental world and the external physical world. Therefore, Vygotsky's theory is widely believed to be an alternative to both the behaviorist and the mentalist approach to the problem of the mind and that of language. A group of linguists working within the field of second language acquisition even claimed that Vygotsky's theory provides the solution that can finally settle the long-standing social-cognitive debate in the study of language teaching and learning.

Despite Vygotsky's unquestionable dedication to the science of psychology, my study of Vygotsky's cultural-historical theory has led me to doubt the almost unanimous consensus on the theoretical contributions that Vygotsky is believed to have made to contemporary scholarship, especially with regard to language studies. My research on the semiotics of Vygotsky's cultural-historical theory shows that Vygotsky's theorization of the development of the human mind as a process of increasing abstraction, and language as a system of abstract meanings independent of concrete human experiences is fundamentally problematic. This is because such theorization not only reifies language into an inhuman system of fixed codes that denies the creativity and agency of individuals engaged in communicative activities, but also takes away both the linguistic rights and responsibilities of the individuals. Furthermore, Vygotsky's psychology, especially his linguistic view, is deeply rooted in a blind belief in naïve realism and rationalism that favor intellect over illiteracy, scientific knowledge over everyday experiences, logic over common sense, etc. In the end, it is not just our history of mental development and our knowledge of the world that have been classified and ranked according to their degree of sophistication, but also us as human beings.

In order to understand the hidden semiotic construct of Vygotsky's cultural-historical theory, this paper chooses a peculiar perspective to place Vygotsky's semiotics against that of Alfred Korzybski, the founding father of general semantics, who shares much of his views on language meaning and its impact on the human mind with Vygotsky. There is no recorded evidence showing that Vygotsky and Korzybski have had any contact with each other. However, Korzybski's theorization of language "meaning" does, as we will see in the following discussion, shed new light on understanding the semiotics of Vygotsky's cultural-historical theory. More importantly, reading Vygotsky together with his contemporaries against the bigger picture of the history of ideas also helps us develop a wider perspective on, and thus a deeper understanding of, whether Vygotsky's cultural-historical theory could really carry us as far as many Vygotskyans believe it could, if it is founded on a rather shaky linguistic basis in the first place?

By bringing these fundamental problems in Vygotsky's psychology to light, I hope to initiate a critical reading and rethinking of not just Vygotsky's psychology, but also its appropriations in contemporary sciences, such as linguistics, communication studies, and educational studies. This paper could be the beginning of a new *perspective* to the studies of human communication and psychology by adopting a different view of language, a view I believe is, first and foremost, liberal.

Vygotskian semiotics and general semantics

It is well known that Vygotsky believes that the semiotic operations of an individual are a process that involves both the internalization of signs and the externalization of psychological workings back into signs again. That is to say, the influence that sign operations have on ontogenetic development of the child moves from the interpsychological level to the intrapsycohlogical level and back onto the interpsycohlogical level again. It is precisely the constant practice of this process that gives rise to the leap in the child's mental development from the elementary or primitive level to the more advanced level.

Vygotsky, being a man of his times, was certainly not the first one to be so fascinated with evolutionism with a semiotic/linguistic twist on thought development in man. I have found some interesting parallels between Vygotsky's conceptualization of the thought-language-behavior relationship and that of a contemporary of his: the founder of general semantics, Alfred Korzybski, who wrote the famous book *Science and Sanity: An Introduction to Non-Aristotelian Systems and General Semantics* around the same time as Vygotsky drafted his *Thought and Language* (i.e. the early 1930s). Perhaps one could say that Korzybski was as interested in psychology, physiology and language as Vygotsky was. Korzybski defines language "as names either for unspeakable entities on the objective level, be it things or feelings, or as *names for relations*", which reminds us of how Vygotsky distinguishes between everyday concepts that are object-related and real concepts that are developed on the basis of everyday concepts or concept-relations. Korzybski gives an example of an experiment that he used to conduct time and again to prove the necessity of such a division within language itself. The experiment is basically about asking the meaning of every word a person says, and then continuing to do so by asking the meanings of words used in definitions this person has already given. Korzybski observes that not long after this process starts, the person being questioned will always end up speaking in circles, i.e. using what needs to be explained to explain the very thing itself. Korzybski thinks that when this result starts to appear, it means that this person has reached the level of *undefined terms*, [1] which is typically accompanied by affective pressure (red face, sweating palms, etc.) and the person giving up by saying: "I know what it means, but I just can't explain" (Korzybski, 1948: p. 21). This represents what Korzybski calls "affective first-order effects," which are interwoven with desires, intentions, feelings, and other affective states, and thus have an objective character (ibid.). Vygotsky would find this utterly agreeable, since he has also demonstrated that it is extremely difficult for young children to define an everyday concept such as "brother," without falling back on some concrete examples of their everyday life experience. As Vygotsky also says, children all know perfectly well everyday concepts like "brother", but they lack the knowledge (or conscious awareness) of the *relations* between these everyday concepts and other concepts (but *not* the relations between these everyday concepts and the concrete *things* they designate), which, according to Vygotsky, is precisely what makes the mental act of defining possible. This similarity between Vygotsky and Korzybski's semiotics is not some superficial coincidence, but has profound common roots in their theorizing of meaning and its relation to thinking. Based on Vygotsky's theorization of functional stratification of language in ontogenesis, there are four stages of concept formation and mental development: syncretism, complexive thinking, conceptual thinking and scientific concepts with the first three stages being biological and the fourth cultural-historical in nature. The biological evolutionary thinking consisting of the primitive forms of syncretic and complexive mental operations will start to appear less frequently in adolescents as they begin to think more frequently in true concepts. The end of stage three in the child's development signifies the completion of a long process of psychological development that moves gradually away from concrete, experiential thinking to more generalized, abstracted forms of thinking, although Vygotsky also notes that all the different phases of psychological development do not necessarily have very clear-cut boundaries with each other, and most of them co-exist with one another like the strata representing different geological epochs coexist in the earth's crust. Whereas the first three stages of psychological development in the child are "natural" or "genetic", the fourth stage of development is fundamentally rooted in the social and cultural environment of the child, because it is realized through the mediation of various external "cultural tools" (such as speech) instead of direct influence that the external environment has on the child and his thinking. In other words, when the child reaches the fourth stage of development, the usual stimulus-response mechanism is interrupted by an externally introduced mediation tool that the child has learned to master, and through such an interruption the child can voluntarily and consciously direct the various stimulation that the environment has on himself. As for the questions of how and why the child comes to take control over the cultural tools (such as speech) at the fourth stage of development, but not in the previous three stages, the answers have a lot to do with the emergence of *conscious awareness* [2] in the child's psychology and also with the general question concerning the relationships between development and educational instruction.

Korzybski does not take a developmental or ontogenetic view in the strict sense of the term, but he "shares" with Vygotsky the idea that meaning is neither homogeneous nor naturally stable in relation to psychological functioning. He says:

> 'Meaning' must be considered as a multiordinal term, as it applies to all levels of abstractions, and so has no general content. We can only speak legitimately of 'meanings' in the plural. Perhaps, we can speak of the meanings of meanings, although I suspect that the latter would represent the un-speakable first order effect, the affective, personal raw material, out of which our ordinary meanings are built.
>
> *Korzybski, 1948: p. 22*

The unspeakable first-order meanings are also called elementalistic meanings by Korzybski, and they are the form of meaning that has an objective character, like what Vygotsky calls the "object-relatedness" of meaning. By contrast, the "meanings of meanings" are also known as non-elementalistic meanings in Korzybski's work, and are very close to what Vygotsky has in mind as the "real concepts" or the "concepts of concepts." For Vygotsky, the same generality of concepts can appear at different levels of structural generalization or abstraction, therefore, meanings, as represented in these inter-conceptual relationships, have different degrees of concreteness and abstractness, depending on which stage of concept development they are in. The differences between everyday concepts and real concepts and how the former are transformed into the latter are recapitulated by Korzybski in his analysis of the relationships between language, thought and behavior, from a point of view that he calls "semantic reaction." It is described as:

> the psycho-logical[3] reaction of a given individual to words and language and other symbols and events in connection with their meanings, and the psychological reactions, which become meanings and relational configurations the moment the given individual begins to analyse them or somebody else does that for him.
>
> *Korzybski, 1948: p. 24*

This point of view might also be used to describe Vygotsky's approach to concept development without causing any serious objection, considering the fact that semantics plays a major role in Vygotsky's cultural-historical theory. For both of them, meaning assumes different functional roles in stimulating different reactions or responses from an individual at different levels or stages of psychophysiological operations, and as we can see both of their theorizations of language-thought relationships are rooted in the good old stimulus-response model. Korzybski defines the term "semantic reaction" to include both the meaning-triggered reflexes and the responses, with the latter being more long-lasting. He says:

> If, for instance, a statement or any event evokes some individual's attention, or one train of associations in preference to another, or envy, or anger, or fear, or prejudice, we would have to speak of all such responses on psycho-logical levels as s.r [i.e. semantic reaction]. A stimulus was present, and a response followed; so that, by definition, we should speak of a reaction. As the active factor in the stimulus was the individual meanings to the given person, and his response had meanings to him as a first order effect, the reaction must be called a semantic reaction.
>
> *Korzybski, 1948: p. 25*

Of course, like Vygotsky, Korzybski must think that his concept of semantic reaction differs fundamentally from Pavlov's oversimplified S-R model, because semantic reaction is "a psycho-logical response to a stimulus *in connection with meanings*" (ibid. Italics added). Here, signs are introduced to "interrupt" the normal psychological reflex and thus transform the process into the much more complex "psycho-logical" process that involves conscious analysis and logical reasoning on the individual's part. Like Vygotsky, who argues that thinking in pure meaning (i.e. in real concepts) is the highest form of rational human thinking, Korzybski also believes that semantic reactions are what leads to true sanity (Korzybski, 1948: p. 35). If we compare how and why Vygotsky thinks that rationality is achieved in an individual's development, and how Korzybski explicates the characteristics of sanity in man, we would find that by conceptualizing meaning and thought in such a hierarchical manner, it is no surprise that they have reached similar conclusions. Vygotsky rejects Piaget's theory that the lack of conscious awareness in children is due to the residue of egocentrism in their thinking, and argues that children's inability to think in concepts is due to the lack of a *system* in their thinking. The *system* of thinking only emerges after a long process of cultural development assisted by external auxiliary signs, which means that the significance of the process of enculturation for the child must necessitate the child's social-cultural environment of education itself. Interestingly enough, the following quote from Korzybski's *Science and Sanity* presents a very similar argument to that of Vygotsky, although the latter might not have taken the same degree of interest in mathematics and other sciences when it comes to the significance of developing a "structure" in thought. Korzybski says:

In fact, without a structural formulation and a Ā [i.e. non-Aristotelian] revision based on the study of science and mathematics, it is impossible to discover, to control, or to educate these s.r [i.e. semantic reactions]. For this reason it was necessary to analyse the semantic factors in connection with brief and elementary considerations taken from modern science. ... In fact, because the objective levels are not words, the only possible aim of science is to discover *structure*, which, when formulated, is *always simple* and easily understood by everyone, with the exception, of course, of very pathological individuals. We have already seen that structures to be considered as a configuration of relations, and that relations appear as the essential factors in meanings, and so of s.r. The present enquiry, because structural, reveals vital factors of s.r. The consequences are extremely simple, yet very important. We see that by a simple *structural re-education* of the s.r, which in the great mass of people are on the level of copying animals in their nervous reactions, we powerfully affect the s.r, and so are able to impart very simply, to all, in the most elementary education of the s.r of the child, *cultural* results at present sometimes acquired unconsciously and painfully in university education.

Korzybski, 1948: p. 29

Vygotsky wrote in *Ape, primitive man, and child: essays in the history of behavior* that the first stage of a child's mental development is primitive in nature. It is not difficult to detect traces of child primitivism in Korzybski's conceptualizing of children's mentality from the above quote. The structure of thinking, for Korzybski, can be discovered through studying the semantic reactions of individuals, because these reactions are stimulated in a systematic way and by what is usually known as "scientific knowledge." This idea is also endorsed by Vygotsky in his argumentation for the significance of education in elevating the human mind onto the higher level of abstract and conceptual thinking: first, the rational man, and ultimately, (as Vygotsky aptly puts it) the super-man. For both Vygotsky and Korzybski, the goal is always for people to assert power and control over nature, society, and their behavior and speech. This, for Vygotsky, is the point where human beings truly acquire their freedom, by being able to master, instead of just using, both natural and cultural tools (such as language) to consciously control and organize their behavior, people Man become truly rational beings and thus differ themselves from even the most intelligent of the animals. Korzybski thinks that the goal is to gain full understanding of all the most humanly important and interesting terms of our language, because most of the tragedies that happen to our life are caused by such an ignorance of, or inability to master, those multiordinal terms (Korzybski, 1948: p. 74). Multiordinal terms are those that "if they can be applied to a statement they can also be applied to a statement about the first statement, and so, ultimately, to all statements, no matter what their order of abstraction is" (Korzybski, 1948: p. 14). These terms thus have different meanings at different levels of abstraction order, and should be understood differently as the situation varies. On the contrary, the confusion of such different orders of abstraction leads to "insanity" of all forms (Korzybski, 1948: p. 74). Korzybski does not restrain himself from lamenting over how our society produces morons and "insane" people, when he thinks it should be producing "geniuses" (Korzybski, 1948: p. 75). It then should be no surprise to find Korzybski's fascination with developing a theory of sanity, which can unveil all the mystery of the human mind and thus help create a better world for mankind to live in, which is, of course, a world composed of "geniuses."

While it is interesting to see how much Korzybski's rhetoric of "geniuses" and Vygotsky's rhetoric of "super-men" echo each other, it would be a mistake to ignore the differences in their respective views. In a sense, Korzybski could be regarded as the "pessimist," who bears the deepest doubt for the semantic abstractions in language. The nervous system of man is so ready to take in whatever stimuli coming from their semantic environment that they oftentimes become confused between reality and symbolism, due to little or improper evaluation. Samuel Hayakawa, one of the close followers of Korzybski claims that for the occurrence of such confusions, the society is to blame: "most societies systematically encourage, concerning certain topics, the habitual confusion of symbols with things symbolized" (Hayakawa, 1974: p. 26). According to Christopher Hutton, the distrust of abstractions and metaphors found in the work of "therapeutic semanticists"[4] such as Korzybski and Hayakawa, leads to the belief that "language must constantly be checked against reality" (Hutton, 1995: p. 87). The flip side of Korzybski's distrust of abstractions and metaphors is the fear of losing grip on the sensual experiences – things we can know for sure. On the other hand, Vygotsky could be seen as the "positivist," who believes that language is a true and reliable reflection of not just the physical world but also the inner world of man. It is not necessarily a one-on-one matching reflection between language and the two worlds. Language is always an abstraction, a generalization, of either the thing or the thought itself, and this idea seems so ubiquitous, in both the academia and the lay world, that the question of "the symbol is not the thing it stands for" does not even come into the picture of discussion. For Vygotsky, what makes the communication circuit of world-language-thought possible is the shared meaning, or the scientific concept. Vygotsky thinks that generalizing reality into a concept may appear to be a process of impoverishment of meaning, when the truth is just the opposite; the process of generalization through speech is only an impoverishment for the *form* of the expression, but a significant enrichment in terms of meaning, because different meanings are integrated into a complex meaning, represented in one single concept.

An excellent example of this communication circuit is the artist Joseph Kosuth's famous "One and Three Chairs," where a wooden chair is placed on the floor against the wall, with a shadow of the chair cast on it; right next to the wooden chair hangs a black-and-white photo of the very same chair in exactly the same size as the real object; on the other side of the wooden chair hangs a board with the definition of the word "chair" extracted from the Oxford English Dictionary. They could be three different chairs, since they have three different forms of representation, yet they are also at the same time the same chair; that is, they all represent the intangible concept "chair." Roy Harris thinks that Kosuth's work ingeniously represents all three kinds of signs; i.e. signs based on resemblance (the real wooden chair and the picture of it in real proportion on the wall), on convention (the dictionary definition of the word "chair") and on concomitance (the shadow of the chair on the wall behind the chair) (Harris, 1996: p. 108). Vygotsky would say that the invisible concept of "chair" only appears after a long period of development for every individual. The process must begin with the child gradually coming to familiarize himself with, and thus understand, each genre representation of the "chair", and then to establish connections between each genre through their similarities and differences, until finally the true concept of "chair" emerges as a result of continuous mental operations of abstraction and generalization in this process. Therefore, for Vygotsky, it is out of question whether the abstracted concept matches with the reality or not, because we human beings are safe by living our lives in the world of abstracted semantic world that exists above the sensual experiences coming directly from the real world, because sensual experiences can vary from individual to individual, yet this condition of human existence necessitates the act of abstracting the most stable, essential and common aspects of human experiences into a system that all human beings share.

Language, science, native realism and rationalism

As we can see, Korzybski and Vygotsky have quite opposite views regarding the implications that the linguistic representation of reality has on human lives. Hutton observes that the modern linguistics as a whole is largely a history of "therapeutic polemic" founded on "naïve realism" (Hutton, 1995: p. 97; p. 88). Although the imminence of distorted reality always looms large, which ultimately jeopardizes rational actions of man, language must accurately reflect reality. However, regardless of whether Vygotsky might disagree with these therapeutic semanticists, Vygotsky's cultural-historical theory is also founded on nothing but the very same naïve realism, except that, for Vygotsky, there already exists a reliable system of shared meaning that not only makes mutual understanding between individuals possible but also provides a reliable conduit between the physical world and the mental world. The shared system of meaning is the cultural product of a society and is passed on from generation to generation. For Vygotsky, this is no simple impartation of knowledge from one generation to the next; it is such a culturally and psychologically significant process that its success marks the very triumph of intelligence over instincts, rationalism over primitivism, and civilization over barbarianism. It is a process of enculturation of the mind, a process whose key lies in a series of functional transformations to the level of fully rational thinking, through the assistance of auxiliary signs such as language. The underlying assumption has already been formulated by Franz Boas around two decades earlier than Vygotsky started to draft his book *Ape, primitive man, and child: essays in the history of behavior*.

[The] important change from primitive culture to civilization seems to consist in a gradual elimination of … emotional, socially determined associations of sense-impressions and of activities, for which intellectual associations are gradually substituted.

Boas, 1965: p. 225

However, for Vygotsky intellect or rational thinking does not come out of the blue, and simply replace sense-impressions to become the dominant form of mental operation. All higher forms of thinking evolve on the basis of lower forms; and since this evolvement is elicited by the stimuli coming from the social-cultural milieu, it is first and foremost a process of adaptation to the environment. Language, being an objective and autonomous sign system that reflects reality, has the ideal internal structure that can mold and shape the child's mind into a similar structure, so that a truthful and rational understanding of reality can be obtained by the time the child becomes an adolescent. In a sense, the auxiliary sign system plays a much more significant role than just assisting the child's communication with other people; nor is it merely a tool that the child uses to achieve higher forms of thinking, as Vygotsky and his followers always say. The sign system itself is at the same time a yardstick, a universal standard in its own right, which defines what the mind comes to be like, or more precisely, what a *rational* mind should turn out to be eventually, because it is the sign system (i.e. language) that structures the mind. Whereas Vygotsky never seems to question what bothers the therapeutic semanticists so much – that language might not be a reliable and objective representation of reality – the therapeutic semanticists are skeptical about the reliability of language in describing the world as it is, they do have an ideal of what they think the human-world relationship *should be* like:

Citizens of a modern society *need* … more than that ordinary "common sense" which was defined by Stuart Chase as that which tells you that the world is flat. They *need to be* systematically aware of the powers and limitations of symbols, especially words, if they are to guard against being driven into complete bewilderment by the complexity of their semantic environment.

Hayakawa, 1974: p. 27, Italics added

For Vygotsky, citizens of a modern society, at least the majority of them, are already equipped with more than just "common sense"; once they have completed their ontogenetic development, they become equipped with conscious awareness so that they are not only capable of understanding symbols *per se*, but also "the powers and limitations of symbols, especially words." But there is more to that. At the point where the individual acquires true conscious awareness and thus starts to think in pure meaning, he no longer acts only in accordance to the stimulation he receives from outside, but actively uses auxiliary cultural tools (such as language) to control his behavior, so as to influence the environment. This, according to Vygotsky, marks the beginning of real human creativity as well as what he calls "free action." Therefore, in a cultural-historical sense, freedom is defined as an individual having conscious control over his/her own behavior, and actively directing it to influence the environment. Freedom is not to be understood as the destruction of or the escape from control; on the contrary, it is to subject all the conscious, semi-conscious and even unconscious processes in man's organisms to the dominance of reason. All these are, according to Vygotsky, within the possibility of development: "The human species ... becomes the subject of the most complex methods of artificial selection and psychological conditioning at man's very own hands" (Vygotsky, 1997a: p. 350). The result to be achieved is a society, where mankind as a whole reaches the fullest of their potentials through organized and rational behavior, an ideal that does resemble, in more ways than the Vygotskians would like to admit, the fictional Walden Two[5] under B. F. Skinner's pen. "'Control' expresses it, I think," as the protagonist and designer of the ideal behaviorist community of Walden Two puts it, "[t]he control of human behavior" through a well-designed behavioral technology (Skinner, 1976: p. 271).

From Vygotsky, to Korzybski, to Boas and now to Skinner, the rhetoric for developing a highly civilized society on the foundation of rationalism (no matter whether it is defined as an intrinsic characteristic of the mind or of the more observable behavior of man) can be found in many forms of narrative in the first greater half of the 20th-century Western intelligentsia. Their obsession with rationality, technology, science, and a hope for a new beginning of society and of humanity is no coincidence, but the result of a certain historical making. In Eric Hobsbawm's book *The Age of Extremes: The Short Twentieth Century 1914–1991*, there is an interesting summary of how some of the greatest Western thinkers of the 20th century understood this century that they had lived through. It is interesting because there is a hidden message that Hobsbawm might have left with intention by picking out the twelve intellectual representatives of the 20th century, among whom are writers, philosophers, anthropologists, musicians, artists, historians and scientists. The message itself is not difficult to come to terms with: while almost all the humanities people recapitulate the 20th century as "the most terrible century in Western history," "the most violent century in human history," "a catastrophe, a disaster," the scientists are characterizing the century as bearing astonishing progress in science and technology, which brings forth a hope for mankind to "always start all over again." (Hobsbawm, 1994: pp. 1–2). It might be argued that the pessimism in the humanities and the rise of hope in the world of sciences are not contradictory to each other, because the latter could be deemed as both an emotional and a logical reaction to all the pain and agony that humanity had suffered during the 20th century. It seems as if the humanities people, at least as represented by the Western intelligentsia, have become disillusioned with the government, the economy, the media, and thus have once again, like their 18th-century forefathers, made the "rational choice" of fetishizing the sciences and technology, which they believe can bring humanity out of its suffering to finally embrace true freedom.

There is something ironic about the kind of rationalism that scientists such as Vygotsky and Skinner worship. Rationalism, when taken to the extremes by its practitioners, turns into precisely what it tries to escape from – irrationality – because it constitutes the blind (and thus in a sense naïve) belief that there are objective approaches to facts, which can be generalized and systemized into an autonomous body of knowledge, independent of concrete sensual impressions and experiences, and that these systems of knowledge later become the guidelines for organized human thinking and behavior. If we recall Vygotsky's theorization of the ontogenetic development of thinking, the process for an individual to become a rational thinking being is precisely such an ideal of subjecting the mind to the guarding social-cultural laws. The paradox that lies within the rationalists' agenda of human engineering is giving credence to a theory of freedom that is nothing more than a euphemism for dogmatized restrictions. What lies underneath such a paradox is the rationalists' deepest fear of chaos, irregularity, and indeed, of things getting out of control. Therefore, for scientists such as Vygotsky and Skinner, as well as those therapeutic semanticists, the chaos and uncontrolled behavior belong to the primitive society that we, as modern men and women, should have long left behind. Citizens of the modern society should arm themselves with the power of science and technology, to rid themselves the tendency of giving their reason and harmony away to the immediacy of any sensual and/or emotional disturbance. Mediation is key: the mediation between thinking and behavior, between the external and the internal world. But if direct influence or engineering of human thinking is impossible (or too inhumane and politically incorrect to ever be considered an option in a civilized society), the only way out would be through the usage of tools. Therefore, freedom of action in cultural-historical theory needs to be understood in a certain way; that is, before the child learns to master the cultural tools, they are captivated by ignorance, animal instincts, and amorphous thinking composed of imagery (i.e. the superficiality of objects and events); but through the application of external tools provided by the social-cultural system, the child gradually becomes liberated from the captivation of primitivism and it is then that the child finally, for the first time in life, becomes intellectualized and consciously aware of his/her own speech and behavior and those of others. To put it in a simple way: *the child, indeed every child, needs to be taught to think*. Then there fits in the significance of education, the concept of the Zone of Proximal Development, scaffolding, etc.

However, if the child needs to be taught to think, then how should we interpret the child's creativity and agency as an independent individual within such a perspective of development? Vygotsky does recognize a certain degree of active agency of human beings as a crucial characteristic that separates man from animals. Vygotsky, following Marx and Engel's basic conceptualization of how labor has changed the developmental course of human species, acknowledges that primitive people enter the kingdom of intellect because they are not only able to use signs, but also to create artificial signs. This is supported by Vygotsky's discussion of primitive people using knots to substitute their natural memory. However, this agency attributed to mankind is restricted to Vygotsky's discussion of the phylogenesis of man as a result of a rather long process of historical development; when it comes to the ontogenetic level, there is not much discussion of individual agency to be found. Vygotsky must discuss the characteristic of active agency in sign creation in the broad sense of the history of human development, because within such a perspective, the social order in question is still in the process of formation. But when it comes to the investigation of the ontogenesis of man, there is less a question of sign creation but more of sign using or sign application, because at this level of discussion, Vygotsky obviously presupposes the completion of the formation of social rules and social order. A good example of this is how Vygotsky assumes the functioning of speech as a well-developed autonomous cultural tool that elicits the individual's mind to escalate the ladder of abstraction.

Vygotsky's presupposition of a complete and self-sustaining system of social order is not an argument that comes out of the blue. Any careful reader of Vygotsky's work should not find it difficult to realize that his cultural-historical theory talks little of the "cultural" or the "social," and he leaves his readers almost no detailed investigation but a few general comments on the relations between social-cultural systems and the formation of concepts in children. As Carl Ratner observes, the omission of the real social systems in which the psychological functions take place is evident in Vygotsky's study of concept formation. Vygotsky claims that there is a new way of using language in adolescence, as compared to young children, but he never gives any analysis of the social basis for this new use of words, and thus he inevitably reduces his social analysis to a semiotic one that "overlooked the real world of social praxis" (Vygotsky, 1997a: p. 103). For a lot of Vygotsky's followers, this is not some theoretical problem or imperfection in Vygotsky's theory, but where they should pick up his ideas to further develop his (or their) theories (Ratner, 2002: p. 11; Daniels, 2008). Yet it might be a good idea for the Vygotskians to ask why Vygotsky does not talk about "the social" in his psychology, which is so indebted to a social-cultural view, before they happily start their own journeys, carrying with them the inheritance of an "unfinished" project from Vygotsky. Rather, they dismissed the necessity of doing so by attributing the lack of theorization of the social aspects in Vygotsky's psychology to his untimely death.[6] Vygotsky could have had the chance to spare more lines on what he meant by "social" and/or "cultural," had he really wished to do so. He did not, because he took them for granted. For Vygotsky, it is simply out of the hands of the psychologist to lay out the various social mechanisms. What more needs to be explained? Most of Vygotsky's empirical studies, aimed at examining how the social and the cultural aspects of a society influence the psychological functioning of an individual, were carried out in experiments in laboratories. The only field work that he ever designed to test his theory is the expedition to Central Asia, but he and Luria considered no social and cultural factors of the peasants being studied and simply went there with the least culture- and context-sensitive methodology imaginable: questioning the peasants with syllogistic questions.

Vygotsky has genuine trust in the advantages of experiments and how they can bring us closer to truth. He praises how the invention of the thermometer has improved our understanding of heat by liberating human cognition from unreliable senses, and how experiments can clarify facts by concentrating on crucial factors and eliminating distracting or uncontrollable elements. Of course, this is true when viewed in a certain sense, but it also speaks a lot about why the real-life cultural relations *per se* do not interest Vygotsky as much as his followers might expect them to. The rationalist would not be willing to lend his science to a methodology that studies social facts in a "butterfly-collecting" fashion. Psychology, according to Vygotsky, must have "a single set of theoretical concepts and explanatory principles" (van der Veer & Valsiner, 1991: p. 143), and, as Vygotsky defines it in *The Historical Meaning of the Crisis in Psychology*, must be a unified science that has its own *Das Kapital* and its own thermometer (Vygotsky, 1997b: pp. 330–331). Then what are the implications of Vygotsky's undertheorizing of social relations and thus taking them as a given? This brings us back to the question of semiotics and individual agency that we mentioned earlier. The best example that demonstrates Vygotsky's readiness to take the social and cultural aspects of human existence as a given is his semiotic views in relation to individual behavior. Language is already a self-sustaining system where meaning is categorized, classified, structuralized into a certain order that favors the abstract over the concrete, the scientific over the lay. This system transforms the thinking operations of the child as the child receives more and more exposure to linguistic interaction with caretakers and/or parents. According to Vygotsky, the child demonstrates increasing agency in his use of language, and his agency peaks during adolescence as he comes to full conscious awareness of the relations between concepts, or in other words, as he becomes the master of his own speech and behavior. However, if we take a close look, the agency in question is an extremely limited concept. As we mentioned earlier, there is no discussion of moment-to-moment sign creation in Vygotsky's theory of how speech affects thinking, and the relation between the individual and the signs is in essence a matter of application. The signs are ready-made so that the child can acquire them as he acquires other skills of communication. It is precisely such a sign-agent relation that makes the functions of signs so important in the formation of rational thinking. To specify the functions of sign operations, their origin, and their interrelations is also to make the structure or system that supports these functions transparent, so the myths that surround the question of human psychology can be resolved. However, in such a framework, the signs are alienated from the individual, inhabiting a separate and autonomous ecology of their own, and the agency that the individual comes to acquire is nothing more than coming to terms with the *a priori* interrelations and the inter-functions between the signs. There is also a paradox in Vygotsky's discussion of agency: if the child's mind is influenced, or re-structured, through internalizing these external relations, what creativity is left to the individual if his conscious awareness is to know how to subject his thought and behavior to certain laws? Isn't such conscious awareness that represents a free mind also under the spell of these invisible yet ubiquitous laws? Aren't the rationalists a bit too eager to trade subjective autonomy of the individual for the sake of "objectivity" granted by some mysterious natural laws?

However, it would be equally naïve to think that freedom is the condition of no control or that creativity is making random rules according to one's own idiosyncratic tastes. It would miss the point to think that our talk of freedom of actions in ontogenetic development here is a choice between either actions subject to natural, objective laws or actions of absolutely no external restraints. At this point, it should be clear enough to see that the problem with Vygotsky's argument of free actions lies in its dependency on a theory of rationalism that it does not need. If one wants to argue for man's obtainment of free actions on the basis of a free mind, it is futile to try to come up with some grand theory that celebrates objectivity and rationality only to hide behind them when such objectivity and rationality need explanations themselves. In order to objectify the study of the mind, the rationalist objectifies the mind by depicting its developmental history into a process of emancipating thinking from sensual constraints and gradually coming to recognize, and thus subordinate itself under, the natural laws of abstraction. The opposite of rationality in Vygotsky's cultural-historical theory is unquestionably the status of enslavement to one's own senses, feelings, and emotions. It is surprising to see such blind fanaticism for rationalism being taken in, equally unquestionably, by Vygotsky's contemporary followers and celebrated as some long-lost "speak of truth," for van der Veer and Valsiner write:

> [Vygotsky's] assertion that we [human beings] should strive for the "intellectualization of all psychological functions" (Vygotsky, 1932i/1982, p. 415) was essentially in line with Spinoza's thinking. … [T]he "capricious" and "fitful" dissipation of energy by "savages" was opposed to the "organized" and "systematic" labor of rational modern man. Rational man acquired dominion over his primitive mental process by making use of various cultural tools.
>
> *van der Veer and Valsiner, 1991: pp. 240–241*

The systemic labor of man, the intellectualization of psychological functions, the passing-on of various cultural tools, the creation of a new human species, and the rest of the magnificent dreams of a "Marxist" scientist unsurprisingly find their ultimate solution in a carefully and scientifically designed program of education. The child must be taught to think, and clearly not in any outlawed manner, but in one that amounts to scientificity. Therefore, it should not be a program that grants everybody the right to be a "qualified" educator and it certainly should not give credence to any method to be applied in the glorious enterprise of enlightening the "pre-intellectual" mind either. For the rationalists, there is always a Grand Canyon between the excellence of *the* scientific method and "the dismal quality of everything else" (Feyerabend, 1987: p. 299). As a result, there arises an irony in the very idea of the rationalists' futuristic dream of universalizing reason and civilization to all mankind through education: the ideal of universal rationality has already pushed a great number of people and cultures to the periphery by classifying modes of thinking and praising some of them (or just one?) while disparaging the rest, before the ideal itself is put to practice through education. The rationalist psychologist's scientific ideal of man in the hope of a universal transformative education is largely a confused one, unconsciously mixed with the ideologies typical of the 1920s- and 1930s-USSR. The revolutionary gurus had to admit the lack of scientific knowledge and intellectual thinking in lower-class workers and peasants, from whose very hands they realized their dream of Bolshevik democracy. Trotsky once addressed a group of educators, saying that man is himself chaotic, so their nature should be changed to create a "new," "improved edition" of man (Joravsky, 1989: p. 205). In response to this educational campaign in the 1920s and 1930s in the USSR, many of the Russian intelligentsia held rather ambivalent opinions towards it (for various reasons, and many of them were thus denigrated as lackeys of capitalism), but there were also quite a number of them, such as Vygotsky, Luria and Leont'ev, who found no serious contradiction in this campaign, either theory-wise or ideology-wise. Another byproduct (or rather, the presupposition?) of such an educational campaign that has also escaped the mind of the rationalist psychologist and educator Vygotsky is the compartmentalization of knowledge, and the abstraction of knowledge into a system of meaning that has been detached from direct experiences of man. However, as Paul Feyerabend sharply and accurately points out that by doing so, "*[t]hey* [i.e. the rationalists] extol the 'rationality' and 'objectivity' of science without realizing that a procedure whose main aim it [sic] is to get rid of all human elements is bound to lead to inhuman actions" (Feyerabend, 1987: p. 299). Vygotsky's resounding argument for the mode of psychological functioning in pure, abstract meaning detached of direct experience seems to belong to a form of naïve realism, and indeed, nothing close to the kind of dialectical materialism that is attributed to Vygotsky by many of his followers today.

This naïve realism, intrinsic in Vygotsky cultural-historical theory, is ever more conspicuous when seen from a linguistic perspective. What is especially interesting is that the objective laws of abstraction that are said to characterize higher forms of thinking come from no other source but a rather simple and crude theory of semantics. Vygotsky distinguishes between sense and meaning: whereas sense is the aggregation of all the psychological reactions, meaning is the most stable part of all (Vygotsky, 1987, p. 277). Such a system of meaning is also independent of the linguistic forms, and this is considered by Vygotsky as the philosophical cornerstone of, and also practical explanation as to, why people are able to learn foreign languages and why language plays such an important role in the development of scientific concepts (or higher forms of psychological function). The development of concepts depends and represents the semantic aspect of speech development, just as the learning of a foreign language relies on the semantic aspect of the native language (Vygotsky, 1987: pp. 179–180). Meaning in the Vygotskian framework of cultural-historical psychology is sorted, trimmed, and wrapped into, as it were, a parcel that can be passed around between individuals. And who does all the sorting, trimming, and wrapping? Certainly not the young child,[7] whose consciousness, especially in the early stages of its development, is still residing in complete darkness. For Vygotsky, there is little doubt that the laws of abstraction are the

natural, historical, and thus objective result of human development as a social species. What goes wrong in Vygotsky's theorization of psychological development is
his failing to understand that the fact that we human beings *can* abstract and gen-
eralize our experiences and represent part of that generalized experiences in the
form of language does not presuppose that there *is* a body of abstract laws that
make possible such psychological, or mental, or cognitive processes, or that language is some tool introduced from outside to organize an individual's experiences.
Let me just say that this is not one of those good old distinctions between theoretical *prescription* and scientific *description* that orthodox methodologists are keen to
play against their critics. Nor am I confounding what Herber Feigl calls the context
of discovery with the context of justification, which, according to Feyerabend, is just a
new twist of the old "prescription-description" tale (Feyerabend, 2010: pp. 150–152).
This is because the natural, objective laws (if there are any), or the generalizations that
we usually call knowledge, are not some carefully wrapped-up parcels we can store
away in our mind, ready for use when the time and situation seem appropriate.
Similarly, signs do not automatically stand in lines next to one another to form a
fixed abstract "system" that exists independently of people's experiences (past or
present, linguistic or non-linguistic), or the specific context where such experiences arise. Vygotsky's psychology is built upon, and thus deeply indebted to, a
modern "language myth" that postulates the legitimacy of three abstractions:

> (i) it abstracts from the identities of both speaker and hearer, (ii) it abstracts
> from the social setting of the speech act, and (iii) it abstracts from the content
> of what is said. By operating these three abstractions, supposedly in the inter-
> ests of providing a model with maximum generality, linguistics in effect
> decontextualizes language. Speech is isolated in a theoretical vacuum, in which
> neither speaker nor hearer is entitled to any linguistic rights, being themselves
> not persons but anonymous stand-ins.
>
> *Harris, 1996: p. 153*

This also points out an intrinsic self-contradiction in Vygotsky's psychology; that is,
if during the processes of language/speech development and thought development
of the child, language is to become an ever more abstract, autonomous, decon-
textualized, and thus inhuman, system that functions according to its own laws, the
developmental processes also inevitably becomes a process of stripping away (first
and foremost) the individual's linguistic and conceptual freedom, which is just the
opposite of what Vygotsky claims, i.e. such development gives the individual
freedom. It is beyond the scope of this thesis to discuss what freedom is, but there
should be little doubt that freedom constitutes rights and responsibilities. But in
Vygotsky's cultural-historical theory, language is *nobody's* language; the individual
does not, and indeed cannot, claim ownership of language to be part of his/her
own experiences, because to grasp the true meaning of language means to lose all
subjective and human connections with it. It is quite effortless to imagine what
would happen when language is *homeless*: people would blame language for crimes

that it does not commit, when it is really *our* fault, and *our* problem, just as the therapeutic semanticists did. It seems that one of the biggest mistakes in Vygotsky's theoretical legend is failing to recognize that freedom is important, not because it can cling to some ultimate Truth that is beyond the ordinary man, but precisely because it is human, and it is human be to free. As Feyerabend sharply points out:

> The attempt to increase liberty, to lead a full and rewarding life, and the corresponding attempt to discover the secrets of nature and of man, entails ... the rejection of all universal standards and of all rigid traditions ...
>
> *Feyerabend, 2010*

And this must start, therefore, by changing the way people understand language as well as their relationship towards language: they are not muppets controlled by the language rules, but active agents who can do things with words. Children, too, have linguistic capacity and responsibilities that need recognition, and not as some primitive forms of psychological reactions that awaits the grace of civilization and intellectualization. It might be revealing to take a look at how Gilles Deleuze once described children's linguistic behavior:

> Children never stop talking about what they are doing or trying to do: exploring milieus, by means of dynamic trajectories, and drawing up maps of them. ... The trajectory merges not only with the subjectivity of those who travel through a milieu, but also with the subjectivity of the milieu itself, insofar as it is reflected in those who travel through it. ... Parents are themselves a milieu that children travel through: they pass through its qualities and powers and make a map of them. They take on a personal and parental form only as the representatives of one milieu within another. But it is wrong to think that children are limited before all else to their parents, and only had access to milieus afterward, by extention [sic] or derivation. ... There is never a moment when children are not already plunged into an actual milieu in which they are moving about ...
>
> *Deleuze, 1997: pp. 61–62*

We can see that the relationship of the parent and the child here is quite different from that discussed in a Vygotskian framework. The child's agency in their development as the "cartographer" is recognized, and for every child the map and the trajectories are different and unique for themselves. The parents are not guiding their children walking down the same paths as all other parents (should) do, i.e. the "scientific" paths; the paths are mapped out by the child himself.

Conclusion

We have come to the end of a long discussion of Vygotsky's cultural-historical theory, starting from his semiotics, his semantics, to his belief in naïve realism, rationalism, and all the way to his futuristic view on a transformative educational program, and then back to how all these ideas rest on a naïve view of language. Vygotsky's semiotics reifies language into a system of fixed codes that resembles a pyramid of meaning constructs with the bottom being the most random and sense-related kind and the top the most sophisticated and abstract kind. This reification comes in handy in supporting a psychology that believes the development of the mind repeats the trajectory of language development. What Vygotsky fails to see is that our senses and past experiences play an inseparable role in every step of our communicative activities. Speech or verbal communication is only one of the many forms of communication, and no form is necessarily superior to the others. The fact that language does have an audible phenetic system as well as visual writing system may trick us into believing that language is the kind of knowledge that one can internalize, store away, and retrieve from memory to be applied to real-life communicative scenarios, when it is in fact the kind of knowledge that needs a lot of improvisation in the here-and-now. The idea of improvisation with language happens to be very nicely summed up by someone[8] I came across in my random shuffling of the New Yorker one day. Apollo Robbins is a professional magician of what the New Yorker columnist Adam Green calls "supernatural ability," a true legend in the circle of magic. He "pickpockets" and "steals" things from people in the most mysterious ways, and his spectacular thefts have drawn the psychiatrists, neuroscientists, and the military to study his methods, in the hope of unraveling the nature of human attention. When asked how he does his tricks of taking things from people without their awareness, the magician says: "What I'm doing is taking inventory and making sight maps and getting a feel for who these people are and what I'm going to do with them. I'm a jazz performer – I have to improvise with what I'm given." Robbins's way of describing his tricks of "pick-pocketing" is fascinating from a linguist point of view, because with words, we human beings (including children) do exactly the same things during communication. We improvise with what we are given in the flow of communication; it is not just the words, but also our understanding of the context, our previous experiences of communication, the fact that we can (or cannot) hear and see the other party we are communicating with, our emotions, imagination, prediction, and so on that enable us to achieve such improvisation that makes sense to others as well as ourselves. Such first-order communicative activities can only be improvised because no one can both stay in and out of such communicative moments at the same time, and no one can see the "whole picture" but to complete the hidden or unforeseeable part of the situation with one's past experiences and prediction, before one comes up with an answer that he/she thinks or hopes the other person understands. It is through this rather complicated, not entirely-describable improvisation process with language that meaning is born, and not through some semantic system that exists prior to the communicative activities.

I have argued against Vygotsky's view that 1) language is the mirror of the mind, the idea that meaning develops along a path of achieving abstractness that is only obtained by disregarding everyday life experiences; 2) the theorization of abstract thinking in line with the laws of logic as superior over reasoning that is based on common sense and knowledge of everyday life; and 3) the sub-theorization that this distinction of thinking/reasoning is made possible on the basis of the degree of abstractness as reflected in the meaning of language. If the sociocultural theorists today truly are aiming at a new approach to studying language acquisition, language development in children, etc., it is crucial to give a much more critical rethinking of the linguistic implications of Vygotsky's cultural-historical theory than what they have done to date: a critical view that could start from a more liberal understanding of language. I say it is a "liberal" view, because it is not any school of thought/theory – there is no such thing as "liberal linguistics" for sure; it is more of a perspective, or an attitude that testifies to no specific methodology but requires certain presuppositions or premises to be identified as "liberal." Many of these premises have already been mentioned and discussed in this paper, such as 1) viewing language and linguistic behaviors as contingent, heterogeneous – or as Geertz put it "shamelessly and unapologetically ad hoc"; 2) meaning as context[9] – and experience-bound; 3) linguistic actants as responsible "linguistic experts"[10] of their language in their own right, and so on. It is true that to start from these premises makes it much more difficult to establish a scientific practice to study human language, behavior and thinking than to start with more fine-grained prescribed laws of what language is. But in this context, to sacrifice the premises, even in the name of science, would lead to even more disastrous consequences (such as, to take the linguistic rights and responsibilities away from the linguistic actants, to deny or ignore people's linguistic agency, etc.). It is true that linguistics has a long history of conceptualizing language as a system of rule-governed units – verbal, audible and visual, starting from the descriptive forefathers back in the 18th century. But as Hutton once sharply pointed out (in a casual conversation with me), "the metalinguistic beliefs of descriptive linguists have left them without a common language to talk to those – such as literary critics or lawyers or historians – who cannot take the relation of form to meaning as a given." In fact, to view language as experience-independent units also leaves them without a common language with the lay people, i.e. the language speakers themselves. Then it becomes almost absurd for these experts still to claim with authority what these lay people's language mean and what that tells about their mind. All in all, much is still taken for granted when it comes to the question of language – meaning, words, grammar, etc. – in the study of Vygotsky's cultural-historical theory. If practitioners in psychology have tossed the question of language to the philosophers from the outset of their research, then I believe to get back to this question is of crucial importance to the outlook of their discipline, because once they do, they will find that they are setting themselves on a completely different route of exploration that may eventually shed new light on the human conditions under inspection. To end with the words of a wise man regarding our discussion of language (although he is referring to a different "question"):

The question concerns all of us – and all of us must participate in their solution. The most stupid student and the most cunning peasant [or the most uneducated of them too?], the much honoured public servant and his long-suffering wife; academics and dog catchers, murderers and saints – they all have the right to say: look here, I, too, am human; I, too, have ideas, dreams, feelings, desires; I, too, have been created in god's image – but you never paid attention to my world in your pretty tales … The relevance of abstract questions, the concept of the answers given, the quality of life adumbrated in these answers – all these things can be decided only if everyone is permitted to participate in the debate and encouraged to give her or his views on the matter.

Feyerabend, 1987: p. 308

Notes

1 Korzybski thinks that it is impossible to try to provide a definition for every word, because further definitions can always be pushed for, yet they will eventually run into undefined terms. He says: "If we enquire about the 'meaning' of a word, we find that it depends on the 'meaning' of other words used in defining it, and that the eventual new relations posited between them ultimately depend on the m.o meanings [i.e. multi-ordinal meanings] of the undefined terms, which, at a certain given period, cannot be elucidated any further" (Korzybski, 1948: p.21)

2 Conscious awareness is defined by Vygotsky as "an act of consciousness whose object is the activity of consciousness itself" (Vygotsky, 1987: p. 190).

3 Korzybski distinguishes between "psychological" and "psycho-logical," because he believes that the latter catches the essences of human sanity by considering both the differences and connections of the "emotional" and the "intellectual" aspects of human thinking.

4 The term "therapeutic semantics" is discussed by John Lyons, in *Semantics* (1977), Vol. 2, Cambridge: Cambridge University Press (as quoted in Hutton, 1995: p. 86).

5 Some might argue that even Skinner himself has made it clear through the mouth of Mr. Frazier in *Walden Two* that Walden Two as the ideal society under a behaviorist's design is different from a communist society, and has even listed four weaknesses of Russian communism with examples. However, my argument here lies more in the point that their theoretical resemblance arises out of their shared belief in creating an ideal society populated with rational individuals through human engineering, and much less (if at all) in reference of Walden Two to the actual USSR back in its heyday; the latter is not the same as the world found in a Communist scientist's books.

6 Vygotsky's untimely death could have prevented him from further developing his theory, but the unfinished project was not going anywhere near a socially-indebted investigation of human behavior. If we refer to the historical facts, Vygotsky signed himself up for medicine courses at university, and was even offered a chance to set up a sub-section under the All-Union Institute of Experimental Medicine in Moscow towards the end of his life (van der Veer & Valsiner, 1991: p. 17). And there was a clear turn in his interest of study in the final years of his life to psychiatry and clinical psychology, where questions of pathological cases such as schizophrenia, aphasia, Alzheimer's, etc. were to be explored (van der Veer & Valsiner, 1991: p. 75). Therefore, there was no sign that Vygotsky was even thinking of turning towards the "social" side of psychology in the last few years of his life.

7 The child, of course, actively engages in communication with the things and people around him, but the point to bear in mind is that for Vygotsky, the child does not *make*

the rules; they *play by the rules* (e.g. the relations between concepts, etc.) that already exist before the child comes into the flow of communication.

8 See the following article, accessed 02/08/2013 online: http://www.newyorker.com/reporting/2013/01/07/130107fa_fact_green.

9 It is true that it is debatable as to how important the role of "context" has been in Vygotsky's semantics. Some scholars argued that Vygotsky had certainly realized that language is context-dependent in his later works, and this argument is not unfounded, since Vygotsky did talk about the social and cultural origin of language on various occasions. However, I have my reservations as to whether the prominence that Vygotsky had given to the idea of "context" in discussion of language and meaning can truly overrule the fixed-code tendency in his semantics or language view in general, which theorizes meaning in humans' speech and thought development as a process of functional development towards, strangely enough, context-independent abstractness.

10 For more details on the idea of a "linguistic expert," see Harris's discussions of "Everybody is a linguist" in *Introduction to Integrational Linguistics* (1998), Oxford: Pergamon Press.

References

Boas, F. (1965). *The mind of primitive man* (Rev. edn.). New York: Free Press.

Daniels, H. (2008). Reflections on points of departure in the development of sociocultural and activity theory. In B. van Oers, W. Wardekker, E. Elbers, & R. van der Veer (Eds.), *The transformation of learning: Advances in cultural-historical activity theory* (pp. 58–75). Cambridge: Cambridge University Press.

Deleuze, G. (1997). *Essays: Critical and clinical*. (D. W. Smith & M. A. Greco, trans.). Minneapolis, MN: University of Minnesota Press.

Feyerabend, P. (1987). *Farewell to reason*. London & New York: Verso.

Feyerabend, P. (2010). *Against method* (4th edn.). London & New York: Verso.

Hobsbawm, E. (1994). *The age of extremes: the short twentieth century 1914–1991*. London: Abacus.

Harris, R. (1990b). The dialect myth. In J. A. Edmondson, C. Feagin and P. Mühlhäusler (Eds). *Development and diversity: language variation across time and Space: a Festschrift for Charles-James N. Bailey*. (Dallas, TX: Summer Institute of linguistics). Arlington, TX: University of Texas. Summer Institute of Linguistics publications in linguistics, 93, pp. 3–19.

Harris, R. (1996). *Signs, language and communication: integrational and segregational approaches*. London & New York: Routledge.

Hayakawa, S. I. (1974). *Language in thought and action*. London: George Allen & Unwin Ltd.

Hutton, C. (1995). The critique of primitive belief and modern linguistics. *Journal of literary semantics: An international review*. XXIV/2 August, pp. 81–103.

Joravsky, D. (1989). *Russian psychology: a critical history*. Oxford: Blackwell.

Korzybski, A. (1948). *Science and sanity: An introduction to non-Aristotelian systems and general semantics* (3rd. edn.). Lakeville, CT: International Non-Aristotelian Library Pub. Co.

Luria, A. R., & Vygotsky, L. S. (1992). *Ape, primitive man, and child: essays in the history of behavior* (E. Rossiter, trans.). New York: Harvester Wheatsheaf.

Lyons, J. (1977). *Semantics*, Vol. 2, Cambridge: Cambridge University Press (as quoted in C. Hutton, 1995, p. 86).

Ratner, C. (2002). *Cultural psychology: Theory and method*. New York: Kluwe Academic Plenum.

Skinner, B. F. (1976). *Walden Two*. Indianapolis, IN & Cambridge: Hackett Publishing Company, Inc.

van der Veer, R. & Valsiner, J. (1991). *Understanding Vygotsky: a quest for synthesis.* Oxford: Blackwell.

Vygotsky, L. S. (1987). The development of Scientific Concepts in children. In R. W. Rieber & A. S. Carton (Eds.). *The collected works of L. S. Vygotsky,* Vol. 1, (pp.167–241). New York: Plenum Press.

Vygotsky, L. S. (1991). *Thought and language,* (5th edn.). A. Kozulin (Ed.). Cambridge, MA: MIT Press.

Vygotsky, L. S. (1997a). *Educational psychology.* (R. Silverman, trans.). Boca Raton, FL: St. Lucie Press.

Vygotsky, L. S. (1997b). *The collected works of L. S. Vygotsky* Vol. 3. R. W. Rieber & J. Wollock (Eds.). New York: Plenum Press.

4

VYGOTSKY'S "SIGNIFICANT OTHER"

Alexander Luria's contribution to the development of Vygotsky's ideas

Eli Lamdan

This chapter is somewhat exceptional compared to other chapters of this book. It is the only chapter not directly devoted to the life and work of Lev Vygotsky, but to another well-known psychologist – Alexander Romanovich Luria. Their personal and intellectual relationships were so close that it is impossible to talk about the former without talking about the latter. Both were among the most famous Soviet psychologists, but their life pathways were so different. Vygotsky died of tuberculosis in 1934 when he was not yet 38 years old and had been active for only a decade in the field of psychology. Luria, on the other hand, lived a rich life and died in 1977 at the age of 75 and after almost 60 years of a rich scientific career. Luria, who during his long career gained renown throughout the world, was also one of those who acted to glorify Lev Vygotsky's name and disseminate his ideas. The question that interests us here is what did Luria contribute to the development of Vygotsky's ideas during their common work?

The meteoric rise of Alexander Luria

Alexander Luria was born in 1902 in the city of Kazan, outside of the Pale of Settlement, to an acculturated Jewish family that was well integrated into Russian society.[1] His father, Roman Albertovich, was an internist who studied in Kazan University and started his medical career in the city and, to a limited extent, a research career as well. His mother, Eugenia Victorovna Haskina, was a practicing dentist, which was not very common at the time. The Luria family represented a certain segment of Russian Jewry. It was the outcome of a hesitant and inconsistent attempt to integrate Jews into Russian society, which the historian Benjamin Natans called "a selective integration."[2] Therefore, Luria's family was an integral part of what is known as the Russian intelligentsia.

The revolution that broke out in 1917 changed Russia radically and brought its peoples into an unprecedented social turmoil.[3] In the new nascent order there was a strong need for educated and talented people to rebuild life in Soviet Russia. In this period, previously discriminated social groups, such as educated and acculturated Jews, had an opportunity for unprecedented social mobility. During this period, Roman Luria's medical career rose enormously and the young Alexander made his first steps, full of self-confidence and enthusiasm, in the field of psychology.[4]

During his studies at Kazan University's Faculty of Social Sciences, Luria was active in the local Organization for Social Sciences and initiated the publication of at least one translated book.[5] He also did some work in the local *Narkomiust*.[6] After graduating, Luria took a part in two scientific projects in Kazan. He joined the local Institute for Scientific Organization of Labor (*KINOT*) and founded the Kazan Psychoanalytic Circle.

Luria joined *KINOT* in 1921, shortly after its establishment. He was involved there in psychophysiological experiments and in psychotechnics.[7] He also served as an academic secretary of the institute and initiated the publication of a short-lived journal *Voprosy psikhofiziologii, refleksologii i gigieny truda*. This journal, officially edited by the famous Vladimir Bekhterev from Petrograd, was Luria's first experience in "scientific enterprise".[8]

In 1922 Luria established the Kazan Psychoanalytical Circle. Luria's interest in psychoanalysis was an expression of his ambition to overcome the shortcomings of classical experimental psychology.[9] In the establishment of the psychoanalytic circle Luria revealed some of his characteristic traits – enthusiasm, initiative, the ability to establish wide contacts and the desire to connect his scientific endeavor to the transnational context.

Luria announced the establishment of the circle to Sigmund Freud and received his blessing and permission to translate Freud's *Massenpsychologie und Ich-Analyse*. Circle's meetings were a combination of a seminar for studying psychoanalysis and initial attempts to present original works. Reports on its activities appeared regularly in *Internationale Zeitschrift für Psychoanalyse*. [10]

Luria's varied activity in Kazan eventually led him to Moscow. Following the consolidation of the Kazan circle with the nascent Russian Psychoanalytic Society in Moscow, Luria was invited to the capital and soon became the secretary of the Russian Psychoanalytic Society.[11] At the same time, his psychophysiological work seems to have impressed Konstantin Kornilov, the new director of the Moscow Psychological Institute.[12] Kornilov invited Luria to join the institute, and appointed him to its academic secretary. It is quite possible that their acquaintance took place in the first all-Russian Congress of Psychoneurology, held in Moscow in January 1923.[13] Thus Luria found himself in one of the two most important intellectual centers of Russia, its new-old capital.

Luria brings Vygotsky to Moscow

Luria started his career in Moscow in two different institutions – the Psychoanalytic Society and the Institute of Psychology. The Psychoanalytic Society soon became a secondary place of his activity. He continued, by virtue of his position, to publish articles in *Internationale Zeitschrift für Psychoanalyse* and participated in society's activities. However, most of his efforts seem to have been directed toward Kornilov's Institute of Psychology.

Luria's admission to the Institute was part of Kornilov's attempt to recruit new staff following the dismissal of his teacher Georgi Chelpanov. In this process, Kornilov used a quasi-Marxist discourse to justify the dismissal of Chelpanov and his own personal promotion. He introduced reactology, his theory based on the stimulus-response model, as the Marxist theory of psychology. But, in fact, there was no difference between that and classical psychophysiology.[14]

Luria enthusiastically joined Kornilov's reactological project. He tried to combine his interest in psychoanalysis with the psychophysiological methods used at the Institute. He combined the classical associative experiment, identified primarily with Carl Jung, with a measure of strength and form of a simple motor response attached to a verbal response (an association).[15] This attempt also coincided with Luria's adoption of the Marxist discourse and his claim that psychoanalysis was consistent with Marxism. The result was that despite his interest in "the whole personality" in its social context, Luria presented a mechanistic and biological conception of mind and behavior.[16]

As an academic secretary, Luria was a member of the Institute's administration and certainly had an ability to influence the recruitment of new staff. Thus he had a significant role in bringing Vygotsky to Moscow. Luria met Lev Vygotsky at the Second All-Russian Congress of Psychoneurology, held in January 1924 in Petrograd. Luria was there as part of his Institute's delegation. It would not be unreasonable to speculate that perhaps one of his goals at the Congress was to seek new talents for the Institute.

Vygotsky's interest in psychology was relatively new, but one of his lectures at the congress was particularly pretentious.[17] Vygotsky criticized reflexology for its disregard of the problem of consciousness. He presented himself as the extreme of reflexologists, one who goes all the way with the materialist approach and applies it to the question of consciousness. Vygotsky's lecture attracted Luria's and his associates' attention. All in all, Vygotsky criticized their competitors for the "Marxist psychology" brand and defended the independence of psychology as a science distinct from the physiology of reflexes. As a result, Luria arranged Vygotsky's move to Moscow. And indeed, within a short time Vygotsky joined the Institute of Psychology as a researcher.

Luria expands Vygotsky's circle

Studies in recent years have changed significantly the way we understand Vygotsky's place in psychology.[18] According to these studies, it is impossible to speak of a Vygotskian theory in psychology, but of constantly developing and changing ideas that did not suffice to crystallize into a systematic theory. Furthermore, it is impossible to speak of the "Vygotsky School," but rather of a network of intellectual connections and collaborations that can be called the "Vygotsky Circle." As

Anton Yasnitsky pointed out, it would be more correct to speak of the "Vygotsky-Luria Circle".[19] This is because of all Vygotsky's collaborators, the relations with Luria were closest and lengthiest and because Luria contributed a lot to establishing at least part of Vygotsky's professional ties.

When Vygotsky arrived in Moscow, Luria served as secretary of the Russian Psychoanalytic Society. Luria's activity in the Psychoanalytic Society attracted Vygotsky as well, such that he increasingly became interested in psychoanalysis. It was expressed, for example, in his *Psychology of Art* and his and Luria's introduction to Freud's *Beyond the Pleasure Principle*. [20]

One of the most interesting personalities with whom Vygotsky became acquainted through Luria was Sabina Spielrein. Spielrein was a well-known psychoanalyst and a physician who returned to Russia after many years in Europe.[21] In the relatively short time she spent in Moscow, she could be, and surely was, a source of the most up-to-date psychoanalytic thinking. Her ideas about the connection between childish thinking, aphasia and dreaming could serve as inspiration for the evolving ideas of Vygotsky and Luria. Interestingly, Spielrein for some time closely worked with Jean Piaget, and even analyzed him in Geneva in the early 1920s. So, she could serve as a "bridge", or a common source of inspiration, between Piaget on the one hand and Luria and Vygotsky on the other, in their common interest of thought and speech and their development.[22]

Like many other scholars and specialists in the 1920s, Luria worked in several places. Partly this situation stemmed from a lack of educated specialists and partly from their need to earn a living. In Luria's case we probably can add his wide research interests. That is how he found himself working in three other places – the Psychological Laboratory of the Academy of Communist Upbringing, the Moscow University's Clinic for Nervous Diseases and the special laboratory he established at the Moscow District's Prosecutor's Office. For the building of the Vygotsky-Luria Circle, the first two were of great importance.

Luria founded the psychological laboratory at the Academy of Communist Upbringing, apparently in 1925. During the first two years Luria and his students studied verbal associations of children in an attempt to characterize the development of their speech and thinking.[23] Later, around 1927, this was the place where a group of Luria's and Vygotsky's students began to carry out research in "instrumental psychology" or "cultural development of the child."

Another new research area for Luria was medicine. His interest in medicine is not surprising – his father was a known physician, many of his associates to the psychoanalytic circle in Kazan were medics or medical students and he himself studied medicine for a short time in Kazan.

It is unclear how Luria was accepted to conduct experiments at the Clinic for Nervous Diseases, but his work there began apparently in 1925. At the time Luria joined the clinic, it was directed by Grigorii Rossolimo.[24] Rossolimo was a neurologist with a special interest in psychology, so it is not surprising that he made room in his clinic for a psychologist with an interest in medicine.

Luria's main associate at the clinic was Mark S. Lebedinskii. Lebedinskii was a physician who dealt with issues of public health and preventive medicine.[25] After getting acquainted with Luria, he adopted Luria's combined motor method and used it widely in his research.[26] In their joint research, Luria and Lebedinskii applied this method to patients with various diseases, including hysteria, neurasthenia, aphasia, and Parkinson's disease.[27] They tried to show that Luria's method would enable them on the one hand to diagnose various diseases, assuming that every neurological or psychiatric disorder has unique a behavioral pattern, and on the other, to learn something about the neuropsychological mechanism behind these disorders. Later on, Lebedinskii continued to cooperate with Luria and Vygotsky in the study of aphasia and other neurological diseases.

From Luria's connection to the clinic, Vygotsky also had his first experience in clinical psychological research. It is quite possible that, in this case, Luria was also the one who helped Vygotsky integrate into clinical work. Here they conducted experiments with aphasia and Parkinson's disease patients, in order to examine hypotheses stemming from Vygotsky's instrumental theory.[28]

These examples show that Luria was central to the construction of Vygotsky's network of collaborations. Of course, Vygotsky also had connections and activities that had little to do with Luria, but Luria not only helped to create Vygotsky's network of contacts, he also, as described below, was an active participant in, and sometimes even precursor to, Vygotsky's intellectual development.

Luria as one of the "importers" of the Gestalt theory

From the very beginning, as we can learn from his involvement in the psychoanalytic movement, Luria tried to position his work in an international context. Until 1925, however, Luria had no personal contacts with scientists outside of Soviet Russia. This year, he joined his father on a business trip to Western Europe.[29] This trip was an important milestone for Alexander Luria. There he got an opportunity to meet colleagues and create some personal connections. One place he visited and one group that Luria met there became very important for his intellectual development – his visit to the Berlin Institute of Psychology, where Gestaltism flourished at the time, and where Kurt Lewin's research team was based.

When Luria arrived in Berlin, the Gestalt school was already a significant and well-known current in the field of psychology. It was already long after the pioneering works of the three founders of the school – Max Wertheimer, Wolfgang Koehler and Kurt Koffka – were published.[30] They had already established the Gestalt psychology journal, *Psychologische Forschung*, and at that point went beyond the local German discourse.[31]

Gestalt theory attracted Luria's attention. The Gestaltists, emerging from the German experimental and philosophical traditions, criticized classic experimental psychology for being too atomistic and mechanistic in its approach. They emphasized the importance of whole and organized structures with intrinsic meaning that cannot be reduced to their components. All this was of great interest to Luria, given his thinking on the "whole personality" and similar criticism toward classical psychology that he adopted earlier. Luria first found in psychoanalysis the answer to his interest in the "whole personality". But psychoanalysis lacked an experimental tradition, which was important to Luria, and he attempted to integrate it into Kornilov's reactological project that actually suffered from the same shortcomings as classical psychology.

In this context, Kurt Lewin's Gestalt approach to the study of personality was of particular interest to Luria. Questions of will, intention, needs, and affect stood at the center of his and his students' experiments.[32] Interestingly, the problematics here were somewhat close to that of psychoanalysis, but the theoretical framework was quite different. According to Lewin's dynamic theory of personality, what motivates man to act are his needs and quasi-needs. In addition, a personality operates within an environment, as it appears for it, which constitutes the psychological field. In this field, different things exert forces of attraction and repulsion depending on one's needs.

In the summer of 1925, during his visit in Berlin, Luria could not meet Kurt Koffka or Wolfgang Kochler, because both of them were abroad at the time.[33] But Luria could meet Max Wertheimer, and he certainly met some members of Lewin's team, and perhaps even Lewin himself. During Luria's visit, Lewin's team dealt with various aspects of his dynamic theory of personality. Tamara Dembo, one of his Russian-speaking students, was studying anger, and Luria took part in her experiments as a subject.[34]

Lewin's research style, his use of experiments to investigate the dynamics of the human mind and behavior, left a great impression on Luria. This makes sense given Luria's interest in the "whole personality" on the one hand and his evaluation of the experimental approach on the other. Lewin's theory and methodology constituted, for Luria, a kind of alternative to psychoanalysis as a source of inspiration and a reference point for the development of his own psychological work.[35]

Upon his return from Germany, Luria presented his enthusiastic view of the Gestalt school in the philosophical-ideological journal *Pod znamenem marksizma*. [36] Luria presented Gestalt psychology here as coinciding with the dialectical materialism. At each stage of the rise in complexity, Luria argued, emerges a new "closed system", which creates "new qualitative unity." This closed system consists of the organism and its environment, and only through this prism one can understand behavior. Luria rejected the argument that complex behavior can be explained as a sum of reflexes, as Pavlov's school or American behaviorists tend to do. He advocated, in the approach he attributed to Gestalt psychology, that complex behavior is "goal-directed" – a "meaningful" ("*osmyslennoe*") adaptation to the environment. Luria's methodological conclusion was that psychological experimentation should be designed as a "meaningful action" ("*osmyslennoe deistvie*") and be as close as possible to real-life conditions. Lewin's experiments were described here as an example of the realization of this methodological conclusion.

In a book published two years later, Luria expanded these claims.[37] About half of the book was dedicated to the criticism of behaviorism, with its "mosaic" and atomistic approach. The other half of the book was devoted to the Gestalt theory. Its great advantage, according to Luria, is the conception that "psychic processes, more than processes of another order, are holistic and structurally framed".[38] Luria presented a brief review of various studies on perception, animal behavior and human behavior, along with general works on the structural and holistic approach. His review left no doubt as to his sympathy for this psychological approach.

It is well known that Vygotsky also became interested in Gestalt psychology at about the same time.[39] Thus, for example, Vygotsky wrote a preface to the translation of Koffka's article published in 1926, apparently at the initiative of Luria and Vygotsky.[40] In this preface, Vygotsky prophesied in a militant and blunt political language that with time the gap between the evolving Marxist psychology and the Gestalt psychology would widen. It should be said that Vygotsky was wrong, at least regarding himself and his associates. In the years to come, there was some convergence between Gestalt psychologists and the Vygotsky-Luria Circle. This was largely due to Luria's work.

Luria's use of Gestaltist ideas in his study of affective reactions

Beyond the favorable review of Gestaltist ideas for the Russian audience, these ideas gradually began to infiltrate Luria's research. For example, in his first studies at the Academy of Communist Upbringing on the development of children's verbal associations, Luria found that the first type of adequate reactions to verbal stimuli is predicative reaction, i.e. associations that complement a meaningful expression. Only later during development do true associations appear. Luria interpreted these results as evidence for the primacy of holistic processes, in the spirit of Gestalt theory.[41]

In 1928 Luria published a long article dedicated to his main experimental technique at the time – the combined motor method.[42] One of the interesting points here is Luria's argument for the decision to combine a voluntary motor response with the verbal associative experiment. Luria argued that in order to reflect a process in the central nervous system (a verbal reaction) through a peripheral process (a motor reaction), one should unite them within a unified system with an active set (*ustanovka*). The verbal association and the voluntary movement together comprise a system that Luria called a "motor gestalt". Luria also called this system "a stable behavioral structure" and argued that the activity of the movement allows it to stand out against other peripheral processes. He analogized it to the prominence of a form against its background in Gestalt psychology.

In 1928 Luria published another article in which he proposed a classification of all possible behaviors.[43] One interesting point here is that it proposes another meaning of the concept of reaction. A reaction here is a holistic behavioral act, and not necessarily a reflex-like response. Regarding acquired behavior, along with the existence of conditional reflexes, Luria recognized the existence of automatic behavior derived from "learning from above", from intellectual behavior in response to new and complex situations, similar to apes from Koehler's experiments. This type of behavior is characterized by the delay of reaction, planning and organization of behavior. The last type of behavior is the lack of adequate response to a super-complex situation. This is, according to Luria, an affective behavior, defined here as disorganized behavior.

In addition, we can see concrete impact of Kurt Lewin's ideas on Luria's research during this period.[44] First, Luria adopted Lewin's concept of conflict – a conflict between forces that act on a person in his psychological field and influence his behavior here and now.[45] For Luria it was the main mechanism of an affect. Second, Lewin's influence is also evident, and explicitly stated, in the construction of experiments. The main idea here was to create a task for a subject that would give rise to opposing tendencies for actions, or create a conflict between a task and subject's ability to perform it.

These are just a few examples showing that there were significant influences from Gestalt psychology very early in Luria's career. Luria's study of affective behavior coincided with his participation in Vygotsky's "instrumental psychology". At a certain stage, Luria began to combine insights from these two projects. This, along with Luria's increasing exposure to the new trends in psychology, influenced Vygotsky's original project. But before we discuss it, we shall turn to Luria's part in the "instrumental psychology" project.

Luria and the "Instrumental Psychology" project

To a large extent, one may say that "instrumental psychology" was Luria's and Vygotsky's joint project, even though the initial idea was surely Vygotsky's. Vygotsky and Luria spoke first about their theory in two subsequent presentations at the first All-Union Congress of Pedology in December 1927.[46] Luria also published an article about it in a Western journal, and later Vygotsky published another one under similar name in Russian and in English.[47] A detailed discussion of instrumental psychology is beyond the aims of this article. I will try to clarify here only the role of Luria in this project.

Luria enthusiastically joined Vygotsky's "instrumental psychology" project, or in his other name, the study of cultural development of the child. Most of the studies were carried out in Luria's laboratory at the Academy of Communist Upbringing. The only study from that period published as a monograph was Aleksei Leontiev's *Development of Memory*.[48] Luria himself conducted a study on the development of writing that was related to Leontiev's study.[49] In Leontiev's study children were trained to remember words or phrases using "auxiliary tools or signs" – cards with pictures (pictograms) – that were more or less related to the words. Luria, on the other hand, investigated how children develop their own signs or tools to meet the memory task and tried to show the stages of this process. All this fell within the central paradigm of instrumental psychology – in the course of ontogenesis natural psychological functions are transformed into cultural psychological functions through external auxiliary tools or signs.

In addition, Luria played a significant role in the integration of their experimental studies with relevant Western studies and the generalization of their theory of cultural development. Apart from the English article mentioned above, Luria published an article on the development of children's thinking and wrote the chapter on child development in his joint book with Vygotsky, *Essays in the History of Behavior.* [50] Luria tried to place their theory within the context of contemporary European psychology and made extensive use of the ideas and findings of various psychologists.

Luria composed the "natural" state of the child, before the formative influence of a culture, from various sources. He combined Freudian ideas about infant's very beginning of life, Erich Jaensch's findings on children's perception and memory and Jean Piaget's ideas and findings on children's thought. Luria introduced a child as a primitive and egocentric creature, who cannot distinguish between past and present, fantasy and reality, desirable and obtainable. [51]

This primitive state of the child, as defined by Luria, is the starting point for the transformation from a natural behavior to cultural. This transformation is based on the use of auxiliary means – "tools" or "signs". So, according to Vygotsky and Luria, cultural behavior is characterized by an instrumental psychological act. The basic scheme of this act is "stimulus-sign-reaction". One can see that this is a slight modification of the behaviorist/reactological scheme "stimulus-reaction". Despite an attempt to break the S-R model and introduce additional complexity in the form of a tool or a sign, it remained open to an atomistic and mechanistic interpretation that views the behavioral act as a passive sum of responses to specific stimuli. Despite the tension between this scheme and Luria's more holistic aspirations, he tried to combine their instrumental research with notions from Lewin's dynamic theory.

In discussing the cultural development of attention, Luria suggested that such an instrumental mechanism is probably responsible for the creation of quasi-needs, or "cultural drives" as Luria called them, which play an important role in organizing and performing voluntary actions according to Kurt Lewin. [52] In another case, in discussing the development of abstract thinking, Luria recognized the structural influence of the situation field – form, arrangement and context of the object – on children's counting, relying again on Lewinian concepts. [53] Interestingly, here he didn't use the instrumental mechanism in order to explain the transformation of "primitive counting" (i.e. dependent on the visual field) into abstract counting (i.e. liberated from the domination of the visual field), and only noted that this "cultural method" appears "under the influence of school and the cultural environment" and "emancipate" the child from "the visual field". However, these references to Lewin remained somewhat contradictory to the central idea and scheme of instrumental psychology.

Another problem is particularly evident in Luria's presentation of cultural development in their *Essays*. Luria presented cultural development as the development of distinct specific functions. Each psychological function undergoes a somewhat mechanistic transformation, using tools-signs, into a cultural function, without any obvious connection to other functions. Despite the aspiration to understand personality as a whole and criticism of atomistic and mosaic classical psychology, the human psyche is described as a kind of mosaic of psychological functions.

By 1929 the study of cultural development had progressed and appeared to support Luria's and Vygotsky's premises. In the study on problem solving conducted by Rosa Levina, they even observed a phenomenon that seemed important and interesting.[54] She found that the egocentric speech, well known from Piaget's research, increases when dealing with difficult problems. In Luria's and Vygotsky's interpretation, egocentric speech was instrumental in child's thinking, and its internalization at a later stage is the origin of the inner speech of the verbal thinking. They considered it sufficiently important discovery and chose it as representative of their work for Luria's presentation at the Ninth International Congress of Psychology.[55]

Along with what appeared to be the success of the project, difficulties were also discovered. In 1929 Vygotsky became skeptical about the course in which their research developed.[56] In a letter to his student and associate, Aleksei Leonetiev, Vygotsky complained about problems and inaccuracies in his joint book with Luria. He insisted that it was time to stop and rethink everything. He proposed dealing with the difficulties by "the most rigorous, monastic regime of thought; ideological seclusion, if necessary".[57]

Luria, on the other hand, was presented with an opportunity to deal with these difficulties in completely the opposite way. In 1929 he received an invitation to attend the Ninth International Congress of Psychology held at Yale University in New Haven, CT, USA. Participation in the congress exposed him to the most recent developments in psychology. It was an opportunity to deepen existing academic contacts and create new ones. All of this provided Luria with sources of inspiration that greatly influenced his subsequent joint work with Vygotsky.

Luria at the Ninth International Congress of Psychology

The Ninth International Congress of Psychology, the first outside Europe, was held at Yale University in New Haven. Luria received the invitation to participate in the congress sometime during the first half of 1929. However, his participation was apparently only confirmed by Soviet authorities at the last moment.[58] Luria joined the Soviet delegation, the largest in the interwar period, after several members also participated in the international physiological congress held in Boston, MA, a little earlier.[59]

Luria presented two talks at the congress. The first talk, "The new method of expressive motor reactions in studying affective traces", presented Luria's study of affect.[60] Before the congress Luria had published two articles in German on this issue (and another one after the congress), but it was its first presentation in English.[61] Luria lectured at the session of legal psychology (sub-session diagnosis) because the presentation was devoted to his experiments with criminals. Luria presented the second talk, co-authored with Vygotsky, "The function and fate of egocentric speech", at the session of developmental psychology.[62] During the same session, Kurt Lewin presented his research on the impact of environmental forces on a child's behavior.[63] For Luria it was an opportunity to renew their acquaintance and to deepen their contact.

Beyond the sessions where Luria presented his work, he was deeply interested in many other talks at the congress. His notebook of summaries shows that he paid a lot of attention to general theoretical issues.[64] In addition to participation in the congress, Luria stayed in the USA for almost a month and conducted a brief tour of several important east coast academic centers.[65] In addition to the Yale University and the institutions of New York City, he also visited Boston, MA, and Worcester, MA, hometown of Clark University. At least part of that time he spent with Kurt Koffka, who for several years worked in the USA. It is not clear how and when they met, but their contact was already close enough for them to share accommodations and travel together. In Boston, Luria surely visited the Harvard Psychological Clinic.[66] There he met Henry Murray, whose interests were closely aligned to Luria's. Luria even lectured twice on his method at Harvard, and there he met the well-known physiologist Walter Cannon.[67] Furthermore, Luria visited an American-Jewish philosopher, Horace Kallen. Kallen first met Luria during his visit to the Soviet Union in 1927.[68] During Luria's visit to the USA in 1929, Kallen helped him to obtain a contract for publishing his as yet unpublished book, *The Nature of Human Conflicts.* [69]

Luria left New York for Europe on 10 October 1929, but stayed in Europe for a while. First in the Netherlands, he attended a lecture in Utrecht by Adhémar Gelb, an associate of Kurt Goldstein in their ground-breaking studies of brain damage. He also met in Amsterdam a Dutch psychopathologist of Russian-Jewish origin, Anton Abraham Grünbaum, whose presentation in New Haven impressed him a lot.[70] From there he apparently continued to Berlin, where he planned to meet with Kurt Lewin again and perhaps also with his friend, the famous Soviet film director Sergei Eisenstein. Luria returned to Moscow during the first week of November, laden with experiences, new ideas and new contacts.[71]

Luria's insights and experiences from his long trip were summed up in two articles published within a relatively short period of time.[72] The shorter one was published in the journal *Nauchnoe slovo*, and the second, a more detailed one, in the more ideological journal *Estestvoznanie i marksizm*. Luria devoted both articles to criticism of American psychology and to reviewing the most promising trends in psychology.

Along with a certain assessment of the scope, importance, and investment in psychological research in the USA, Luria was critical of American psychology in general. He characterized American psychology in three words – "pragmatism, empiricism, mechanism." He argued that the average American psychologist is not interested in the question of "why" but rather in "what and how" questions. This leads him to the naivest empiricism and from it to the search and measurement of various quantitative data and to the examination of correlations between them. Luria called these studies "measuring science" or "extensional research" and treated them disparagingly as "statistical etudes." In the more theoretical and experimental sector of American psychology, Luria recognized the rise of behaviorism, acknowledging its lack of uniformity and the existence of other views among American psychologists.[73]

The evaluation of American psychology was for Luria an integral part of the way he experienced the congress and his insights from it. Luria perceived the congress "as a demonstration of the basic principles of modern American behaviorism and as spontaneously growing and emerging, from all sides, trends of overcoming its primitive views, its mechanistic worldview."[74] Luria identified these trends in various fields of research: neurology, physiology, psychopathology and developmental psychology.[75]

For example, the work of the American psychologist Karl Lashley was of special interest for Luria. Lashley conducted a series of experiments which showed that the removal of different parts of the cortex did not significantly impair the ability of conditional learning. Lashley's conclusions were mainly directed against attempts to localize complex skills in specific areas of the cortex. For Luria, this was evidence of a change in basic assumptions in psychology:

> The concept of the brain as a system of neuronal units, which forms the basis for reflexive acts, begins to give way to a completely different view of the brain as a holistic regulating mechanism, with a well-known integrative function and functioning according to completely unique dynamic principles.[76]

Luria also refers to Walter Cannon's studies on cats whose sympathetic nervous system have been removed. In these experiments, Cannon questioned the prevailing view that this system is responsible for an emotional activity. In this context Luria wrote:

> The atomistic principle of understanding the mechanism of behavior, which is based on the idea of the separate action of individual "responsible" systems, is being replaced by a different principle – the dynamic principle that mandates including any specific system in the activity of the whole organism ...[77]

In the field of psychopathology, Luria mentioned the works of Kurt Goldstein and Adhémar Gelb, but discussed in detail the work of Anton A. Grünbaum. Luria noted that Grünbaum's approach perceives aphasia not as the result of damage to a specific area of the brain, but rather as the result of damage to the brain as a whole system.

Luria presents Grünbaum's recent research in the field of human motion, especially with the apraxia patients, as further evidence of the impossibility of understanding human functions as the sum of elements, motor elements in the case of motion. The same, according to Luria, is true for psychological functions – "any psychological function can be understood and correctly studied, only by deriving it from the whole system of basic attitudes of personality."[78]

Luria argued that concepts such as set (*ustanovka*), organization and structure, which express the new approach, have penetrated even the discourse of psychologists such as Edward Thorndike, who represented for him a distinct mechanistic approach. These holistic concepts and principles "found their brilliant development," as Luria put it, in one of the main evening lectures by Wolfgang Köhler. Luria drew his conclusions from Köhler's lecture:

> The principle of association should be replaced by the principle of organization, and this is not only a psychologically descriptive term, it is a concept that is adequate for a number of physiological and general biological laws. The activity of man and animal consists precisely in an organization, regulation of his own activity aimed at adapting to the environment and mastering this environment, and this process cannot be understood at all in terms of association, but only in terms of organization of a holistic system of behavior.[79]

This principle of organization was expressed, according to Luria, in a most remarkable manner in Kurt Lewin's work. His lecture at the congress presented the application of his field theory to children's behavior. Lewin also introduced an innovative use of short films for analysis of behavior, which made a great impression on Luria. For him it was a successful alternative to understanding behavior as the sum of innate and acquired reflexes. Luria noted that:

> Behavior is regulated here not by a system of separate reflex movements, but by the structure of the influencing field, on the one hand, and the structure of child behavior (the dominant role of the optical apparatus), on the other.[80]

Luria introduced the Lewinian approach as a "step forward towards a holistic explanation of behavioral rules." However, Luria argued that Lewin's approach (as with the Gestalt school in general) is physicalistic, because it ignores "the complex holistic nature of behavior of the historical human." At the same time, Luria constrained his criticism. According to him, Lewin's concept of psychological field can also contain "social sets (*ustanovki*) of the personality," and so to include the social dimension in the understanding of mind and behavior.

Luria's criticism of the Gestalt school also seems to be intentionally exaggerated. Interestingly, Luria criticized Lewin only in the ideological *Estestvoznanie i marksizm*, and not in a more solid journal *Nauchnoe slovo*. This does not necessarily indicate Luria's dishonesty, but the criticism of Lewin, could certainly be a preventive defense from unfair judgment by ideological purists.

To sum up Luria's journey to the USA, he had returned to Russia with three major achievements. First, he became an acknowledged member of the transnational psychological community, having established personal contacts and opened up future possibilities for collaborations. Secondly, these contacts almost immediately allowed him to obtain a contract for the publication of his first foreign language book. And finally, Luria returned from the visit with a deeper understanding of holistic concepts, which would enable both him and Vygotsky to revise significantly their work.

From instrumental psychology to psychology of functional systems

One of the most interesting moments in the development of Vygotsky's thought is the theoretical turn that occurred in 1930. This turn was proclaimed in his lecture at the Clinic for Nervous Diseases, "On psychological systems."[81] After three years of research of psychological functions through instrumental method, and more than a year of doubts about it, Vygotsky changed his mind. He stated that:

> the entire issue resides not just in the changes within the functions, but in the changes in the connections and in the infinitely diverse forms of development that develop from this. It resides in the development of new syntheses in a certain stage of development, new central functions and new forms of connections between them. We must take interest in systems and their fate.[82]

I claim that Alexander Luria played a significant role in this theoretical turn. We have already seen how such a systemic thought was reflected in Luria's insights from his trip abroad. In addition, as I shall try to show here, Luria fully expressed this new thinking in his book, *The Nature of Human Conflicts*. Though the book was published in New York in 1932, its Russian manuscript was sent to Liveright publishing house much earlier. Luria decided to rewrite extensive parts of the manuscript he already had, and to add a few new experiments, some of them with Vygotsky's participation.[83] Finally, the book was ready in July 1930, several months before Vygotsky's famous lecture.[84]

The theoretical and methodological introduction of the book dealt mainly with the concept of organization.[85] Luria presented two approaches to the problem of organization of the nervous system and behavior. The first, which he rejected, was identified in Russia most of all with Pavlov's work, known as the "switchboard model," and is essentially an associative approach that uses the concepts of excitation and inhibition. In contrast to this approach, Luria presented an alternative view:

> The structure of the organism presupposes not an accidental mosaic, but a complex organisation of separate systems. This organisation is expressed paramountly in a functional correlation of these systems, in that they do not combine one with the other in an accidental way, but they unite as very definite parts into an integrated functional structure.
>
> The basic features of this total structural organisation of behaviour is a functional inequality of the different systems entering into it; certain systems appear as governing and regulating, others as subordinate, executing one or another function. It is clear that the significance of these in the system of organisation is not always the same, and the whole activity of the organism can be understood only as a dynamic system, a conditioned activity of its component parts.[86]

Using this approach, Luria presented his study of affect in the first two parts of the book.[87] What interests us here in particular is the integration of this new systems approach with the ideas of the cultural and social development of the child. Luria dealt with it in the third part of the book. This part suffered from a poor translation, which apparently disturbed the acceptance of these ideas in that time.[88] In the introduction he laid his premise on the developmental dimension of his work.

> The forms of organisation of behaviour in the first stages of this development are certainly something else than those forms of organisation which differentiate more complex behaviour, and we can the sooner say this development proceeds along the path of dominating the primitive laws, rather than along the path of simple repetitions of them in their new stages ... The genesis of organised human behaviour is through the development and inclusion of all the new regulating systems, which overcome the primitive forms of behaviour and transfer them to that which is a new and a more systematised organisation.[89]

Luria has shown in his experiments that the behavioral acts of children are very different from those of adults and resemble affective states and conflictive situations. Luria's conclusion from all these experiments was that the childish activity at the early stages of development is diffuse, impulsive and immediate, like affect or neurosis. Luria suggested that there is a connection between the "diffuse structure of child neurodynamics" and other phenomena indicated by various psychologists.[90] For example, he links it to the larger dependence of children in the environmental field during their behavior in Lewin's experiments and to the primitive nature of childish thinking, as Piaget described it.

Here, as well as in the discussion on affect and conflict, Luria suggested the existence of a mechanism responsible for the separation between the regulatory and executive systems of activity. This mechanism, "a functional barrier," emerges during development and is damaged in affective and pathological states. Based on the studies of Hughlings Jackson and Henry Head, Luria suggested that the functional barrier is related to the organizing function of the new and higher layers of the nervous system and the organizing role of the speech. Various pathological states such as hysteria, oligophrenia and aphasia, were very central in his argumentation.[91] Luria concluded from them, using simple reactions experiments alongside clinical analysis, that the functional barrier mechanism is "the systems of internal speech or the analogous systems of the auxiliary stimuli," hence it is "not a natural mechanism but one of cultural origin."[92] Speech emerges here as the regulatory system that mediates every behavioral act.

Luria devoted the last chapter of the book to the problem of mastering behavior, or to the ancient problem of will and voluntary action.[93] He rejected the concept of volitional action as a simple and primary act, as well as the concept of will as an illusion behind which there are only needs and drives. Again, he mentioned Lewin's theory as the right direction towards the explanation of will. Lewin understood a volitional action as a formation of quasi-needs that cause "tension" in the psychic system whose discharge leads to an action. It seems that Luria completely accepted Lewin's model, but was more interested in the formation process of these "artificial needs" than in their mode of operation. At this point he proposed a synthesis between Lewin's dynamic theory and Vygotsky's instrumental theory.

> ... [Volitional] behaviour is a compound product of psychological growth, in the process of which the primitive, natural forms of behaviour are complicated by new cultural ones, and as a result of this there is elaborated a new relation of the personality to its own behaviour ... Whilst in the first stages of his development the human was able to act only on the surroundings, making instruments which helped him to gain the mastery over the external situation – in his further growth he began to elaborate those artificial stimuli that enabled him to think of himself as an object of action and that aided him in controlling his own behaviour ... The development of the voluntary processes comes about as a result of the elaboration of the various forms of behaviour, the mobilisation of the Quasi-Bedürfnisse to achieve his ends. Voluntary behaviour is the ability to create stimuli and to subordinate them; or in other words, to bring into being stimuli of a special order, directed to the organisation of behaviour.[94]

One can see that Luria repeated here the ideas of *Etudes in the History of Behavior*, but in a more holistic version. Instead of dealing with psychological functions, Luria referred here to behavioral acts and their structural organization with a speech as a regulatory system. Luria conducted a series of experiments, mainly in a clinical setting, in order to corroborate this claim. As he wrote to Horace Kallen, and in the book, his purpose was to make the hysteric be calm, the Parkinson's patient move quickly and the child control his diffuse behavior.[95] In all these situations, Luria claimed to demonstrate an improvement in the performance of motor tasks by some external auxiliary means, but mainly and better through the use of loud or internal speech.

To summarize this part, one can see that Luria was somewhat ahead of Vygotsky in changing attitudes toward the higher psychological functions of man. The new ideas that Luria had brought from his trip abroad caused him to make new experiments and rephrase old ideas. Vygotsky was to some extent involved in these experiments. Thus, it is at least possible to say that they worked together on this important turning point in Vygotsky's thought.

The Central Asian expeditions of 1931–1932

After finishing the work on *The Nature of Human Conflicts*, Luria's next major project was ethno-physiological research.[96] In *Etudes on the History of Behavior*, Luria and Vygotsky focused on three lines of human development: biological, cultural-historical and ontogenetic, in which the two previous phases are intertwined in the child's development. If in the last field they conducted some original research, the others were entirely based on Western psychologists and anthropologists. Therefore, the project can be understood as their attempt to examine their views on the historical evolution of psychological processes. In addition, the modernizing and developing impulse of the Stalinist Great Turn, especially toward the undeveloped regions of the Soviet Union, enabled the flourishing of ethnopsychological research, which was driven by the same basic values – progress, development and change.

The idea dates back to 1929, when Vygotsky visited Tashkent, Uzbekistan, where he did several experiments of which almost nothing is known. Luria, for his part, sought ways to find Western funding and partners for an ethno-psychological research expedition to one of the country's remote regions. Under the conditions of the Great Depression that broke out at the end of 1929, the chances for that were negligible. Therefore, the expedition finally went to Uzbekistan in the summer of 1931 with only Soviet funding and scientists.

The purpose of the study was:

> to investigate the variations of thought and other psychological processes in people living in a very primitive economic and social environment, and to record those changes which develop as a result of the introduction of higher and more complex forms of economic life and the raising of the general cultural level.[97]

In other words, Luria's research was based on a vulgar Marxist premise. According to his hypothesis, those living in the traditional, "feudal", Central Asian society will show a primitive structure of mental processes. On the other hand, those who went through the Soviet socialization processes, industrialization and collectivization, received some education and leaped straight to the "socialist society" will show mental processes characteristic of civilized and modern humans.

Luria divided his subjects into several groups according to their involvement in the new emerging order.[98] On the one hand there were men and women living the traditional way of life. On the other side were residents of new *kolkhozes* who were uneducated, or poorly educated, social activists, and those who studied at a local institution for elementary school teachers training. Luria and his team examined their psychological processes such as perception, abstraction, reasoning, problem solving, imagination, and self-esteem. In all of these processes Luria found differences between the "primitive" and the "progressive" groups. The former presented thinking based on a concrete experience, while the latter had already shown the beginnings of abstract thinking.

The results excited Vygotsky, perhaps even more than Luria. His letters to Luria during the first expedition reveal this clearly.

> This is now the best part of our work – and the new part in the best meaning of the word.[99] ... I am literally writing to you in *Emphase* [utter excitement] – in an enthusiastic state that one does not often experience ... Our new path

has been conquered for us (by you), not just as an idea, but also in practice – in the experiment[100] ... For our research, this is a huge decisive step forward and a pivotal change to a new point of view. But this expedition would also be an event for any context of European research.[101]

Luria himself was also enthusiastic about the results. While still in Uzbekistan, he wrote to Horsley Gantt, his translator, and was already planning his next book.

As far as I know, this is the first experimental psychological expedition organized in order to study structural characteristics of the psyche at different historical stages ... During this time, we collected materials of an exceptional interest, forcing us to reconsider several of the most fundamental psychological views, and in the coming years I will turn to you for assistance in the publication of a new book in America. It will be an experimental study of the historically developed structures of the human mind.[102]

At the end of the journey Luria reported on the expedition in Western academic journals and through personal correspondence.[103] From his letter to Köhler we learn that Luria considered of great importance the experiments of perception generally, and experiments in optical illusions particularly.[104] Perhaps because perception was often perceived as more "natural" and less influenced by social and cultural factors. Luria told Köhler that his primitive subjects almost did not succumb to optical illusions, a consequence he attributed to their social environment. Luria, who did not give up the cooperation with Western scientists, tried to convince Köhler to join the next expedition, and expressed the hope that Kurt Koffka and Kurt Lewin would join. Either way, in April 1932, Koffka's participation had already been resolved.[105]

In the summer of 1932 Koffka joined Luria's second expedition to Central Asia. He first visited Moscow, where he met Vygotsky, who even served as an interpreter of one of Koffka's lectures.[106] In the field studies, Koffka was responsible for the perception experiments. Contrary to previous findings, Koffka found that "with very few exceptions the men and women examined by us succumbed to the optical illusion."[107] This does not necessarily mean that Koffka received completely opposite results, but he certainly interpreted differently some negative results. He claimed that:

Naïve, social subjects who treated the experimenter on a footing of equality and did not regard the experiment as a test of their ability had the illusion without exception. Only when the subjects were suspicious, staring a long time at the patterns before making their judgments, the illusions failed to appear with some though by no means with all patterns, in accordance with well-known facts.[108]

This difference in interpretation was due to Koffka's different basic premises. Two of the most important were the consideration the whole psychological field (or the behavioral environment) of the subjects, and the meaning of the whole situation for them.[109] These concepts were not entirely unknown to Luria and Vygotsky, but they failed to take them into account here. Perhaps as an outsider, Koffka could see things differently that were transparent and self-evident to Luria and his team.

Thus, Luria also noted the suspicious attitude of some people, especially in the traditional, remote communities, but referred to it as a kind of folklore, an exotic scenery, and nothing more. Koffka on the other hand took it seriously. From his letter to his student, Molly Harrower we learn that a group of the security authorities (*OGPU*) accompanied them, especially in the remote areas.[110] Taking into account that acts of resistance to the Soviet regime still occurred occasionally and the division of the region into national republics encountered difficulties, and even active armed resistance, due to the multi-ethnic character of the region, one can understand the suspicion toward a team of Europeans, accompanied by security personnel, who turn to them with meaningless questions and tasks.[111]

Koffka's unequivocal conclusion apparently led Luria to rethink his premises. He published only a brief report on the second expedition, which included Koffka's conclusions that he sent independently, and no book on the subject was published at the time.[112] One indirect piece of evidence of Luria's discontent with the results can be found in Vygotsky's letter to him.

> I keep thinking and I will continue to do so for as long as I am not convinced of the contrary that you ... have proven, in experiments, the phylogenetic existence of a layer of complex[ive] thinking, and, dependent on that, distinct structure of all basic systems of the psyche and of all main forms of activity and − in perspective − even that of consciousness. Is this really that meagre that you are dissatisfied with the results of the two expeditions?[113]

So, Luria was the first to understand Koffka's criticism and to realize that their research needed some revision. It seems that this whole episode and the close acquaintance with Koffka were among the causes of the second important turning point in Vygotsky's thought. From this period Vygotsky started to deal with the semantic organization of consciousness and, in this context, with the question of meaning and sense, in addition to the principle of structural organization of the psyche.

The unfinished theory and the birth of the Genius

In the short time that Vygotsky had to live, he did not develop his new ideas into a complete theory. Most of these ideas remained in archival documents and only few of them expressed in his last book *Thought and Speech*.[114] All this time Vygotsky continued to work closely with Luria, especially with regard to their, now common, interest in the neurological clinic. As we have seen, the interest in neurology was not new for Luria. He expressed interest in combining experimental and clinical research even before he traveled to the congress in New Haven, and this tendency increased after it, inspired by works of Goldstein, Gelb and Grünbaum.

Between the two trips to Central Asia, Luria, together with a group of Vygotsky's associates, moved to Kharkov, perhaps with the idea of creating an institutional base there. The move was also connected to the hostile atmosphere and unfair ideological criticism that Vygotsky and Luria experienced in Moscow. In Kharkov, Luria was appointed head of the psychological sector of the Ukrainian Psychoneurological Academy and Mark Lebedinskii head of clinical psychology department. There, with the increased interest in the neurological and psychiatric clinic Luria and Vygotsky started their medical training, planned extensive clinical research and made some preliminary works.[115]

At the same time, similar work was done in Moscow, mainly by two students of Kurt Lewin, Gita Birenbaum and Bluma Zeigarnik. Both of them returned from Berlin during 1930–1931 and entered the Vygotsky-Luria Circle, probably thanks to Luria's contacts with Lewin. They started to work in the clinical department of the Institute for Higher Nervous Activity of the Communist Academy and conducted research on aphasiaand other pathological states.[116]

As we know, Vygotsky planned to publish an edited volume and a series of publications from these works, but it wasn't realized. Vygotsky was also asked to join the new All-Union Institute for Experimental Medicine and to establish a department of clinical psychology, but he died before he could take this position. After his death, Luria took this position and headed this department from 1934 to the end of 1936. These clinical studies were very important for the research of semantic organization of consciousness, because they dealt with various disturbances of semantic functions in human speech.

Vygotsky died from tuberculosis in the summer of 1934. However, Luria's role in relation to him did not end. Here ends the story of Vygotsky the scientist and the man and begins another story. I tried to show throughout the article that the relationship between Vygotsky and Luria was a relationship between equal associates, and at certain points Luria even had a leading role in their joint work. However, the myth of Vygotsky tells us a story of the Genius and the Teacher, and Luria played a significant role in its construction.

Immediately after Vygotsky's death many of his associates and disciples acted to commemorate him.[117] Luria's role in these activities was central. He wrote obituaries in Russian and English and organized a major volume in the memory of Vygotsky, with participation of internationally known scientists, although this ultimately wasn't realized.[118] In the context of Stalinist culture, and Stalinist science in particular, which emphasizes the importance of the leader and the cult of the founding father, the logical result was the cult of "Vygotsky the Genius."[119] I do not argue that all Soviet scientists, or even psychologists, accepted this view of Vygotsky. Of course, it was far from the myth built around Pavlov. But it was the same model that Vygotsky's associates and disciples have accepted.

Joseph Stalin died in 1953. Decades later, after the Stalinist period was over, Luria resumed and developed further his wide international contacts. In this period, he was instrumental in the "export" of the Vygotsky myth abroad.[120] Luria made a huge effort to promote the translation of Vygotsky's texts and his image as an important figure in the history of Russian psychology. Presumably his motivation was complex. Luria and others could thus achieve a higher status in the Soviet scientific system. In addition, his sincere appreciation to Vygotsky, to the man he considered his teacher, played a role in his motivation. Ultimately, Luria was very successful in this last contribution to Vygotsky.

Notes

1   Elena A. Luria, *Moy otets A. R. Luria* (Moscow: Gnozis, 1994), 5–15.
2   Benjamin Nathans, *Beyond the Pale: the Jewish Encounter with Late Imperial Russia* (Berkley, CA: University of California Press, 2002).
3   Stephen A. Smith, "The revolutions of 1917–1918," in *The Cambridge History of Russia: The Twentieth Century*, ed. Ronald Grigor Suny (Cambridge: Cambridge University Press, 2006).
4   On Roman Luria's medical career see: Anonymous, "Professor Roman Albertovich Luriia," *Trudy Kazanskogo gosudarstvennogo instituta usovershenstvovaniia vrachei* 1 (1929): 5–8, and archival documents in GARF, f. 4737, op. 2, d. 1510, l. 2–5.
5   Lujo Brentano, *Opyt teorii potrebnostei* (Kazan: Gosizdat, 1921).
6   GARF, f. 4737, op. 2, d. 1509, l. 19
7   Alexander R. Luria, "K metodam psikhotekhnicheskogo issledovaniia. Opyt – model'." *Sbornik biuro nauchnoi organizatsii truda g. Kazan'* 1 (1922): 3–15; Alexander R. Luria, "Refleksologicheskii metod v issledovanii vnushaemosti (K voprosy o vnushennom utomlenii)," *Voprosy psikhofiziologii, refleksologii i gigieny truda* 1 (1923): 43–54; Alexander R. Luria, "Utomliaemost' rabochikh slovolitni," *Voprosy psikhofiziologii, refleksologii i gigieny truda* 1 (1923): 91–104.
8   Aleksandr R. Luriia, *Etapy proidennogo puti* (Moscow: Izdatel'stvo MGU, 1982), 13–14.
9   Aleksandr R. Luriia, "Printsipy real'noi psikhologii (o nekotorykh tendentsiiakh sovremennoi psikhologii)," in *Psikhologicheskoe nasledie: Izbrannye trudy po obshchei psikhologii*, eds. Zhanna M. Glozman, Dmitrii A. Leont'ev and Elena G. Radkovskaia (Moscow: Smysl, 2003), 295–383; Luriia, *Etapy proidennogo puti*, 11–12; Aleksandr R. Luriia, "Puti rannego razvitiia sovetskoi psikhologii: dvadtsatye gody po sobstvennym vospominaniiam," in *Psikhologicheskoe nasledie: Izbrannye trudy po obshchei psikhologii*, eds. Zhanna M. Glozman, Dmitrii A. Leont'ev and Elena G. Radkovskaia (Moscow: Smysl, 2003), 261.
10   Alexander R. Luria, "Kasaner Psychoanalytische Vereinigung (Sitzungsbericht)," *Internationale Zeitschrift für Psychoanalyse* 9 (1923): 239; Alexander R. Luria, "Kasaner Psychoanalytische Vereinigung (Rußland)," *Internationale Zeitschrift für Psychoanalyse* 8 (1922): 523–525; Alexander R. Luria, "Kasaner Psychoanalytische Vereinigung (Sitzungsbericht)," *Internationale Zeitschrift für Psychoanalyse* 9 (1923): 114–116; Alexander R. Luria, "Kasaner Psychoanalytische Vereinigung (Sitzungsbericht)," *Internationale Zeitschrift für Psychoanalyse* 9 (1923): 238–239; Alexander Luria, "Sitzungsbericht der Kasaner Psychoanalytischen Vereinigung," *Internationale Zeitschrift für Psychoanalyse* 9 (1923): 543–544.
11   Aleksandr M. Etkind, *Eros nevozmozhnogo. Razvitie psikhoanaliza v Rossii* (Moscow: Gnoziz, 1994), 189–190.
12   Luriia, *Etapy proidennogo puti*, 15.
13   Luria, "Kasaner Psychoanalytische Vereinigung (Sitzungsbericht)," 114.

14   Sergei A. Bogdanchikov, *Proiskhozhdenie marksistskoi psikhologii: Diskussiia mezhdu K. N. Kornilovym i G. I. Chelpanovym v otechestvennoi psikhologii 20-kh godov* (Moscow-Berlin: DirectMedia, 2014).

15   Aleksandr R. Luriia and Aleksei N. Leont'ev, "Issledovanie ob"ektivnykh simptomov affektivnykh reaktsii (Opyt reaktologicheskogo issledovaniia massovogo affekta)," in *Problemy sovremennoi psikhologii*, ed. Konstantin N. Kornilov (Leningrad: Gosizdat, 1926), 47–99.

16   Aleksandr R. Luriia, "Psikhoanaliz kak sistema monisticheskoi psikhologii," in *Psikhologia i marksizm*, ed. Konstantin N. Kornilov (Moscow-Leningrad: Gosizdat, 1925), 47–48.

17   Lev S. Vygotskii, "Metodika refleksologicheskogo i psikhologicheskogo issledovaniia," in *Problemy sovremennoi psikhologii*, ed. Konstantin N. Kornilov (Moscow-Leningrad: Gosizdat, 1926), 26–46.

18   For the most recent studies see: Anton Yasnitsky and René van der Veer, eds., *Revisionist Revolution in Vygotsky Studies* (London: Routledge, 2016).

19   Anton Yasnitsky, "Unity in diversity: the Vygotsky-Luria circle as an informal personal network of scholars," in *Revisionist Revolution in Vygotsky Studies*, eds. Anton Yasnitsky and René van der Veer (London: Routledge, 2016), 27–49.

20   Aleksandr R. Luriia and Lev S. Vygotskii, "Predislovie" in *Po tu storonu printsipa udovol'stviia*, Zigmund Freid (Moscow: Sovremennye problemy, 1925), 3–16; Lev S. Vygotskii, *Psikhologiia iskusstva* (Moscow: Iskusstvo, 1965).

21   Etkind, *Eros nevozmozhnogo*, 129–170.

22   Marie J. Santiago-Delefosse and J.-M. Oderic Delefosse, "Spielrein, Piaget and Vygotsky: Three Positions on Child thought and Language," *Theory & Psychology* 12 (2002): 723–747.

23   Aleksandr R. Luriia, ed., *Rech' i intellekt v razvitii rebenka* (Moscow: Akademiia kommunisticheskogo vospitaniia, 1927); Aleksandr R. Luriia, ed., *Rech' i intellekt derevnskogo, gorodskogo i besprizornogo rebenka* (Moscow: Gosizdat, 1930).

24   Richard Satran, "G. I. Rossolimo (1860–1928) Neurologist and Public Benefactor," *Journal of the History of the Neurosciences: Basic and Clinical Perspectives* 16 (2007): 65–73.

25   A. G. Naishtat and Mark S. Lebedinskii, *Gigiena obshchestvennogo rabotnika (Gigiena aktivista)* (Moscow: Mozdravotdel, 1928).

26   Mark S. Lebedinskii, "Sopriazhennyi motornyi metod issledovaniia intellektual'nykh reaktsii," *Zhurnal nevropatologii i psikhiatrii imeni S. S. Korsakova* 6 (1928): 723–734; Mark S. Lebedinskii, *Razvitie vysshei motoriki u rebenka* (Moscow: Uchpedgiz, 1931).

27   Aleksandr R. Luriia and Mark S. Lebedinskii, "Sopriazhennaia motornaia metodika v issledovanii nervnobol'nykh," in *Nevrologiia: Trudy kliniki nervnykh boleznei MGU, sbornik 2* (Moscow: Izdatelstvo MGU, 1928), 66–96.

28   See below.

29   Luriia, *Moy otets*, 43–44.

30   On Gestalt psychology see: Mitchell G. Ash, *Gestalt Psychology in German Culture: holism and the quest for objectivity* (Cambridge: Cambridge University Press, 1995).

31   The first publication of Gestalt psychology in the United States is: Kurt Koffka, "Perception: An introduction to the Gestalt-theorie," *Psychological Bulletin* 19 (1922): 53–585. http://psychclassics.yorku.ca/Koffka/Perception/perception.htm.

32   Alfred J. Marrow, *The Practical Theorist: The Life and Work of Kurt Lewin* (New York: Basic Books, 1969), 29–47.

33   Anton Yasnitsky, "A transnational history of 'the beginning of beautiful friendship': the birth of the cultural-historical Gestalt psychology of Alexander Luria, Kurt Lewin, Lev Vygotsky and others," in *Revisionist Revolution in Vygotsky Studies*, eds. Anton Yasnitsky and René van der Veer (London: Routledge, 2016), 204.

34   Mikhail G. Iaroshevskii, "V shkole Kurta Levina: Iz besed s B. V. Zeigarnik," *Voprosy psikhologii* 3 (1988): 172–179.

35   In the absence of Luria's testimony on the subject, I base this possibility on the testimony of an American student of Kurt Lewin who expressed himself in a similar vein. See: Marrow, *The Practical Theorist*, 51–52.

36 Aleksandr R. Luriia, "Printsipial'nye voprosy sovremennoi psikhologii," *Pod znamenem marksizma* 3–4 (1926): 129–139.
37 Aleksandr R. Luriia, *Sovremennaia psikhologiia v ee osnovnykh techeniiakh* (Moscow: Rabotnik prosveshcheniia, 1928).
38 Luriia, *Sovremennaia psikhologiia v ee osnovnykh techeniiakh*, 37.
39 René van der Veer and Jan Valsiner, *Understanding Vygotsky: a Quest for Synthesis* (Oxford: Blackwell, 1991), 155–182.
40 Kurt Koffka, "Samonabliudenie i metod psikhologii," in *Problemy sovremennoi psikhologii*, ed. Konstantin N. Kornilov (Leningrad: Gosizdat, 1926), 176–191.
41 Luriia, "Rechevye reaktsii rebenka," 27–36.
42 Aleksandr R. Luriia, "Sopriazhennaia motornaia metodika i ee primenenie v issledovanii affektivnykh reaktsii," *Problemy sovremennoi psikhologii* 3 (1928): 45–99; Alexander Luria, "Die Methode der abbildenden Motorik bei Kommunikation der Systeme und ihre Anwendung auf die Affektpsychologie," *Psychologische Forschung* 12 (1929): 127–179.
43 Aleksandr Luriia, "O sisteme psikhologii povedeniia," *Psikhologiia* 1 (1928): 53–65.
44 Aleksandr Luriia, "Eksperimental'nye konflikty u cheloveka," *Problemy sovremennoi psikhologii* 6 (1930): 97–137; Alexander Luria, *The Nature of Human Conflicts or Emotion, Conflict and Will. An Objective Study of Disorganization and Control of Human Behavior* (New York: Liveright, 1932), 205–330.
45 Marrow, *The Practical Theorist*, 62.
46 Lev S. Vygotskii, "Instrumental'nyi metod v psikhologii," in *Osnovnye problemy pedologii v SSSR*, ed. Aron B. Zalkind (Moscow: Rabotnik prosveshcheniia, 1928), 158–159; Aleksandr R. Luria, "K metodike imstrumental'no-psikhologicheskogo issledovaniia," in *Osnovnye problemy pedologii v SSSR*, ed. Aron B. Zalkind (Moscow: Rabotnik prosveshcheniia, 1928), 159.
47 Alexander R. Luria, "The Problem of Cultural Behavior of the Child," Journal of Genetic Psychology 35 (1928): 493–506; Lev S. Vygotskii, "Problema kul'turnogo razvitiia rebenka," *Pedologiia* 1 (1928): 58–77; Lev S. Vygotski, "The Problem of Cultural Development of the Child," Journal of Genetic Psychology 36 (1929): 415–432.
48 Aleksei N. Leont'ev, *Razvitie pamiati. Eksperimental'noe issledovanie vysshykh psikhologicheskikh funktsii* (Moscow: Uchpedgiz, 1931).
49 Aleksandr R. Luriia, "Materialy k genezisu pis'ma u rebenka," in *Voprosy marksistskoi pedagogiki*, ed. Anonymous (Moscow: AKV, 1929), 143–176.
50 Aleksandr R. Luriia, "Puti razvitiia detskogo myshleniia," *Estestvoznanie i marksizm* 2 (1929): 97–130; Lev S. Vygotskii and Aleksandr R. Luriia, *Etiudy po istorii povedeniia: obez'iana, primitiv, rebenok* (Moscow-Leningrad: Gosizdat, 1930).
51 Vygotskii and Luriia, *Etiudy po istorii povedeniia*, 126–133.
52 Vygotskii and Luriia, *Etiudy po istorii povedeniia*, 176–183.
53 Vygotskii and Luriia, *Etiudy po istorii povedeniia*, 184–191.
54 Roza E. Levina, "Idei L.S. Vygotskogo o planiruiushchei rechi rebenka," *Voprosy psikhologii* 4 (1968): 105–115.
55 See below.
56 For a more detailed discussion see: Anton Yasnitsky, *Vygotsky. An Intellectual Biography* (London & New York: Routledge, 2018).
57 Correspondence from Vygotsky to Leontiev, 23 July 1929, in Lev S. Vygotskii, "Pis'ma k uchenikam i soratnikam," *Vestnik MGU. Seriia 14. Psikhologiia* 3 (2004): 18.
58 Correspondence from Vygotsky to Leontiev, 2 July 1929, in Vygotskii, "Pis'ma k uchenikam i soratnikam," 17; Correspondence from Robert M. Yerkes to Luria, 5 October 1929, MS-569, Box 30, Folder 558, Robert Mearns Yerkes papers, Manuscripts and Archives, Yale University Library, New Haven, CT, USA.
59 Anton Yasnitsky, "Ob izoliatsionizme sovetskoi psikhologii: zarubezhnye konferentsii 1920–30-kh gg.," *Voprosy psikhologii* 3 (2010): 101–112.
60 Alexander Luria, "The new method of expressive motor reactions in studying affective traces," at the Ninth International Congress of Psychology held at Yale University,

New Haven, CT, 1–7 September 1929, ed. J. M. Cattell (Princeton, NJ: Psychological Review Company, 1930), 294–296.

61 Luria, "Die Methode der abbildenden Motorik bei Kommunikation der Systeme und ihre Anwendung auf die Affektpsychologie"; Mark S. Lebedinsky und Alexander Luria, "Die Methode der abbildenden Motorik in der Untersuchung der Nervenkranken," *Archiv für Psychiatrie und Nervenkrankheiten* 87 (1929): 471–497; Alexander Luria, "Die Methode der abbildenden Motorik in der Tatbestandsdiagnostik," *Zeitschrift für angewandte Psychologie* 35 (1930): 139–183.

62 Lev S. Vygotsky and Alexander Luria, "The function and fate of egocentric speech," at the Ninth International Congress of Psychology held at Yale University, New Haven, CT, 1–7 September 1929, ed. J. M. Cattell (Princeton, NJ: Psychological Review Company, 1930), 464–465.

63 Kurt Lewin, "Die Auswirkung von Umweltkraften," at the Ninth International Congress of Psychology held at Yale University, New Haven, CT, 1–7 September 1929, ed. J. M. Cattell (Princeton, NJ: Psychological Review Company, 1930), 286–288.

64 A notebook "9-i mezhdunarodnyi kongress po psikhologii 1929," Luria Family Archive, Svistukha village, Moscow, Russia.

65 Anton Yasnitsky, "Rekonstruktsiia poezdki A. R. Lurii na IX mezhdunarodnyi psikhologicheskii kongress," *Voprosy psikhologii* 4 (2012): 86–93.

66 Correspondence from Luria to Henry Murray, 9 January 1930, Series HUGFP 97.6, Box 12, Papers of Henry A. Murray, 1925–1988, Harvard University Archive, Boston, MA, USA.

67 Correspondence from Luria to Kallen, 29 September 1929, MS-1, Box 19, Folder 18, Horace M. Kallen Papers, American Jewish Archives, Cincinnati, OH, USA.

68 Horace M. Kallen, *The Frontiers of Hope* (New York: Arno Press, 1977), 289 (first published in 1929).

69 See the correspondence between Kallen and Luria – MS-1, Box 19, Folder 18, Horace M. Kallen Papers, American Jewish Archives, Cincinnati, OH, USA; RG 317, Series V, folder 780, Papers of Horace M. Kallen (1882–1974), YIVO Institute for Jewish Research, New York, USA.

70 A notebook "Doklady i referaty 1929, 1930, 1931," in the Luria Family Archive, Svistukha village, Moscow, Russia.

71 Yasnitsky, "Rekonstruktsiia poezdki A. R. Lurii na IX mezhdunarodnyi psikhologicheskii kongress," 90.

72 Aleksandr R. Luriia, "Mezhdunarodnyi kongress psikhologov v Amerike (1–7 sentiabria 1929)," *Nauchnoe slovo* 4 (1930): 83–99; Aleksandr R. Luriia, "Puti sovremennoi psikhologii," *Estestvoznanie i marksizm* 2–3 (1930): 61–102.

73 Luria, "Mezhdunarodnyi kongress psikhologov v Amerike," 84–90; Luria, "Puti sovremennoi psikhologii," 62–74.

74 Luria, "Mezhdunarodnyi kongress psikhologov v Amerike," 91.

75 Luria, "Puti sovremennoi psikhologii," 74–95.

76 Luria, "Mezhdunarodnyi kongress psikhologov v Amerike," 94.

77 Luria, "Puti sovremennoi psikhologii," 83.

78 Luria, "Puti sovremennoi psikhologii," 86.

79 Luria, "Mezhdunarodnyi kongress psikhologov v Amerike," 93–94.

80 Luria, "Puti sovremennoi psikhologii," 93.

81 Lev S. Vygotskii, "O psikhologicheskikh sistemakh," in *Sobranie sochinenii, tom I: Voprosy teorii i istorii psikhologii*, eds. Aleksandr R. Luria and Mikhail G. Iaroshevskii (Moscow: Pedagogika, 1982), 109–131.

82 Lev S. Vygotsky, "On psychological systems," in *The Collected Works of L. S. Vygotsky. Vol 3: Problems of Theory and History of Psychology*, eds. R. W. Rieber and J. Wollock (New York: Plenum, 1997), 102.

83 Correspondence from Luria to Kallen, 7 February 1930, RG 317, Series V, folder 780, Papers of Horace Meyer Kallen (1882–1974), YIVO Institute for Jewish Research, New York, USA; Correspondence from Luria to Kallen, 31 March 1930 and 14 June

1930, MS-1, Box 19, Folder 18, Horace M. Kallen Papers, American Jewish Archives, Cincinnati, OH, USA.

84 Correspondence from Luria to Kallen, 5 July 1930, MS-1, Box 19, Folder 18, Horace M. Kallen Papers, American Jewish Archives, Cincinnati, OH, USA.

85 Luria, *The Nature of Human Conflicts*, 3–39.

86 Luria, *The Nature of Human Conflicts*, 6–7.

87 The vast majority of these experiments were done before Luria's trip to the USA. See above the short discussion of Luria's study of affect.

88 See the translator's admission of this fact – Luria, *The Nature of Human Conflicts*, X.

89 Luria, *The Nature of Human Conflicts*, 9–10.

90 Luria, *The Nature of Human Conflicts*, 356–359.

91 Luria, *The Nature of Human Conflicts*, 367–397.

92 Luria, *The Nature of Human Conflicts*, 394–395.

93 Luria, *The Nature of Human Conflicts*, 397–428.

94 Luria, *The Nature of Human Conflicts*, 401.

95 Luria, *The Nature of Human Conflicts*, 403.

96 Eli Lamdan and Anton Yasnitsky, "Did Uzbek Have Illusions? The Luria-Koffka controversy of 1932," in *Revisionist Revolution in Vygotsky Studies*, eds. Anton Yasnitsky and René van der Veer (London: Routledge, 2016), 175–200.

97 Alexander Luria, "Psychological Expedition to Central Asia," *Science* 74 (1931): 383–384.

98 Aleksandr R. Luriia, *Ob istoricheskom razvitii poznavatel'nykh protsessov* (Moscow: Nauka, 1974), 27.

99 Correspondence from Vygotsky to Luria, 20 June 1931, in Georg Rückriem, *Lev Semënovič Vygotskij. Briefe/Letters. 1924–1934* (Berlin: Lehmanns Media, 2009), 262.

100 Correspondence from Vygotsky to Luria, 11 July 1931, in Georg Rückriem, *Lev Semënovič Vygotskij*, 264.

101 Correspondence from Vygotsky to Luria, 1 August 1931, in Georg Rückriem, *Lev Semënovič Vygotskij*, 266.

102 Correspondence from Luria to Horsley Gantt, 17 August 1931, Series III, Box 48, Folder 28, The W. Horsley Gantt Collection, Medical Archives of the JHMI, Baltimore, MD, USA.

103 Alexander Luria, "Psychological Expedition to Central Asia," *Science* 74 (1931): 383–384; Alexander Luria, "Psychologische Expedition nach Mittelassien," *Zeitschrift für Angewandte Psychologie* 40 (1931): 551–552; Alexander Luria, "Psychological Expedition to Central Asia," *Journal of Genetic Psychology* 40 (1931): 241–242; Correspondence from Luria to Kallen, 29 October 1931, MS-1, Box 19, Folder 18, Horace M. Kallen Papers, American Jewish Archives, Cincinnati, OH, USA.

104 Correspondence from Luria to Wolfgang Köhler, 3 December 1931, American Philosophical Society Archive, Philadelphia, PA.

105 Correspondence from Luria to Kurt Lewin, 9 April 1932, in Alexandr Metraux, "Alexandr Lurijas Briefe an Lewin," *Mittteilungen der Luria-Gesellschaft* 9 (2002): 36–37.

106 Kurt Koffka, "Preodolenie mekhanisticheskikh i vitalisticheskikh techenii v sovremennoi psikhologii," *Psikhologiia* 3 (1932): 59–69.

107 Koffka, quoted in Alexander Luria, "The second psychological expedition to Central Asia," *Journal of Genetic Psychology* 44 (1934): 257.

108 Koffka, quoted in Luria, "The second psychological expedition to Central Asia," 257.

109 While still in Central Asia, Koffka had started to write his *Principles of Gestalt Psychology*. For his general view and basic assumptions for psychological research, with references to the expedition, see Kurt Koffka, *Principles of Gestalt Psychology* (New York: Harcourt, Brace and Co., 1935), 3–68.

110 Correspondence from Kurt Koffka to Molly Harrower, 1 July 1932, in Molly Harrower, *Kurt Koffka: An unwitting self-portrait* (Gainesville, FL: University of Florida Press, 1983), 150.

111 Arne Haugen, *The Establishment of National Republics in Soviet Central Asia* (New York: Palgrave Macmillan, 2003).

112   On the socio-political context of this, see Lamdan and Yasnitsky, "Did Uzbek Have Illusions?" 188–193.

113   Correspondence from Vygotsky to Luria, 17 August 1932, in Georg Rückriem, *Lev Semёnovič Vygotskij*, 274–275.

114   René van der Veer and Anton Yasnitsky, "Vygotsky the published: who wrote Vygotsky and what Vygotsky actually wrote," in *Revisionist Revolution in Vygotsky Studies*, eds. Anton Yasnitsky and René van der Veer (London: Routledge, 2016), 73–93; Ekaterina Zavershneva, "Vygotsky the unpublished: an overview of the personal archive (1912–1934)," in *Revisionist Revolution in Vygotsky Studies*, eds. Anton Yasnitsky and René van der Veer (London: Routledge, 2016), 94–126.

115   Some of them: Mark S. Lebedinskii, "Psikhologicheskii analiz sluchaia afazii," *Sovetskaia psikhonevrologiia* 9 (1933): 49–58; Aleksandr R. Luriia, "K voprosu o psikhologicheskom issledovanii raspada rechevykh funktsii. Doklad na konferentsii UPNA. Zasedanie 27 noiabria 1932-go g.," *Sovetskaia psikhonevrologiia* 9 (1933): 161–162; Lev S. Vygotskii, "Psikhologiia i uchenie o lokalizatsii," in *Pervyi vseukrainskii s"ezd nevropatologov i psikhiatrov. Kharkov, 1934. 8–14 iiunia*, ed. L. L. Rokhlin, (Kharkov: Knizhnaia fabrika imeni G. I. Petrovskogo, 1934), 34–41.

116   Bluma V. Zeigarnik, "K probleme ponimaniia perenosnogo smysla predlozheniia pri patologicheskikh izmeneniiakh myshleniia," in *Novoe v uchenii ob agnozii, apraksii i afazii*, ed. Anonymous (Moscow: OGIZ, 1934), 132–146; Gita V. Birenbaum, "K voprosu ob obrazovanii perenosnykh i uslovnykh znachenii slova pri patologicheskikh izmeneniiakh myshleniia," in *Novoe v uchenii ob agnozii, apraksii i afazii*, ed. *Anonymous* (Moscow: OGIZ, 1934), 147–164.

117   Yasnitsky, *Vygotsky. An Intellectual Biography*.

118   Aleksandr R. Luriia, "Prof. L. S. Vygotskii 1896–1934," *Sovetskaia nevropatologiia, psikhiatriia i psikhogigiena* 4 (1935): 165–169; Alexander Luria, "Professor L. S. Vygotsky (1896–1934)," *Journal of Genetic Psychology* 46 (1935): 224–226; Alexander Luria, "L. S. Vygotsky," *Character and Personality* 3 (1935): 238–240.

119   On Stalinist science see: Nikolai Krementsov, *Stalinist Science* (Princeton, NJ: Princeton University Press, 1997). On Stalinist science in psychology see: Anton Yasnitsky, "The archetype of Soviet psychology: from the Stalinism of the 1930s to the 'Stalinist science' of our time," in *Revisionist Revolution in Vygotsky Studies*, eds. Anton Yasnitsky and René van der Veer (London: Routledge, 2016), 3–26.

120   René van der Veer and Anton Yasnitsky, "Translating Vygotsky: some problems of transnational Vygotskian science," in *Revisionist Revolution in Vygotsky Studies*, eds. Anton Yasnitsky and René van der Veer (London: Routledge, 2016), 143–174.

5

A HISTORY OF THE SOCIAL CONSTRUCTION OF THE "CULTURAL-HISTORICAL"

Peter Keiler

> The word is a philosophy of the fact; it can be its mythology and its scientific theory.
> *Lev S. Vygotsky*

Introduction

General remarks

As one of the co-founders of Critical Psychology, which took its rise in the context of the radical student movement of the late 1960s and early 1970s in the Federal Republic of Germany (FRG) and West Berlin, the author of the present paper has been engaged in the study of the so-called "cultural-historical" approach in Soviet psychology since the mid-1970s. In the beginning, like all of West German psychologists with a Marxist (non-Maoist) orientation at that time, he was deeply impressed by the German version of A.N. Leontiev's book *Problems of the development of the psyche [Problemy razvitiia psikhiki]*, which in a licensed version and with a detailed foreword by Klaus Holzkamp and Volker Schurig was published in 1973 in the FRG. (The original version had already been available in the German Democratic Republic – GDR – since 1964).[1] For about a decade this book, appearing in several editions, was celebrated as a testimonial of "cultural-historical theory" in its hitherto best elaborated version (cf. Holzkamp & Schurig 1973; Keiler 1976; Keiler 1981a), determining not only the public's attitude towards L.S. Vygotsky but also the common use of the terminology conveyed by the book, which at that time was uncritically accepted as reliable and compulsory. In 1979 the present author, animated by the lecture of the German version of E.A. Budilova's *Philosophical problems in Soviet Psychology [Filosofskie problemy v sovetskoi psikhologii]*, started to engage in the controversy between Leontiev and S.L. Rubinshtein, an enterprise that subsequently led him to a detachment from Leontiev's views, encouraging him to undertake a more detailed study of the "cultural-historical" approach, especially in its historical connections, with a concentration on the materialist traditions in the history of psychology in the last two centuries.

Taking advantage of the opportunity to realize independent (not granted, not censored) research work on his own account, in the mid-1980s the author came to some surprising insights: for instance, that Leontiev not only in his orientation to the paradigm of "activity" [deiatel'nost', "Tätigkeit"] but also in the elaboration of his famous concept of "objectivization-appropriation" [opredmechivanie-prisvoenie, "Vergegenständlichung-Aneignung"], had beyond doubt been influenced by Rubinshtein and his Marxist interpretation (inspired by the German tradition of theories on the "objective spirit"). This insight shed new light not only on Rubinshtein's later critiques of Leontiev but also on the relation of both of them to Vygotsky, especially on Leontiev's role as the keeper of the "holy grail" and "perfectioner" of Vygotsky's approach. On the other hand, in the late 1980s and early 1990s the author became more and more fascinated by Vygotsky's affinity with the psychological aspects of the work of the German philosopher Ludwig Feuerbach, which has left so many marks in Vygotsky's own writings, though not always recognizable as such at first glance.

The most important findings of this critical-historical research were published in a series of papers and two books, gaining the author the reputation of being a "myth buster" (cf. Keiler 1988a, 1988b, 1991, 1996, 1997/31999, 2002, 2008, 2010a, 2010b, 2015, 2017). However, the respective research work would not have been possible without the remarkable change in the conditions of access to pertinent source material – a change that had already begun in the 1980s. New material was introduced, freely accessible to the public. First they were only in Russian – six volumes of *Sobranie sochinenii [Collected works]* of Vygotsky (1982–1984), and two volumes of *Izbrannye psikhologicheskie proizvedeniia [Selected psychological works]* of Leontiev (1983); then also in German – two volumes of *Ausgewählte Schriften [Selected works]* of Vygotsky (cf. Wygotski 1985/1987); and since the end of the 1980s also in English – six volumes of Vygotsky's *Collected works* (1987–1999), Vygotsky and Luria's *Studies in the history of behavior* (cf. Luria & Vygotsky 1992), a *Vygotsky Reader* (1994), Vygotsky's *Pedagogical psychology* (1997), and, last but not least, a compilation of Vygotsky critiques from the 1930s, edited by R. van der Veer (2000). This new material opened up broader perspectives for a qualified critical examination of "legends" and reception traditions, finding support in the analysis of the re-published (and in some cases first published) early work of Leontiev (cf. Leont'ev 2001, Leont'ev 2003a, Leont'ev 2006).

This perspective has assumed a new quality, establishing the project of publishing the *Complete Collected Works of Lev Semenovich Vygotsky* in 15 volumes (cf. ISCAR NEWS 2008, Vol. 6, No. 2, pp. 7 ff.) in order to replace the six volumes of *Sobranie sochinenii*, which, along with the *Collected works*, have become the subject of severe criticism in recent years (cf. for instance van der Veer 1997a; van der Veer & Yasnitsky 2011). In more or less close relation to this project, during the last decade there has been a lot of archival and "textological" work, trying to restore what might be called the "authentic" legacy of Vygotsky (cf. Zavershneva 2009; Zavershneva 2010a;

Zavershneva 2010b; Zavershneva 2010c; Yasnitsky 2010; Kellog 2011; Kellog & Yasnitsky 2011; Mecacci & Yasnitsky 2011; Yasnitsky 2011a; Zavershneva 2012a; Zavershneva 2012b; Zavershneva 2012c; Zavershneva & Osipov 2012; Zavershneva & van der Veer 2018) – an ambitious enterprise in the context of which Vygotsky's aphorism about "the word" being "the philosophy of the fact" was gaining programmatic significance: how authentic, or "honest," is the commonly used terminology? What is the reality behind (or covered by) the established shibboleths?

Subject of the paper and applied method

In the present paper, the main accent is put on the question of the legitimacy of the commonly used labels "cultural-historical theory" and "cultural-historical school," emphasizing in addition the concept of the "higher psychological functions" as the main topic of Vygotsky's research program between 1927/1928 and 1934 (the year of his death). In sections 1–7, the method will be mainly empirical-historical. That is, based on the original literature (Russian and English texts from the 1920s and 1930s) and on the respective correspondence, it will be documented *who, when,* on *which occasion,* and *with what intentions,* called (denominated, designated) *what how.* This will be complemented by two interval sections (2 and 4) presenting some general reflections and additional information about the conceptions sustained by Vygotsky as the *spiritus rector* [2] (as is generally accepted) of the theories under investigation between 1927/1928 and 1934, accentuating the period between 1928 and 1932, which is commonly associated with the idea of the genesis and development of *the* "cultural-historical theory" (cf. for instance as "trendsetters" van der Veer & Valsiner 1991). Section 8 is dedicated to a résumé of the findings elaborated in paragraphs 1–7, and in addition gives a survey of the development of the discourse after the "rediscovery" of Vygotsky during the "thaw" of the late 1950s. Lastly, in section 9 there will be a critical conclusion of the findings of the foregoing sections.

Because of the "sensibility of the matter" (Feuerbach) it was necessary to include a lot of annotations with comments, explications, and additional information, the real significance of which perhaps may be recognized only in reading the whole paper a second time.

The author is deeply indebted to René van der Veer and Anton Yasnitsky for providing copies of a good quantity of the original historical sources (Russian texts) referred to and quoted from in the present paper, thus not only furthering this paper but also those that still are in preparation and will give a more detailed account of some topics that in the present paper have only been outlined. To mention their help in every single case separately would have required a considerable number of additional annotations.

1. Development of the autochthonous[3] terminology until 1932

The two earliest pertinent documents, freely accessible to the public, date from 1929, the year in which Vygotsky's "instrumentalism," inspired by Spinoza's and

Hegel's high appreciation of the "tool"[4] and characteristic of the period from 1928 until 1930, had already found its full expression. Thus, in the context of his letter to A.N. Leontiev dated the 15th of April 1929, Vygotsky first speaks of "our theory" (quoted in Puzyrei & Vygotsky 2007, p. 23), then gives the information that he wants to "convene a 'conference' in spring or summer of people working with the instrumental method" (ibid.),[5] finally saying: "I am sincerely happy about your joys: The study of Korsakov's psychosis is *very* interesting; in general, pathology + cultural psychology (divergence) is the *principal* means of analysis …" (quoted in Puzyrei & Vygotsky 2007, p.23).

On the 23rd of July the same year (i.e. three months later), Vygotsky in another letter to Leontiev writes by way of introduction: "I wholeheartedly share your sentiments. There is some benefit to a situation in which I[nstrumental] P[sychology] winds up in the category of unprofitable pursuits" (ibid., pp. 25 f.; insertions in brackets by Puzyrei).[6] Later on, expressing some second thoughts, he adds: "Let us explain that studying cultural psychology is no joke, not something to do at odd moments or among other things, and no grounds for every new person's own conjectures" (ibid., p. 26). And as footnote there is a remark, referring to Vygotsky's collaborators at the Institute for Experimental Defectology, L.V. Zankov and I.M. Solov'ev: "In a moral sense, I hold them fully responsible for their departure from cultural psychology …" (ibid., footnote).

From that, one gets the impression that Vygotsky in the summer of 1929 still wanted to see the project pushed ahead in collaboration mainly with Luria and Leontiev (at that time it was more ridiculed than attacked, but was nevertheless misunderstood by the colleagues); he wanted it to be subsumed under a more generally conceived current of research and theorizing (in the broadest sense "cultural-psychologically" oriented), but with the specification that "means-stimuli," or "psychological tools," play a central role (cf. Vygotski 1929; A.N. Leont'ev in *Sobr. soch.*, Vol. 1, pp. 23–27, resp. in *Coll. works*, Vol. 3, pp. 19–23; and Leont'ev 2003b, p. 63 f., p. 134).[7]

An early contribution to the specification of the terminology then can be found in the author's short foreword to Leontiev's book *The development of memory [Razvitie pamiati]* (subtitled: "Experimental investigation of the higher psychological functions"[8]), dated the 8th of July 1930. Here Leontiev writes by way of introduction:

> The present work is an attempt at a monographic investigation, starting with *the theory of the historical development of the higher forms of behavior* [teoriia istoricheskogo razvitiia vysshikh form povedeniia] as it has been first formulated by L.S. Vygotsky and has been developed further in recent years by us together with A.R. Luria.
>
> *Leont'ev 2003b, p. 32 transl. and italics by P. Keiler*[9]

In the introduction to his article, separated out of the book and published in the *Journal of Genetic Psychology* in 1932[10] as the third and last within a series, edited by

Luria and Vygotsky under the title "Studies on the cultural development of the child", Leontiev states:

> ... in other words, we must create a general theory of the social[11] and historical development of behavior. Such a theory of social genesis ("the theory of cultural development") was first formulated and brought forward by L.S. Vygotsky.[12] His theory forms the basis of the present experimental-psychological sketch.
>
> *Leontiev 1932, p. 54*

In his ample foreword to Leontiev's book, apparently penned in September of 1930,[13] Vygotsky adopts Leontiev's terminology in writing:

> In this sense Leontiev's methodological work is determined by our central idea: the idea of the historical development of human behavior, the historical theory of the higher psychological functions [istoricheskaia teoriia vysshikh psikhologicheskikh funktsii]. From the viewpoint of this theory, the historical origin and the development of the higher psychological functions of man, and especially that of the higher functions of memory, is the key to understanding their essence [prirody], their composition, their structure, their way of functioning, and at the same time the key to the whole problem of a psychology of man, which is trying to determine adequately the true human content of this psychology.
>
> *Vygotskii 2003, p. 31; transl. and insertion in brackets by P. Keiler*[14]

So it seems, Vygotsky, when penning this, either did not yet have knowledge of the criticism that had been formulated by A. Frankel in his review of *Studies in the history of behavior* – a review that was entitled "Against the eclecticism in psychology and pedology" and was published apparently in August 1930 (for more details cf. Cole 1979, pp. 208 f.) – or he assessed Frankel's criticism at this moment as only marginal, as an event that did not need comment.[15]

The situation was completely different when Vygotsky and Leontiev, more than one and a half years later, were forced to co-author a self-critical enclosure to the book, which was the necessary condition for its release. Publication finally took place in 1932,[16] the book having indeed already gone to press in the late spring of 1931 (cf. A.A. Leontiev 2005) but having been withheld because of the growing criticism of the conceptions of the Vygotsky-Luria group uttered within the broader context of an assessment of the "leading" psychological theories (cf. below, section 3).

In that enclosure, it is first indicated that since the book had been completed ("more than two years ago") there had been "significant additions and modifications" to "the basic psychological conception" guiding Leontiev's investigations, that is "the conception of the historical development of the higher psychological functions [kontseptsii istoricheskogo razvitiia vysshich psikhologicheskikh funktsii]," an indication that later on is explicated in the following way:

In its essence the so-called [tak nazyvaiemaia] theory of the historical (or cultural-historical) development in psychology [teoriia istoricheskogo (ili kul'-
turno-istoricheskogo) razvitiia v psikhologii] denominates the theory *of the
higher psychological functions* (logical memory, voluntary attention, speech-
thinking [rechevoe myshlenie], volitional processes, etc.) – *nothing more, and
nothing less.* The origin and development of the higher psychological functions,
their structure and their composition, their way of functioning and their
mutual connections and interdependencies, the laws that govern their course
and fate – all this constitutes the exact content and the true topic of these
investigations.

*Vygotskii & Leont'ev 2003a, pp. 199 f.; transl. and insertions in brackets by P.
Keiler*[17]

In all probability, Leontiev had not only co-signed the self-criticism but was really
its co-author. However, that he in no way was content with the conclusions that
Vygotsky had drawn from it can be deduced from his letter to Vygotsky, dated the
5th of March 1932. In it he not only expresses his preoccupation with the course
of revision ("significant additions and modifications") adopted by Vygotsky but also
discloses his own orientation: "the return to the initial theses and their development along new lines" (cf. A.A. Leontiev 2005, p. 35, p. 37).[18] At this, his call for
a return "to the roots" even takes on an imploring, dramatic character as he
reproduces exactly the terminology that Vygotsky had used in his letter dated the
23rd of July 1929: first, he quotes word for word from those passages in which
Vygotsky had used formulations such as "cultural psychology" and "i[nstrumental]
p[sychology]" (cf. Leont'ev 2003f, p. 232), and later (within the scope of his criticism of Luria and the explication of his own position) he uses the grammalogue
"CP" for "Cultural Psychology" several times (cf. ibid., pp. 233 ff.).

Given all that, Leontiev's appeal was definitely "out of time." Factually, the
original terminology, which was apt to provoke misunderstandings (cf. above,
footnotes 6 and 14), had already been left behind by Vygotsky more than a year
before the joint self-criticism was penned. Thus, the survey of the contents of
chapter 10 of his *Pedology of the adolescent [Pedologiia podrostka]*, written in the second
half of 1930 and published in the first half of 1931, already presents the *short form*
"Theory of the development of the higher psychological functions [Teoriia razvitiia vysshikh psikhologicheskikh funktsii]" (cf. Vygotskii 1931, p. 214; resp.
Vygotsky 1994, p. 185).

2. Intermediate reflections

Concerning the conceptions held by Vygotsky in the period from 1928 until 1931,
the most adequate (and most authentic) denominations are: "theory (conception)
of the cultural (historical) development of the higher psychological functions," or
more precisely "theory of the cultural-historical determined origin and development of the higher psychological functions." The short form – "theory of the

development of the higher psychological functions" – is also possible, as long as the (behaviorism-oriented) formulation "theory of the social [societal] and historical development of (human) behavior," or "theory of the historical development of the higher forms of behavior," is not preferred. The latter is a variant which has been used by Vygotsky, as well as by Leontiev,[19] whereas the denomination "theory of cultural development," as used by Leontiev as well as by several critics, indeed seems "acceptable" (because of its reference to the title of the series of articles which, under the editorship of Luria and Vygotsky, had been published in the *Journal of Genetic Psychology*).[20] However, it has the disadvantage of obscuring the differences with other (earlier or later) variants of an unspecifically conceived "culture-psychology [Kulturpsychologie]" or "ethnopsychology." This becomes even more problematic when, with reference to the Vygotsky-Luria-Leontiev approach, denominations such as "cultural psychology" or "theory of cultural-psychological development" are used (cf. above, footnotes 6 and 14).

For all that, the *original version*, the "theory of the cultural-historical development of the higher psychological functions" (which A.A. Leontiev much later will call "Vygotsky's 'classical' cultural-historical conception" [cf. Leontiev 2005, p. 43]), can be identified by four essential characteristics:

1. The basic idea that in the psychological development of the child there are two lines (the "natural" and the "cultural") which at a certain point of ontogenesis meet and merge into each other in such a way that it is difficult to distinguish them and follow the course of each of them separately;

2. The conviction that in the process of the transformation of the natural ("lower" ["nizshikh"], elementary) psychological processes in culturally determined "higher" psychological functions, "means-stimuli" or "psychological tools" play the decisive role;[21]

3. The assumption that the genesis of the "higher" (specifically human) psychological functions (logical memory, voluntary attention, speech-thinking [rechevoe myshlenie], volitional processes, etc.) comes to pass in four stages, whereby the last one can be characterized as "ingrowing," or "interiorization" (interiorizatsiia) of the means and methods with which the child is "mastering" (i.e. controlling, organizing) her (his) behavior;

4. The application of the "method of double stimulation," also called the "instrumental method" („Werkzeugmethode").

This *original version* of the "theory of the cultural historical development of the higher psychological functions" which may be qualified as "instrumentalistic," is documented in Luria's "The problem of the cultural behavior of the child" (1928), Vygotsky's "The problem of the cultural development of the child" (1928, 1929), "The genetic roots of thinking and speech" ([1929]; cf. *Coll. works*, Vol. 1, pp. 101–120), "Fundamental problems of contemporary defectology" ([1929] cf. *Coll. works*, Vol. 2, pp. 29–51), "The instrumental method in psychology" ([1929?] cf. *Coll. works*, Vol. 3, pp. 85–89), Leontiev's *The development of memory* ([1931/32], cf.

Leont'ev 2003b),[22] and Vygotsky & Luria's *Studies in the history of behavior* ([1930], Luria & Vygotsky 1992). From this original came *two revised versions.*

The *first revision* – documented in Vygotsky's oral presentation from the 9th of October 1930 on "psychological systems" (cf. *Coll. works*, Vol. 3, pp. 91–107), in the fragment (later entitled by the editor) "Concrete human psychology" (cf. Vygotskii 1986, resp. Vygotsky 1989),[23] and in the 16th chapter ("assignment") of *Pedology of the adolescent* ([1931] cf. *Coll. works*, Vol. 5, pp. 167–184) – is characterized by:

1. the renunciation of the principle of the unilinear formation of the higher psychological functions and the turn to a systemic point of view, taking into account the mutual connections and interdependencies of the functions;
2. the formulation of the basic principle that every higher function was originally shared between (at least) two persons, that it was a reciprocal psychological process;
3. concordant with this basic principle, a reformulation of the concept of interiorization. As every "higher" form of behavior, or "higher" psychological function in its origin is a *social* (sotsial'naia) form of behavior, it must at first have the character of an external operation. That is, the functions of memory, thinking, and attention (to mention only three) in their origin are external operations, including the use of external signs, being a particular form of social relation, a form that cannot be realized without signs. Thus, the sign originally is a means of influencing others and only later becomes a means of affecting oneself. In the course of development every external function is interiorized, that is, it loses the traits of an external operation and is converted into an internal one.

The *second revision* (essentially realized under the pressure of the growing criticism), as it is documented in the theoretical-methodological part of the (later so-called) *History of the development of the higher psych[olog]ical functions* (cf. Vygotskii 1960, resp. *Coll. works*, Vol. 4, pp. 1–119) – i.e. the very part which was probably re-elaborated in 1931[24] – is characterized by the following additional modifications:

1. the attempt to give a new interpretation of the basic idea of the two lines and their "mergence" in the course of the psychological development of the child by a reference to the concept of "systems of action," as it had been introduced by the zoologist H.S. Jennings at the beginning of the century;
2. the strict conceptual differentiation between tools and signs (an indirect self-criticism of the concept of "psychological tools");
3. a stronger accentuation of the *social* aspects of culture compared with its *"real"* (i.e. oriented in material things) aspects.

That said, it is difficult to incorporate the findings of that famous study entitled "Tool and symbol in child development," written to be included in C.

Murchison's *Handbook of Child Psychology*, and co-authored by Vygotsky and Luria (cf. Vygotsky & Luria 1994). The difficulty is that in the pertinent literature this study is commonly dated 1930[25] – i.e. *before* the definite re-elaboration of the theoretical-methodological part of the *History of the development of the higher psych [olog]ical functions* – a dating that does not fit with Guillaume and Meyerson's (1930) significant observation that chimpanzees in their use of "tools" resemble aphasics. This observation, which is referred to for the first time in "Tool and symbol" (cf. Vygotsky & Luria 1994, pp. 111 f.), despite its utmost systematic importance,[26] is not mentioned in the "History" monograph but only reappears in 1934 in the context of Vygotsky's foreword to the Russian edition of K. Koffka's book *The fundamentals of psychical development* (cf. *Coll. works*, Vol. 3, p. 208).[27] On the other hand, Jennings' concept of "systems of action," which is characteristic of the "History" monograph (cf. *Coll. works*, Vol. 4, p. 20, p. 38, p. 63, p. 201, p. 244), neither reappears in "Tool and symbol" nor in other later works by Vygotsky. Hence, the dating of "Tool and symbol" to 1930 must be put in doubt (in this sense cf. the Vygotsky bibliographies in *Sobr. soch.*, Vol. 6, p. 371; *Coll. works*, Vol. 6, p. 292; and Vygodskaia & Lifanova 1996, p. 402), although the correct declaration cannot be more precise than "with the highest probability *after* the definite re-elaboration of the first five chapters of the *History of the development of the higher psych[olog]ical functions*."[28]

In regard to the common practice also to subsume under the label of a "conception of *cultural-historical* development" the later work of Vygotsky (1932–1934), in which the *sociality of man in its various forms* is stressed as the essential (inner) condition of his psychological development (as in some of Vygotsky's "early" writings),[29] it has to be repeated here that incorporation can be justified only in the scope of an auxiliary construction (cf. Keiler 1991, 1997/[3]1999, 2002, 2005, 2015). This auxiliary construction is based especially on the remarkable affinity of the later work of Vygotsky to the views of L. Feuerbach and argues that the aforementioned conception of the cultural-historical determination of the development of the specifically human psychological functions has to be understood in a more general sense, as explicated by Feuerbach:

> Thus *man* is the *God of man*. That he is, he has to thank *Nature*; that he is *man*, he has to thank *man*; spiritually as well as physically he can achieve nothing without his fellow-man. … Wit, acumen, imagination, feeling as distinguished from sensation, reason as a subjective faculty – all these so-called powers of the soul are *powers of humanity*, not of man as an individual; they are products of culture, products of human society. Only where man has *contact* and *friction* with his fellow-man are wit and sagacity kindled … and only where man *communicates* with man, only in speech, a social act, awakes reason. To ask a question and to answer are the first acts of thought. Thought originally demands two. It is not until man has reached an advanced stage of culture that he can double himself, so as to play the part of another within himself.
>
> *Feuerbach 1957, p. 83; italics from the German original, FGW, Vol. 5, pp. 166f,*
> *omissions by P. Keiler*

Or, more succinctly: "… man, who arose directly from nature, was still only a pure natural, not a human being. Man [as human] is a product of man, of culture, of history" (FGW, Vol. 10, p. 178; transl. and insertion in brackets by P. Keiler).[30]

At any rate, it has to be recorded that, despite the revisions, the "higher psychological functions" remained the central topic of Vygotsky's research and theorizing until his untimely death in June 1934. This topic had been present implicitly in "early" Vygotsky's struggle with the reflexology of V.M. Bekhterev's and I.P. Pavlov's "theory of higher nervous activity" (cf. Keiler 2002, pp. 79–82, pp. 91–115; resp. Keiler 2015, pp. 63–65, pp. 74–96), at that time still as an undefined counter-concept to "higher nervous activity (behavior) of animals." In 1928–1930 the (behaviorism-oriented) formulations "higher behavior," or "higher" or "cultural forms of behavior" can be assessed as a preliminary attempt to denominate the "key to the whole problem of a psychology of man, which is trying to determine adequately the true human content of this psychology" in a way that was also acceptable to "mainstream" Soviet-Russian "objective psychology."

3. The terminology and arguments of the critics in 1931 and 1932

Vygotsky's clarification – integrated in the self-critical enclosure to Leontiev's book regarding the so-called "theory of the historical (or cultural-historical) development," or the "theory of the historical development of the higher forms of behavior," or simply the "theory of the higher psychological functions" – took place in the context of the growing criticism that, in the aftermath of Frankel's review of the *Studies in the history of behavior*, were put forward against the ideas of the Vygotsky-Luria group. These criticisms, in the context of the discussion on the "reactology" of K.N. Kornilov, had already assumed a new quality in the spring of 1931 which could no longer be ignored.

Thus, for instance, the aforementioned discussion on reactology was brought to a close by a resolution from the Communist Party cell of the Psychological Institute of the Moscow University, which mentions in a depreciatory manner "the 'culturological' [kul'turnicheskaia] theory of Vygotsky and Luria" (cf. "Results of the discussion on reactological psychology," 1931, p. 388; transl. by P. Keiler). Shortly after this Kornilov was removed from his post as the institute's director.

A.A. Talankin, a member of the party cell and a very active participant in the discussion, uses for the first time the phrase "cultural-historical conception," subsuming Vygotsky's and Luria's approach under a more general theoretical current.

Thus, in his oral presentation at the All-Union Congress on Psychotechnics and the Psychophysiology of Labor on the "turnaround on the psychological front" (delivered in May 1931, and later published in the journal *Sovetskaia psikhonevrologiia*), Talankin reproaches the Vygotsky-Luria group for their tendency towards the "uncritical transfer of various Western European psychological theories that are especially fashionable now" into Soviet psychology: "In one period this was Freudianism [frejdizm]; next came Gestalt psychology [Gestaltpsychologie]; then came cultural psychology [kul'turpsikhologiia], and, finally, the current stemming from

Karl Bühler" (Talankin 2000, p. 10; for the original version cf. Talankin 1931, p. 15). He continues: "The conception of *Vygotsky and Luria* is a cultural-historical one [Kontseptsiia *Vygotskogo i Luriia* – kul'turno-istoricheskaia]. Their merit is that they pose the problem of development in Soviet psychology" (loc. cit.).

After this quite positive evaluation (cf. also Vygotsky in his letter to Luria dated the 1st of June 1931, Puzyrei & Vygotsky 2007, p. 33), Talankin, however, criticizes the concept of "psychological tools" as not conforming with the Marxist concept of tools and, further, censures Vygotsky's and Luria's understanding of culture as "crudely mechanistic," reducing culture to "the sum total of things, instruments, and symbols," showing "elements of real [nastoiashego] instrumentalism." At the end of his disclosure he comes to a conclusion which nullifies all previous positive assessments (e.g. that "the *Vygotsky and Luria* group is undoubtedly talented"), stating that "their conception of cultural psychology [kul'turno-psikhologicheskoi kontseptsiei] must be opposed." As it "has not yet been subjected to criticism," it has to be shown that "a Marxist approach to the problem of the development of mental processes [psikhicheskikh processov], on the basis of the history of labor, indeed differs radically from the approach to the problem of development we find in *Vygotsky and Luria* (Talankin 2000, p. 11; resp. Talankin 1931, p. 15).

For us, it is of foremost interest that Talankin's criticism already uses the wording "cultural-historical," but that Talankin does not yet use the formal denomination "cultural-historical theory" for the approach represented by the Vygotsky-Luria group. But that, however, is in a text which cannot be dated exactly, nor do we know the identity of its author. It has been "found among Vygotsky's papers," consists of "19 yellowed typewritten pages," is entitled "Against the cultural-historical perspective in psychology," and the initial letters of the author's first and last names are "A.Sh." (cf. Vygodskaia & Lifanova 1999a, 79). Vygodskaia and Lifanova identify it as a "review" of Vygotsky and Luria's book *Studies in the history of behavior* and admit that they have no knowledge of whether it was published, but declare that they "know with certainty that Lev Semenovich read it" (ibid.). Certain formulations in the text suggest that this review was written in the aftermath of the resolution of the party cell of the Moscow Psychological Institute and Talankin's claim for a serious critique of the Vygotsky-Luria group, thus, was probably in the second half of 1931 or later. That Vygotsky could read it as a typoscript, may mean that it had been submitted to one of the journals of which he was a member of the editorial board, so he had the opportunity to formulate his response before its publication and possibly write a comment or even a replication that could be published together with the review.

For its systematic significance – for the first time the label "cultural-historical theory"[31] is applied intentionally and repeatedly – it seems justified that "outtakes" of the review be reproduced as they have been quoted by Vygodskaia and Lifanova:

> One example of a noncritical perception of various positions in bourgeois psychology is the work of L.S. Vygotsky and A.R. Luria, which has not yet been subjected to any essential criticism.

Positions that are formalistic and idealistic in their essence are combined in a bizarre way with quite a number of mechanistic moments. However, despite all the eclecticism of Luria's and Vygotsky's cultural-historical theory [kul'-turno-istoricheskoi teorii], idealistic positions constitute the core of its methodological principles.

For the cultural-historical theory, the psychological evolution of collective farm workers in Tajikistan [kolkhoznikov tadjikistana] consists solely in their transformation into simply cultured people. The fact that this is a process of transformation of the peasant into an active conscious builder of socialist society is absolutely beyond the ability of the cultural-historical theory to ascertain.

The abstract historicism of Vygotsky and Luria, expressed in the thesis of cultural man in general, proves to be idealist in its essence. This abstract historicism of the authors of the cultural-historical theory emanates from their basic methodological approach to the problem of development.

All works built on the basis of the cultural-historical conception [kul'turno-istoricheskoi kontseptsii] require disregarding the child's active social involvement.

Seen through the eyes of cultural-historical theory, one cannot discover what is most important in the evolution of the mind [psikhiki] of the Tajik collective farm worker [kolkhoznika-tadjika]: one cannot understand what is specific, what is due to the socialist character of restoring the economy and the everyday life of the Tajik village.

Vygodskaia & Lifanova, 1999a, p. 80[32]

That this critical assessment of Vygotsky's and Luria's views certainly came to Vygotsky's attention but ultimately was not published is indicated by the fact that the simple (and close to the jargon of German police reports[33]) shortened form "kul'turno-istoricheskaia teoriia," or "kul'turno-istoricheskaia kontseptsiia," which had been anticipated already by Talankin, was not applied over the next two years within the continuing discussion about the Vygotsky-Luria group. Thus for instance, M.P. Feofanov in his critical article "The theory of cultural development in pedology as an eclectic[34] conception with basically idealist roots," published in the first issue of 1932 of the journal *Pedologiia*, used the formulation "theory of cultural development" 21 times, that is, exactly the same wording that Leontiev used in his paper, published the same year in the *Journal of Genetic Psychology*; Feofanov used this denomination 10 times without quotation marks (cf. Feofanov 2000, p. 12, p. 17, p. 19, p. 20, p. 26, p. 29), using quotation marks 10 times around the term "cultural development" (cf. ibid., p. 17, p. 19, p. 23, p. 24, p. 25, p. 26, p. 29) and once using quotation marks for the complete term (cf. ibid. p. 18).

In the editorial footnote to Feofanov's article, the anonymous editor reproduced the latter variant (i.e. the whole expression "theory of cultural development" put in quotation marks), but, following the wording of the 1931 resolution of the party cell of the Moscow Psychological Institute, the phrase "culturological theory [kul'turnicheskaia teoriia]" is also used – though this time without quotation marks (cf. Feofanov 1932, p. 221).

Only two issues later, in the same journal, a "review" authored by the two Leningrad psychologists R. Abel'skaia and Ia.S. Neopikhonova was published, entitled "The problem of development in German psychology and its influence on Soviet pedology and psychology."[35] It repeated several points of criticism that had already been put forward by Feofanov, mainly with reference to several passages in Vygotsky's *Pedology of the school age* (1928) and those chapters[36] of his correspondence course "textbook" *Pedology of the adolescent*, which had been published in 1929.

The object of reference for both of Vygotsky's "colleagues" was the book published by H. Werner in 1926, entitled *Einführung in die Entwicklungspsychologie*, the "review" of which was taken by them as an opportunity to compare Werner's views with those of Vygotsky, as they were expressed in *Studies in the history of behavior* and in the last part of *Pedology of the adolescent*, released in 1931. It was no secret that the intention of the "reviewers" was not only to criticize Werner's mistakes but to prove that similar mistakes had also been committed in "Soviet pedology and psychology," especially by Vygotsky and Luria.

For us it is of interest that Abel'skaia and Neopikhonova themselves avoid any labeling, but rather speak of "Vygotsky & Luria's book" (cf. Abel'skaia & Neopikhonova 2000, p. 40), "the works of Vygotsky" (ibid., p. 41) or "Vygotsky's writings" (ibid., p. 42). The labeling appears only at the end within an editorial note which is separated from the "review" by a dividing line. Here, in the first instance, it is clarified that Vygotsky and Luria's "theory 'of cultural development'" does *not* represent *the* "Soviet pedology and psychology," as Abel'skaia and Neopikhonova had mistakenly claimed. After that, with reference to Feofanov's article and "further critical articles, to be published in subsequent issues of our journal,"[37] the "afore said theory [ukazannaia teoriia]" is condemned as suffering from "fundamental methodological defects" (cf. Abel'skaia & Neopikhanova 1932, p. 36).

4. Intermediate résumé

As an intermediate résumé we may take as fact that, concerning the labeling of the conceptions sustained by the Vygotsky-Luria group in the period between 1928 and 1930/1931, the general discussion considered neither the denomination variants "historical theory of the higher psychological functions", nor "conception of the historical development of the higher psychological functions," or the "theory of the historical (or cultural-historical) development in psychology," as they had been used by Vygotsky himself in his detailed foreword to Leontiev's book and in the subsequently written self-critical enclosure; nor had it taken into consideration the variant "theory of the historical development of the higher forms of behavior," which had been used by Leontiev in his foreword to the book, or the alternative "theory of the development of the higher psychological functions," as chosen by Vygotsky for the survey of the contents of the 10th chapter of *Pedology of the adolescent*. Rather, in 1932 the label most used by critics was directly concordant with the denomination that Leontiev had chosen in his article, published the same year in the *Journal of Genetic Psychology*, i.e. the "theory of cultural development" – though different in that critics frequently used quotation marks, either to signal the dubiousness of the whole enterprise ("the so-called ...") or to call into question the adequacy of characterizing the developmental processes under investigation as "cultural" (as opposed to "natural") development.

It should also be noted that the criticisms where published at a time when Vygotsky himself had already recognized that the approach under attack had no substance for further development, even in "defused" form, and that qualitatively new perspectives for future research were needed. These perspectives were already outlined *ex negativo* in the enclosure to Leontiev's book and in Vygotsky's 1931/1932 critique of J. Piaget,[38] whereas Leontiev's perspectives were in the "return to the initial theses and their development along new lines"(A.A. Leontiev 2005, p. 37).[39]

Given all that, the publication of Leontiev's book *The development of memory*, originally planned for the end of 1930,[40] indeed signified a decisive "nodal point" in his career. Had it been published in the same year as Vygotsky's and Luria's *Studies in the history of behavior*, the book would likely have been received with great interest on the part of the reading public, serving in later discussions as a point of reference for not talking about the Vygotsky-Luria group but the Vygotsky-Luria-Leontiev group. However, with the delay in the publication of almost two years, the once highly regarded book[41] in the end was nothing more than the proverbial "dead dog," all the more so as Vygotsky and Leontiev, with their published self-criticism, had already anticipated and "neutralized" all possible attacks *ad personam* Leontiev.

5. The official introduction of the label "cultural-historical theory" by P.I. Razmyslov (1934)

If in the literature relevant to the subject there are no reports about official statements concerning the Vygotsky-Luria group and their "theory of cultural development" in 1933, this does not mean that at this time they were out of danger. Rather, the campaign to deny the "theory of cultural development" any right of existence at all continued "behind closed doors",[42] gaining publicity again in the spring of 1934 with the release of a defamatory "general account".

P.I. Razmyslov, in his role as head of a commission of the People's Control, had been tasked with investigating the "ideological premises" of all the research and publication activities hitherto realized by Vygotsky and Luria.[43] In issue No. 4 of the year 1934 in the journal *Book and Proletarian Revolution (Kniga i Proletarskaia Revoliutsiia)*[44] Razmyslov published a final report that had the defamatory label "cultural-historical theory" in its title: "On Vygotsky's and Luria's 'Cultural-Historical Theory of Psychology' [O 'kul'turno-istoricheskoi teorii psikhologii' Vygotskogo i Luria]." In the text itself the long version of the label "cultural-historical theory of psychology" is used six times and once the shortened form "cultural-historical theory," each time enclosed in quotation marks. In one place Razmyslov criticizes Vygotsky and

Luria for discussing the problems of culture in an abstract way from the perspective of a "cultural European" and "in the spirit of idealist, bourgeois, cultural-historical schools [v dukhe idealisticheskikh burjuaznykh kul'tnurno-istoricheskikh shkol]" (Razmyslov 1934, p. 79; resp. Razmyslov 2000, p. 47).

The point of departure of Razmyslov's attack was the reproach, now something of a cliché, that the "cultural-historical theory" was too general and did not take into account the class membership of the children whose development was under investigation. Moreover, in Vygotsky there was no reference to the means of production and other important concepts of communist „Weltanschauung." Razmyslov based his criticism on pertinent statements of Marx and Engels, trying to prove that Vygotsky's key idea about the genesis of human consciousness – i.e. generally speaking, the "higher psychological functions" from social interaction[45] – were wrong and biased to the "sociological thought of the neopositivists," or "neopositivist sociologists, such as Durkheim" (cf. Razmyslov 1934, p. 80 f., resp. Razmyslov 2000, p. 48 f.), while the application of the "foggy" concept of collective throughout Vygotsky's "books on pedology" (ibid., p. 81, resp. p. 49) was also a point of critique:

> Wherever, in our view, he should be speaking of a child's class environment, his production environment, of the influence of school, his Pioneer group, and the Komsomol movement as the conveyors of the influence of the Party and the proletariat on children, or that the categories of thought reflect and sum up the practice of societal production [obshchestvenno-proizvodstvennuiu praktiku], that they are the stages in our coming to know the world, Vygotsky instead speaks simply about the influence of the collective, neglecting to tell us what collective he is speaking about, or what he means by collective.
>
> *Razmyslov 2000, p. 49; clarifying correction in brackets, Razmyslov 1934, p. 81*

Razmyslov was keen to prove that Vygotsky and Luria "from the beginning" and not just in the elaboration of their "cultural-historical theory" had held ideologically dubious positions, quoting as sources of reference passages from their earliest publications, that is from works that had been written in the early and mid-1920s. Thus, Luria was reproached for his overtly articulated sympathy for psychoanalysis in 1925 (ibid., p. 78 f., resp. p. 45 f.), whereas Vygotsky was charged with his early "reflexological" views (ibid., p. 79, resp. p. 46). In this "retrospective," remarkably, much space was given to a critique of Vygotsky's textbook *Pedagogical psychology. Short course [Pedagogicheskaia psikhologiia. Kratkii kurs]*, written in 1923/1924 but published only in 1926 (cf. ibid., pp. 84 f., resp. pp. 54 ff.).

The mere fact that Razmyslov in his all-round attack referred to a text by Vygotsky that had been written before the latter's official entry into institutionalized psychology, whereby Razmyslov connected this reference with the indication that "Vygotsky never extricated himself from his 'left-wing [levatskikh]' mistakes later on" (ibid., p. 85, resp. p. 56), sufficiently shows that the dispute about the research approach developed by the Vygotsky-Luria group, and the results this approach achieved, had now definitely turned into an exclusively political enterprise. A survey of Vygotsky's conceptions driven by scientific criteria was not *en vogue* at all. Rather, it could only have disturbing effects in the course of proving the ideological untrustworthiness of the protagonists of the "cultural-historical" approach, and discredit them as being "conduits for bourgeois influence on the proletariat" (ibid., p. 86, resp. p. 57); even worse, that their "pseudoscientific, reactionary, anti-Marxist and anti-class theory" in practice would lead to "anti-Soviet" consequences (ibid., p. 83, resp. p. 54).

6. Constancy and changes in the autochthonous terminology in 1934 to 1936

It is of utmost importance that we consider a document that was published shortly after Vygotsky's death within the official report on the 1st All-Ukraine Congress of Neuropathologists and Psychiatrists in June 1934 – a document proving that Vygotsky had until his death remained faithful to the very denomination of his own conception, which he had chosen in 1930. Thus, in this paper, submitted to the organizing committee of the congress under the title "Psychology and the teaching on localization," it is his belief that "a system of psychological analysis, adequate from the viewpoint of the teaching on localization, must be based on the *historical theory of the higher psychological functions* [istoricheskoi teorii visshikh psikhologicheskikh funktsii], which is grounded in a theory of the systemic and semantic structure of human consciousness [soznaniia cheloveka]" (Vygotskii 1934a, p. 36; transl., insertion in brackets, and italics by P. Keiler). Just as important as the existence of this document is the fact that Vygotsky, as we know from his postcard to Leontiev dated the 10th of May 1934, had entrusted Leontiev with handing over his paper to the organizing committee (cf. A.A. Leontiev 2005, pp. 45–46; Puzyrei & Vygotsky 2007, p. 49, p. 60), thus Leontiev beyond doubt had knowledge of its contents.

Hence it is noteworthy that the latter, in his official obituary for Vygotsky published in the journal *Soviet Psychoneurology [Sovetskaia psikhonevrologiia]* in November/December 1934,[46] neither reproduces the denomination that Vygotsky had used in his theses for the congress, nor uses the shortened form "cultural-historical theory" that had been introduced *ex officio* by Razmyslov. Instead, he is offering a new variant of the denomination, applicable to "the entire psychological theory" developed by Vygotsky: "the theory of the *societal-historical* ("cultural" – as opposed to "natural," according to the laws of nature ["naturnomu," estestvennomu]) development of man's psyche" (cf. Leont'ev 1934, p. 188; resp. Leont'ev 2003d, p. 242; transl. by P. Keiler).

In fact, just one and a half years later Leontiev, who at that time had himself become the focus of scrutiny, in his (then unpublished) "Materials about consciousness [Materialy o soznanii]"[47] accepted the shortened form "*cultural-historical* theory [kul'turno-istoricheskaia teoriia]" as the label for Vygotsky's ideas, and at the same time maintained his distance from these ideas, qualifying them as "not sustainable from the historical and philosophical point of view" (Leont'ev 2003e, p. 366; transl. by P. Keiler).[48]

For the sake of comparison, we draw upon Luria's obituary, published in March 1935 concurrently in two slightly different versions in *Character and Personality* (Luria 1934/1935) and the *Journal of Genetic Psychology* (Luria 1935);[49] it is notable that the author, freed from the constraints of writing with appraisals of the highest category in mind,[50] manages to avoid all labeling.

Thus, Luria reports that Vygotsky "created a new school with a large number of followers all over the country" (Luria 1935, p. 224), that "modern science is indebted to him for his work on the *genesis of the psychological functions of the child*," and that according to Vygotsky, "the determining factor in the psychological development of the child and in the creation of the complex mechanism of the psyche is the *social development of the child*" (ibid.). Luria also states that "in a number of papers on his experiments, which have now become classical in Russian psychology," Vygotsky "described some of those mechanisms, social by *nature* [51] and indirect in their structure" (ibid., p. 224 f.), and that he "showed that the development of the psychological functions of the child is bound up with a deep change in the mind, with the development of new and intricate relations between the psychical [sic] functions and with the genesis of *new functional systems*" (ibid., p. 225).

> Furthermore: in light of that theory Vygotsky analysed the origin of such complex psychological functions as logical memory, active attention, will, speech, thought, and character, and was the first psychologist to introduce the historical method[52] in the experimental study of these important problems of human activity
>
> *Luria 1935*

Finally, Luria reports that:

> Vygotsky, having begun with the development of the mental functions, worked out his theory about the *meaningful construction of human consciousness, taken as the product of the historical development of the mental functions.*
>
> *Luria 1935*

Indeed, Luria's obituary holds a lot of detailed and interesting (though not in all instances correct)[53] information, but the "new school" created by Vygotsky remains nameless, as does the aforementioned "theory" which later reappears in the wording "his theory" (ibid.).

It is the same with Luria's study on the "development of mental functions in twins," which was published two years later in *Character and Personality*. Here we see all the catchwords and phrases which are characteristic of Vygotsky's theory of the cultural development of the higher psychological functions (cf. Luria 1936/1937, pp. 35 ff.), and we even find a comprehensive list of the literature necessary for a better understanding (ibid., footnote 1), but again, Luria avoids calling this theory by a specific name. That is, he is neither referring to one of the variants of the denomination Vygotsky and/or Leontiev had used, nor is he applying one of those labels the critics had used since 1931. Rather he avoids completely identifying his own position (which is congruent with that of Vygotsky at the general level but not so at the terminological level)[54] by any name whatsoever.

7. The terminology of the "Report on a conference of psychologists in the editorial office of the journal 'Under the Banner of Marxism'" (1936)

Whereas Luria in regard to the denomination of the conceptions in question seems to remain unsettled, Leontiev, as is documented in his "Materials about consciousness," has already accepted the depreciatory label "cultural-historical theory" as apt for Vygotsky's conceptions. In the first half of 1936, when the great "show down" is taking place, he together with Luria, L. Zankov, and D. Él'konin, is subjected to much scrutiny at the notorious "conference of psychologists at the editorial office of the journal 'Under the Banner of Marxism [Pod znamenem marksizma]'" – a "conference" organized and realized prior to the "Pedology decree"[55] under the chairmanship of M.B. Mitin.

Elaborated by a certain "G.F." and published in *Pod znamenem marksizma* in the September issue of 1936, the report on the aforementioned "conference"[56] gives a critical account of the "state of affairs and the tasks of the psychological science in the USSR," discussing one by one all the psychological currents existing at that time, thus, also assessing the conceptions and activities of the Vygotsky-Luria group:

> Another psychological current [napravlenie], which is "in fashion [imeet khojdenie]" ... and requires an expanded Marxist critique, is the Vygotsky-Luria current. This so-called school [shkolka], camouflaging itself with quotations from the classical writers of Marxism-Leninism, de facto is importing non-Marxist theories into Soviet psychology. This school has until now not been duly criticized and still needs to be unmasked. Its representatives – Luria (Medical-genetic institute), Leontiev (Higher communist institute for people's education), Zankov (Institute of experimental defectology), Él'konin (Leningrad pedological institute), and others – are undertaking a great deal of activity [aktivnost'] in defense of this so-called cultural-historical theory [tak nazivaemoi kul'turno-istoricheskoi teorii]. As it is well known, the cultural-historical conception [kul'turno-istoricheskaia kontseptsiia] has achieved its most complete development in the works [trudakh] of prof. Vygotsky, especially in his opus [rabote] "Thinking and speech." The essence of this conception boils down to the assertion that the development of speech, of thinking, and of all other psychical functions [psikhicheskikh funktsii] depends on the functional use of the sign as the decisive and fundamental moment that organizes the whole psychical activity [psikhicheskuiu deiatel'nost'] of the individual. The sign, which in complete alienation from the productive

activity of men [v polnom otryve ot proizvodstvennoi deiatel'nosti liudei] is becoming the source and driving force of the development of man's psyche [psikhiki cheloveka], takes on an overtly mystic character.

G.F. 1936, p. 92; transl., insertions in brackets, and omissions by P. Keiler

According to G.F., the "methodological error of such a conception" lies in that:

the author conceives the human psyche [chelovecheskuiu psikhiku] as an immanently developing process, beyond the relationships of social classes, beyond men's productive activity. As the mechanists don't understand that the internal contradictions are the source of automotion, as they take for granted the external side of the developmental process, the representatives of the cultural-historical school [kul'turno-istoricheskoi shkoly] take for granted the inner side of development as opposed to the external side. The cultural-historical school in psychology [Kul'turno-istoricheskaia shkola v psikhologii] has its roots in the philosophy of subjective idealism. Its representatives … don't conceive the psychical functions [psikhicheskie funktsii] as a unified [edinyi] complicated dialectical process of the reflection of the objective reality in human consciousness, but as a process of domination [ovladeniia] of the individual's inner psychical functions [vnutrennimi psikhicheskimi funktsiiami] by the individual. Prof. Vygotsky has not understood the determining role of productive activity in the formation, in the genesis of speech and thinking of men.

G.F. 1936, p. 93; transl., insertions in brackets, and omissions by P. Keiler

G.F. concludes with this assessment: "This theory of prof. Vygotsky must be criticized very severely – as an idealist, anti-Marxist theory in psychology, doing much harm to practice" (ibid., p. 94; transl. by P. Keiler).

Subsequent to this assessment of Vygotsky's conceptions, the ominous G.F. (who A.A. Leontiev identified as F.I. Georgiev [cf. Leontiev 2005, p. 60]) reports on the scrutiny Leontiev and Luria received at the "conference," and gives the following résumé:

Professor Leontiev, as one of the representatives of the cultural-historical theory [kul'turno-istoricheskoi teorii], considered it unnecessary to criticize his own theoretical conception, to disclose concrete mistakes in his work. His behavior is a typical example of how not to act in respect to the most important questions of the psychological front.

G.F. 1936, p. 94; transl. and insertions in brackets by P. Keiler

And in regard to Luria, G.F. stated:

It has to be said that prof. Luria, as a representative of the cultural-historical theory [kul'turno-istoricheskoi teorii], likewise considered it unnecessary to criticize his own erroneous theoretical conception at the conference. In his works as well as in his presentation at the conference, prof. Luria in his considerations of the child's development and learning proceeds from the idea that the sign is the determining factor in the development of the child's psychical activity [psikhicheskoi deiatel'nosti].

G.F. 1936; transl. and insertions in brackets by P. Keiler

It would be of little use (and in fact "a little bit late") to give a counter-assessment of G.F.'s characterization of Vygotsky's views (essentially only reproducing and summing up in a compact and accessible manner the reproaches that had been uttered already by former critics). At any rate, his "report on a conference of psychologists at the editorial office of the journal 'Pod znamenem marksizma'" was published in September 1936. This has to be considered in effect the birth of the myth of *the* "cultural-historical school" and the term "cultural-historical theory" (unanimously propagated by representatives of that "school"), having achieved its "most complete development" in Vygotsky's book *Thinking and speech*. (Thus *Thinking and speech*, as it were, is declared the "manifesto" of *the* "cultural-historical" approach).[57] In addition, the "official" (mainstream) terminology applied by G.F. to Vygotsky's conceptions and topics of research would serve as a warrant to negate Vygotsky's own non-interchangeable terminology; thus, thereafter the wording "(higher) psych*ological* functions" would no longer appear, but instead "(higher) psych*ical* functions" would be used whenever Vygotsky's research and theorizing is talked about (cf. Rudneva 1937; Luriia & Leont'ev 1940; Rubinshtein 1940; Rubinshtein 1946);[58] occasional reminders that the correct term should be "psych*ological* functions" (cf. Brushlinskii 1968, p. 5; Iaroshevskii & Gurgenidze 1982, p. 441; and the subject indices in Vygotskii 1956, p. 515 and *Sobr. soch.*, Vol. 1, 479) will appear as mere epiphenomenons, having no consequence at all. That said, the influence of G.F.'s "standards" on the subsequent discourse was all the more enduring as they worked, so to speak, "subterraineously;" the "report" was a much-used source but its existence was usually not mentioned, thus G.F.'s distortions of Vygotsky's conceptions were not subjected to overt counter-criticism or refutation (cf. e.g. Luriia & Leont'ev 1940; Leont'ev & Luriia 1956; Leont'ev, Luriia & Teplov 1960; Leont'ev 1967; Leontiev & Luria 1968, Leont'ev 1982).

8. Résumé of findings and survey of the development of the discourse after the "rediscovery" of Vygotsky in 1956

Summing up, it can be said that, *according to first order sources*, Vygotsky himself subsumed his own conceptions under the following designations:

1929 – "I[nstrumental] P[sychology]," "cultural psychology" (cf. letters to Leontiev from April and July of that year);

1930 – "historical theory of the higher psychological functions [istoricheskaia teoriia vysshikh psikhologicheskikh funktsii]" (cf. foreword to Leontiev's book *The* *development of memory* [subtitled: "Experimental investigation of the higher psychological functions"]);

1930/1931 – "theory of the development of the higher psychological functions [teoriia razvitiia vysshikh psikhologicheskikh funktsii]" (cf. survey of the contents of the 10th chapter of *Pedology of the adolescent*);

1931/1932 – "conception of the historical development of the higher psychological functions [kontseptsiia istoricheskogo razvitiia vysshikh psikhologicheskikh funktsii]," "the so-called [tak nazyvaemaia] theory of the historical (or cultural-historical) development in psychology [teoriia istoricheskogo (ili kul'turno-istoricheskogo) razvitiia v psikhologii]," "theory *of the higher psychological functions* [teoriia *vysshikh psikhologicheskikh funktsii*] (logical memory, voluntary attention, speech-thinking [rechevoe myshlenie], volitional processes, etc.)" (cf. the self-critical enclosure to Leontiev's book, signed also by Leontiev);

1934 – (shortly before Vygotsky's death) "historical theory of the higher psychological functions [istoricheskaia teoriia vysshikh psikhologicheskikh funktsii]" (cf. paper entitled "Psychology and the teaching on localization," elaborated for the 1st All-Ukraine Congress of Neuropathologists and Psychiatrists).

Thus, the "core" of a correct denomination of Vygotsky's theoretical approach, which can generally be accurately applied as a label to *all variants* of this approach between 1928 and 1934, is "theory of the higher psych o l o g i c a l functions." But while generally valid, in each concrete case the label needs a specification, according to the respective subject of investigation or the specifically accentuated characteristic of the respective study. Thus, the conception guiding Vygotsky's patho-psychological research in the last years of his life, could be specified as "theory about the *disintegration* of the higher psychological functions," whereas the original version (1928–1930) should be characterized as "instrumentalistic."

The label "cultural-historical theory [kul'turnogo-istoricheskaia teoriia]," as used in the relevant literature, was linguistically seen as a *solecism* (cf. above, footnote 31), introduced in the mid-1930s by adversaries of Vygotsky (Razmyslov 1934; G. F. 1936). Opponents attributed to the Vygotsky-Luria group (then declared by G. F. the "cultural-historical school") an affinity with any (unspecified) representatives of German „Kulturpsychologie" (cf. Leont'ev, Luriia & Teplov 1960, p. 3), condemning the "cultural-historical" approach in the same breath as the most gruesome political-ideological failures. In 1956, the year of the 20th congress of the Communist Party in the USSR and also what would have been Vygotsky's 60th birthday, this label was declared quasi-sacrosanct by Leontiev and Luria. In their introduction to Vygotsky's *Selected psychological investigations [Izbrannye psikhologicheskie issledovaniia]* (the publication of which was the starting point for the official "rediscovery" of Vygotsky),[59] seeking refuge from criticism of their work they made the inaccurate but momentous assertion that *Vygotsky himself* had "originally designated his psychological conception as cultural-historical theory of the psyche [pervonachal'no nazyval svoiu psikhologicheskuiu kontseptsiiu kul'turno-istoricheskoi teoriei psikhiki]" (cf. Leont'ev & Luriia 1956, p. 7, transl. by P. Keiler).[60]

Indeed, in the following years there were several attempts to introduce (or reanimate) other denominations – "theory of cultural-historical development" (Leont'ev 1959), "theory of cultural development" (Leont'ev, Luriia & Teplov 1960), "theory of the development of the higher psychical functions [teoriia razvitiia vysshikh psikhicheskikh funktsii]" (Leont'ev, Luriia & Teplov 1960; Petrovskii 1967a),[61] "theory of the historical development of the higher psychical functions" (Petrovskii 1967b), "theory of the higher psychical functions" (Bruschlinski 1967), "cultural-historical theory of the 'higher' psychical functions [kul'turnogo-istoricheskaia teoriia 'vysshikh' psikhicheskikh funktsii]" (Brushlinskii 1968;[62]Budilova 1972, "higher" not in quotation marks), "teaching [uchenie] on the development of the higher psychical functions" (Budilova 1972). However, none of these variants won recognition within the general discourse, just as the designation that Rubinshtein had used in both editions of his textbook *Fundamentals of general psychology [Osnovy obshchei psikhologii]* had failed, though it came closest to the autochthonous terminology: "theory of the cultural development of the higher psychical functions [teoriia kultur'nogo razvitiia vysshich psikhicheskikh funktsii]" (cf. Rubinshtein 1940, pp. 69 f.; Rubinshtein 1946, pp. 102 f.). The fact that the Rubinshtein variant has been completely disregarded, as has the attempt of first Brushlinsky and later Budilova to introduce the "hybrid" version "cultural-historical theory of the higher psychical functions," can be assessed as a symptom of not only the struggle for hegemony in Soviet psychology in the late 1960s and 1970s, but also the struggle for the mere preservation of Rubinshtein's legacy (which despite all divergencies with Vygotsky's conceptions, even "in the very hard times" always included an appreciation of his merits);[63] it was a struggle that ultimately did not favor the "Rubinshteinians."

On the other hand, it is quite conspicuous that the topoi "cultural-historical theory" and "cultural-historical school" are neither used by Luria in his afterword to the second volume of *Sobr. soch.*, nor by D. Èl'konin in his afterword to the fourth volume, nor by È.S. Bein, T.A. Vlasova, R.E. Levina, N.G. Morozova, and J.I. Shif in their afterword to the fifth volume.[64] Whereas Luria (who not only in 1956 but once more in 1968 had co-signed the assertion that Vygotsky *himself* had designated his conception as "cultural-historical theory"[65]) in his afterword only talks informally about "Vygotsky's general psychological theory [obshchepsikhologicheskoi teorii L.S. Vygotskogo]," or "this general theory [toi obshchei teorii]" (cf. *Sobr. soch.*, Vol. 2, p. 466). Èl'konin in one place uses the term "theory of the higher psychical functions [teorii razvitiia vysshich psikhicheskikh funktsii]" (*Sobr. soch.*, Vol. 4, p. 386) and in another speaks about the "theory of the higher psychical processes [teoriia vysshich psikhicheskikh protsessov]" (*Sobr. soch.*, Vol. 4, p. 393), and Bein, Vlasova, Levina, Morozova, and Shif use the wording "general psychological theory of the higher psychical functions [obshchei psikhologicheskoi teorii vysshikh psikhicheskikh funktsii]" (*Sobr. soch.*, Vol. 5, p. 335). Furthermore, in Luria's autobiography we even find the autochthonous terminology completely restored. Here, he first uses the denomination "his [i.e. Vygotsky's] theory of the development of higher psychological functions in children" (Luria 1979, p. 126;

insertion in brackets by P. Keiler) and later he talks about Vygotsky's "general theory of the sociohistorical origins of higher psychological functions" (ibid., p. 156).[66] Apparently, it was Leontiev, or the "Leontiev group," within the Vygotsky-Luria-Leontiev school (Davydov & Radzikhovskii 1985, p. 35) or the Vygotsky-Leontiev-Luria school (Zinchenko 1985, pp. 103–104), that was responsible for the adoption and canonization of the allochthonous labeling (cf. Leont'ev 2003d; Zaporojets 1959/1965; Leont'ev 1967; Leont'ev 1982; A.A. Leontiev 2005). Acknowledging that Vygotsky's work was a precursor first to Leontiev's "neo-cultural-historical" approach as represented in his *Problems of the development of the psyche*, [67] and later on for Leontiev's variant of "activity theory", by the late 1960s the term had begun to lose its pejorative character (cf. e.g. Leont'ev 1967; Iudin 1978; Davydov & Radzichovskii 1980a; Davydov & Radzichovskii 1980b; Leont'ev 1982), and in the 1970s, when "the concepts formulated by Vygotsky" had become "widely accepted," it formed the "basis for the main school of Soviet psychology" (cf. Luria 1979, p. 52),[68] and advanced to a shibboleth with international acceptance – a tendency from which the author of the present paper, firmly integrated in the genesis and the development of Critical Psychology throughout the 1970s,[69] also could not escape.

9. Final conclusions

The commonly used label "cultural-historical theory [kul'turno-istoricheskaia teoriia]" is no "autochthonous" denomination for the theoretical conceptions developed by Vygotsky in the years 1927/1928 to 1934 (the year of his death) within the context of a widespread cooperational network. That is, it was neither used by Vygotsky himself nor created in the sphere of cooperation with research workers directly associated with him in the various fields of his activity. Likewise, the designation "cultural-historical school [kul'turno-istoricheskaia shkola]" does not reflect the genuine self-concept of the respective researchers (that is Vygotsky and his more or less intimately associated colleagues). Rather, both denominations were originally introduced by critics in the mid-1930s as labels with defamatory connotations. Later on, within the scope of a defense mechanism that psychoanalysts would call "identification with the aggressor," these labels were "accepted". Furthermore, in the aftermath of the "thaw" when the once "beaten" turned out to be "victorious", they became commonly used shibboleths which (by repression of their disgraceful origin and a systematic falsification of their history) nowadays seem to have lost completely their formerly negative connotations. However, they remain quite problematic in several aspects. Thus, the overall denomination "cultural-historical theory," besides not being Vygotsky's original wording, does not reflect adequately either the variety of the "universe" of Vygotsky's ideas or the process of differentiation and the sometimes dramatic shifts that took place in the development of Vygotsky's theoretical conceptions in the period from 1927/1928 until his last working phase in the spring of 1934. Similarly problematic is the collective concept of the "cultural-historical school" which is confusing in its vagueness and therefore should be likewise abandoned as a misleading denomination. First, being a collective concept, it gives space to arbitrariness in regard to who should be counted in and who not. By contrast, Yasnitsky (2010, p. 6) adequately speaks of a "huge network of protagonists," referring to 33 more women and men besides Vygotsky, finishing this enumeration with the phrase "to mention but a few." Second, on the one hand idolizing the "leading figures" and on the other degrading the "rank and file" to mere supernumeraries (often banished into anonymity, sometimes being victims of a transmogrification of their names),[70] the easy-to-use label "school" systematically obscures the differences between the various scientists who collaborated with Vygotsky at different times, at different places, in different institutions, with different intensity and intimacy, and, not to forget, with different affinity to his ideas – differences which consequently led to "competing research agendas of different groupings within the larger network of Vygotskian scholars" (ibid.).[71] Thus, as it is understood, confusion will by no means be avoided by simply leaving behind the label "cultural-historical school" and using instead the label "Vygotsky-Leontiev-Luria school" or the counter-variant "Vygotsky-Luria-Leontiev school." Even the circumscribing term "Vygotsky's circle" – as it had been adopted by the present author from E. Scheerer some 35 years ago (cf. Keiler 1981b, p. 118, p. 127) and as it is actually favored by Yasnitsky – has to be used with reservation. For in its literal sense it only covers a Vygotsky-centered constellation of collaboration and/or adherence, and does not include such symmetric social relationships as kinship and friendship or correspondence, nor those relationships of cooperation in which Vygotsky was not the intellectual or organizational "center" – each of these relationships affecting in its own way the development of "Vygotskian" ideas. (For the respective references see Keiler 2002, p. 37, p. 226, p. 383; resp. Keiler 2015, p. 25, p. 199.) Thus, further positive work on this concept (and the corresponding terminology) is still required.

Notes

1 In 1964 the German translation of the 1956 version of L.S. Vygotsky's *Myshlenie i rech'* was also published in the GDR, a licensed version of which was published in the FRG five years later but at that time was not attracting the interest of many psychologists.

2 Going further, calling him the "founder of the cultural-historical school" (cf. Engeström 1988, p. 68), is already mystifying.

3 "Autochthonous" properly means "stemming from this very land itself" (from the Greek *autos* meaning "itself, self" and *chton* meaning "earth, soil"). In the present context the term means "either used by Vygotsky himself or created in the sphere of cooperation with research workers directly associated with him in the various fields of his activity".

4 Apparently, Vygotsky, who already in his youth had shown an interest in Hegel's philosophy of history (cf. Dobkin 1982, p. 26), had been inspired to engage more intensively with Hegel's philosophy of the spirit by a closer reading of K. Bühler's *Die geistige Entwicklung des Kindes [The mental development of the child]* (cf. Bühler[4] 1924, especially pp. 429 ff.), taking place in 1927/28, itself having been inspired by K. Koffka's *Die Grundlagen der psychischen Entwicklung [The fundamentals of psychical development]* (cf. Koffka [2]1925). The latter book propagated a "historico-cultural" orientation as compulsory not

only for developmental psychology but for psychology in general (cf. ibid., pp. 1 f.) and, along with Bühler's work, also stressed the importance of the investigations of K. Groos, W. Köhler, L. Levy-Bruhl, W. Stern, M. Wertheimer, and J. Piaget, thus being a kind of "catalyst" for the development of Vygotsky's own approach.

5   In his article about the cultural development of the child, submitted to the *Journal of Genetic Psychology* for publication on the 20th of July 1928, Vygotsky introduced this term as a substitution for the hitherto used denomination "(functional) method of double stimulation" (cf. Luria 1928, pp. 495 f., p. 505; Vygotski 1929, p. 430, p. 433). N.B.: In the German version of the abstract of Vygotsky's article this method is called „Werkzeugmethode" (cf. ibid., pp. 433 ff.).

6   The facts Vygotsky is referring to in his cryptic allusion (which is apt to provoke misunderstandings) are explicated by A.R. Luria in his autobiography, as well as by K.E. Levitin in his Book *A Dissolving Pattern [Mimoletnyi uzor]. Reflections on the Life and Work of A.R. Luria.* Thus, Luria reports: "In the early years of our collaborative work, our theoretical stance met with little understanding or enthusiasm. People would ask: 'Why cultural psychology? Every process is a mixture of natural and cultural influence. Why historical psychology? One can deal with psychological facts without being interested in the behavior of primitive peoples. Why instrumental psychology? We all use instruments in our experiments.'" (Luria 1979, p. 52) And Levitin writes: "Luria recalled, not without sarcasm, what Kornilov said: 'Well, just think, >historical< psychology – Why should we study various wild men? Or >instrumental.< Indeed, every psychology is instrumental; I also use a dynamoscope.' Even the director of the Institute of Psychology did not understand that the question had nothing at all to do with the instruments psychologists use, but the means, the tools, that man himself uses to organize his behavior." (quoted in Levitin 1998, p. 51)

7   This orientation is expressed very clearly in the *Studies in the history of behavior [Etiudy po istorii povedeniia]*, co-authored by Luria and published in the first half of 1930. Here, at the end of the second chapter (entitled "Primitive man and his behavior") Vygotsky identifies his own conception, explicated "in its essential aspects [v ee glavnykh momentakh]," as the "third [tret'ia]" of three "theories of cultural-psychological development [teorii kul'turno-psikhologicheskogo rasvitiia]" presented and discussed in this chapter (the first being that of Taylor & Spencer, and the second that of Levy-Bruhl). Thus, the specificity of his own approach lies in the assumption "that the basic components of the psychological development of primitive man are to be found in the development of technique, and the corresponding development of social structure [sotsial'nogo stroia]" (quoted in Luria & Vygotsky 1992, p. 84; insertion in brackets from the Russian original: Vygotskii & Luriia 1930, p. 120). In this context the term "higher psychological functions [vysshie psikhologicheskie funktsii]" is also introduced (cf. ibid., p. 62; Luria & Vygotsky 1992, p. 44), marking the opposite of the "natural psychological functions [estestvennykh psikhologicheskikh funktsii]" (cf. Vygotskii & Luriia 1930, pp. 66, resp. Luria & Vygotsky 1992, p. 46).

8   The second title page is in German and gives as a subtitle „Experimentelle Untersuchung der höheren psychologischen Funktionen" (cf. the facsimile in Leont'ev 2001, p. 64).

9   "Linguistically", this wording is a fusion of the two denominations that Leontiev had used as synonyms in his oral presentation on the development of children's arithmetical thinking (11th of October 1929): "theory of higher behavior [teoriia razvitiia povedeniia]" and "theory of the historical development of the child [teoriia istoricheskogo razvitiia rebenka]" (cf. Leont'ev 2003c, p. 208).

10 As can be deduced from the list of references, consisting of 23 titles, including Luria & Morozova's "Instrumental reaction in children" and Vygotsky & Luria's "Essays on the history of the behavior" (cf. Leontiev 1932, p. 81), the article had already been submitted for publication in 1930.

11 Here it is not clear if "social" means "social" or "societal", as the original (book) version does not contain this passage.

12 In a footnote Leontiev refers to the "bibliography at the end of this article."
13 In his letter to Leontiev, dated the 31st of July, Vygotsky says: "I found out that the book is 'scheduled' for the four[th] quarter, and that I can hand in the preface in September" (Puzyrei &Vygotsky 2007, p. 30; insertion in brackets by Puzyrei).
14 Vygotsky's preliminary reflections, resulting in this detailed statement, are documented in a short memorandum which is preserved in the Vygotsky family archive and runs as follows: "NB! We are missing a name, a designation. It should not be a signboard (intuitivism). Not instrum., not cultural, not signif[icative], not struct., etc. Not only because of the blend with oth[er] theories but also because of the int[e]rnal lack of clarity, e.g., the idea of analogy with instr. = only scaffolding, dissimilarity is more essential. Culture: but where is culture itself from (it is nonprimordial, and this is hidden). So: 1) for the method the designation meth. of d[ou]ble stimulation. 2) for the theory as a whole a) psychol. of higher functions, i.e. b) histor. psychology or c) histor. theory of higher psychol. f[u]nctions. Because the central concept for us is the concept of higher function: it contains a theory a) of its development, b) of its psychol. nature; c) of the method of its investigation." (quoted in Zavershneva 2010a, p. 30).
15 So far, the "handwritten notes," reported by Vygodskaia & Lifanova (1999b, p. 3), in which Vygotsky under the title "Distortions in the review," and probably referring to Frankel's review, "refutes the reviewer's mistaken statements" have to be dated later.
16 Cf. Rückriem 2001, p. 408; A.A. Leontiev 2005, p. 27.
17 For a more detailed characterization and assessment of Vygotsky and Leontiev's self-criticism cf. Keiler 2002, pp. 316–323.
18 Later, the quintessence of the letter is characterized in the following way: "He [Leontiev] is worried about the dilution and erosion of Vygotsky's ideas about cultural psychology – or as it was previously called, instrumental psychology – as they spread. Vygotsky does nothing to prevent this and Luria, easily carried away with eclecticism even contributes to this problem. Leontiev is by no means setting himself against Vygotsky, and in the letter there is not a single reference to some alternative; on the contrary, he cites to Vygotsky his own letter written three years earlier, reproaching him for straying from his own principles. Leontiev – together with the 1929 Vygotsky versus the 1932 Vygotsky – appears to be a stronger supporter of Vygotsky than Vygotsky himself, reproaching Vygotsky for inconsistency" (ibid., p. 40 f.; insertion in brackets by P. Keiler). Leontiev's disappointment with Vygotsky can be better understood, if one takes into consideration Vygotsky's enthusiasm about Leontiev's book in particular, and the "state of affairs with our idea for summer 1930" in general, expressed by him in his letter to Leontiev, dated the 31st of July 1930, i.e. when the book already had been passed to the publishing house and Vygotsky was preparing his (original) foreword for it (cf. Puzyrei &Vygotsky 2007, pp. 30 f.).
19 N.B.: in their presentations at the First All-Union Congress for the study of behavior, taking place in Leningrad from the 26th of January until the 1st of February1930, both of them used the formulations "higher behavior," or "higher forms of behavior," whereas Luria preferred the variant "cultural forms of behavior" (cf. Vygotskii 1930; Luriia 1930; Leont'ev 1930).
20 It has to be mentioned here that the title of the series "Studies on the cultural development of the child" had not yet been presented at the time of the publication of Luria's "pilot" article "The problem of the cultural behavior of the child" in 1928, but was introduced only in 1929 in the context of the publication of the English version of Vygotsky's article "The problem of the cultural development of the child;" this had already been published in Russian in 1928 in the first issue of the journal Pedologiia, co-founded by Vygotsky. In 1929, only appearing in an editorial footnote that identifies Vygotsky's article as "second in the series of studies on the cultural development of the child" (cf. Vygotski 1929, p. 415), the title then serves as a general headline for Leontiev's article on the development of the voluntary attention of the child (cf. Leontiev 1932, p. 52).
21 The central statement of the "classical" approach, formulated in Vygotsky's 1929 article "Fundamental problems of contemporary defectology," runs as follows: "The artificial

devices, which by analogy with technology are sometimes called psychological tools, are directed toward mastering behavioral processes – someone else's or one's own – in the same way that technology attempts to control the processes of nature. ... The use of psychological tools modifies the whole course and structure of psychological function[s], giving them a new form." (quoted in *Coll. works*, Vol. 2, p. 44; omission and correction in brackets by P. Keiler; for the Russian version cf. *Sobr. soch.*, Vol. 5, p. 26).

22 No English version is available.

23 As the text analysis shows, this fragment is unmistakably a direct parallel text to the 16th chapter of *Pedology of the adolescent*. Thus, dating it to 1929 (cf. Puzyrei 1986a, p. 51, resp. Puzyrei 1989a, p. 54) cannot be accepted, especially as Puzyrei himself is leading this dating *ad absurdum* in his note no. 25, where he is (indirectly) locating the fragment "in the early '30s" (cf. Puzyrei 1986b, p. 64, resp. Puzyrei 1989b, p. 75).

24 There is some reason to believe that the re-elaboration of the theoretical-methodological part of the *History of the development of the higher psych[olog]ical functions* (consisting of five chapters and originally bearing the title "Treatise on the higher psychological functions [Issledovanie vysshikh psikhologicheskikh funktsii]") was already well advanced before the self-critical enclosure to Leontiev's book was written – the latter, as will be remembered, was subtitled "experimental investigation of the higher psychological functions." Thus, Vygotsky's affirmation that, since Leontiev's book was completed "more than two years ago," there had been "significant additions and modifications" in the "basic psychological conception," guiding the research program of the Vygotsky-Luria group, was not only an evasive defence but well substantiated.

25 Thus, already in the appendix ("register of the works of Prof. L.S. Vygotsky") of the original version of *Myshlenie i rech'* (cf. Vygotskii 1934b, p. 321, p. 323). For the dubious history of the publication of this study (especially in its Russian version) cf. van der Veer & Valsiner 1991, p. 188, and van der Veer and Valsiner in Vygotsky 1994, p. 170.

26 As it is clear to see, this observation for Vygotsky was key to understanding the qualitative difference between the "instrumental thinking" (Bühler's [4]1924 „Werkzeugdenken") of human beings and chimpanzees: the "understanding of mechanical connections and the invention of mechanical means for mechanical ends" (cf. *Coll. works*, Vol. 1, p. 110) is *humanized* by speech.

27 It has to be emphasized here that (the 1925 version of) Koffka's book was not only influential in the elaboration of Vygotsky's "instrumentalistic" approach (cf. above, footnote 4) but, as it is documented in numerous references, served as a permanent source of inspiration for Vygotsky until the end of his career.

28 A. Yasnitsky dates "Tool and symbol" (as it seems to me, correctly) "not earlier 1931, probably 1932" (cf. Yasnitsky 2011, p. 56).

29 Cf. Vygotskii 1924; Vygotskii 1925.

30 Vygotsky's nearness to Feuerbach in this point is demonstrated, though not explicitly mentioned, very nicely in M.G. Iaroshevskii's epilogue to the sixth volume of the *Coll. works*, where he, in regard to the Russian version of "Tool and symbol" ("Orudie i znak v razvitii rebenka"), talks about Vygotsky's conception of the "initial integration of the child into the microsocial community [mikrosotsial'nuiu obshchnost'] in the midst of which occurs the miracle [chudo] of converting his natural, very simple functions into higher, cultural-historical functions," a process, that is "ensure[d]" by "tools and signs, and mainly speech signs" (*Coll. works*, Vol. 6, p. 247; for the Russian version cf. *Sobr. soch.*, Vol. 6, p. 331). The general basis of the argument is of course Feuerbach's "a-historical" (i.e. universally valid) fundamental idea, that "the *essence* of man is contained only in the community, the *unity of man with man*" (FGW, Vol. 9, p. 339; transl. by P. Keiler). In accordance with this idea and following his earlier reflections about culture being "nonprimordial" (cf. above, footnote 14), Vygotsky in his later work conceives culture explicitly as a *derived* phenomenon, as "a result of social life and the concerted activity of man" (cf. *Sobr. soch.*, Vol. 3, p. 145; transl. by P. Keiler).

31 It has to be emphasized here that from the linguistic point of view this label is based on a distortion of words, transmogrifying the correct wording "theory of cultural-historical development."

32 For the original Russian version cf. Vygodskaia & Lifanova 1996, p. 106.

33 Cf. for instance: "suspicious observation" instead of "observation of something suspicious" or the notorious "conspiratorial apartment" (instead of "apartment, rented for conspiratorial purposes").

34 In the Russian original it is, oddly enough, "electric conception [elektricheskaia kontseptsiia]" (cf. Feofanov 1932, p. 221).

35 It can be deduced from the first note in the text that it is the printed version, with few edits, of a report Abel'skaia and Neopikhonova had presented to the Department of Pedology of the Leningrad State Pedagogical Institute – possibly with the intention of undermining Vygotsky's teaching activity, having started there in March of 1932 (cf. Abel'skaia & Neopikhonova 2000, p. 44; van der Veer & Valsiner 1991, p. 380).

36 In the original, these were also addressed as "assignments [zadaniia]" (cf. *Sobr. soch.*, tom 6, p. 370, resp. Vygodskaia & Lifanova 1996, p. 400).

37 Ironically, the announced "further critical articles" ultimately did not appear, as *Pedologiia* closed down later that same year (cf. van der Veer & Valsiner 1991, p.380).

38 The respective "critical investigation" was first published as an introduction to the Russian combined edition of Piaget's *Le langage et la pensée chez l'enfant* and *Le jugement et le raisonnement chez l'enfant* in a single volume, entitled *Speech and Thinking of the Child* (cf. Vygotskii 1932). It was later integrated as second "chapter" in Vygotsky's book *Thinking and Speech [Myshlenie i rech']* which, after considerable editorial delay, was finally released posthumously in the beginning of 1935 (misleadingly dated "1934"), despite the dubious circumstances under which it was compiled.

39 N.B.: The "new lines" followed by Leontiev in the mid-1930s (and disclosed in his 1936 criticism of Vygotsky), consisted of, simplistically, on one hand carrying instrumentalism to its extreme, conceiving even the most elementary and intimate forms of human sociality (e.g. the mother-child-dyad) as instrumental relationships (cf. Leont'ev 1998, p. 121), and on the other hand the inversion of the analogy that had served as the basis of Vygotsky's concept of "psychological tools." That is, Leontiev no longer conceived language as a tool, but conversely treated tools as if they were language, i.e. as a "means by which societal consciousness and thinking is incarnated [oveshchestvlennym]" (cf. ibid.; transl. by P. Keiler).

40 Cf. above, footnote 13.

41 As we can read in G. Rückriem's annotations on Leontiev's curriculum vitae, the book had gained the "GLAVNAUKA 1st prize and the TsEKUBU prize for the best opus of [those presented by] Soviet scientists [in that year]" prior to publication (cf. Rückriem 2001, p. 408; transl. and insertions in brackets by P. Keiler).

42 In this sense we must also consider the "conversation" to which Vygotsky "was summoned by [M.B.] Mitin quite unexpectedly" in November 1933 (cf. Puzyrei & Vygotsky 2007, pp. 47 f.; insertion in brackets by P. Keiler). He apparently later assessed (quite realistically) that this was a maneuver, cloaked as an offer of support, to induce the Vygotsky-Luria group to unmask themselves in writing on their own behalf an article for the leading theoretical-ideological journal *Pod znamenem marksizma [Under the Banner of Marxism]*, of which Mitin was the chief editor.

43 Cf. van der Veer 2000, pp. 5–6. It seems the actual point of contact (or rather, the stumbling-block) was the missing "political correctness" of the results of Luria's psychological expeditions to Uzbekistan in 1931 and 1932, during which the "psychological" effects of the societal transformations realized over the previous 10 years should be clarified, especially if and how the mechanization of agriculture has had an influence on the form of thinking of the people living in this Central Asian part of the Soviet Union (cf. van der Veer 2000, and van der Veer & Valsiner 1991, pp. 253 ff.).

44 From the *Soviet Historical Encyclopedia* (1973–1982) we learn that this journal was in circulation from 1932 until 1940, i.e. for nine years, with 108 issues published. Thus, it was

a monthly journal, so we can assume that the respective issue No. 4 was released in April, that is, still during Vygotsky's lifetime.

45 Referring to "many passages in his [Vygotsky's] works," Razmyslov presents (without mentioning the source) the following quasi-quotation: "Observation of the development of higher psychological functions [vysshikh psikhologicheskikh funktsii] shows that the construction [postroenie] of each of them is rigorously governed by one and the same law, that each higher psychological function [vysshaia psikhologicheskaia funktsiia] appears on the stage [na scene] twice in the process of development of behavior: first as a function of collective behavior, as a form of cooperation and interaction, as a means of social adaptation, i.e. as an interpsychological category [kategoriia interpsikhologicheskaia], and then, second, as a mode of the child's individual behavior, as a means of personal [lichnogo] adaptation, as an internal process of behavior, i.e. as an intrapsychological category [kategoriia intrapsikhologicheskaia]" (Razmyslov 2000, p. 49; for the original Russian version cf. Razmyslov 1934, p. 80). In Vygotsky we find the whole passage in almost identical wording in his article "The collective as a factor of the development of the anomalous child," and also with the introductory statement that on the basis of his own work and the work of his collaborators he had "elsewhere formulated this proposition in the following way: ..." (*Coll. works*, Vol. 2, p. 192).

46 According to A.A. Leontiev, the obituary was "*written* by Leontiev in July" (A.A. Leontiev 2005, p. 53; italics by P. Keiler).

47 For the criteria for dating this material cf. Keiler 2010b.

48 N.B.: Some 40 years later, in his introduction to the first volume of *Sobranie sochinenii* ("The creative path of L.S. Vygotsky"), Leontiev explicitly admitted his "identification with the aggressor" (realized as early as 1936): "It must be said that several psychologists of the 1930s (e.g. Talankin, Razmyslov, and others) had already seen and noted this genuine weakness in the conception of the connection between consciousness and real life which manifested itself in the cultural-historical theory." (*Coll. works, Vol. 3*, p. 31) – cf. van der Veer's comment on this "rather sinister remark" (ibid., p. 373, note [25]).

49 This version, being somewhat more extensive, will be used in the following as the primary source of reference.

50 It is also worthwhile to compare Leontiev's and Luria's obituaries in *this* aspect (cf. Keiler 2002, p. 352 ff., resp. Keiler 2015, p. 317 ff.; and Keiler 2010a, p. 14 ff.).

51 Anticipating misinterpretations, in this context "social" does not mean "societal," and "nature" is the equivalent of "essence," "character."

52 The 1934/35 version puts "'developmental' method" instead of "historical method" (cf. ibid. p. 239).

53 Thus, in the beginning of the obituary Luria states that Vygotsky "died ... at the age of 38" (Luria 1935, p. 224; the 1934/1935 version, p. 238, puts "thirty-eight") – a false report, which later in the secondary literature will be repeated over and over again. (N. B.: Leontiev had given in his obituary the same false report with a slight variation: "in the 39th year of his life [na 39 rodu jisni]" [cf. Leont'ev 1934, p. 190; 1997, p. 46].) And Luria's declaration that Vygotsky had been the "most prominent Soviet psychologist" (cf. Luria 1935, p. 224) or a "leading Russian psychologist" (cf. Luria 1934/1935, p. 238), whose papers had "become classical in Russian psychology," is a "charming exaggeration," perhaps pardonable in the actual context but misleading in the long run, having served as "reliable source" of many of the later myths and legends about Vygotsky and his "school."

54 In the context of his early methodological appointment "that the subject of psychology is the integral psychophysiological process of behavior [tselostnii psikhofiziologicheskhii protsess povedeniia]," which "cannot find full and adequate expression in just the mental part [psikhicheskoi chasti]" (cf. *Coll. works*, Vol. 3, p. 116), Vygotsky "in a unique [svoeobrazno] but principal [principalno] way" made "a distinction between psychical [psikhicheskie] and psychological [psikhologicheskie] processes" (Brushlinskii 1968, p. 5, footnote; transl. by P. Keiler). Based on that (both conceptually and terminologically significant) distinction, from the introduction of the term in 1928 until the end of his

life, he consequently used the form "*psychological* functions" (with the later specifications "higher" and "natural" or "elementary"). On the other hand, Luria seems to treat the terms "psychical functions" and "psychological functions" as synonyms, the use of which is more a stylistic than a conceptual problem, leaving the question open, if the variant "mental functions" means the same as "psychical functions [psikhicheskie funktsii]" or if it corresponds to the Russian term "umstvennoe funktsii" (in German: „geistige Funktionen"), the English term having both meanings. This terminological inconsistency is especially noticeable in the "summary" of the study about the "development of mental functions in twins" (ibid., pp. 46 f.), where we have four times "psychological functions" and twice "higher mental functions." Thus, it fits well in the picture that Luria on the one hand is talking about "complex psychological processes" and on the other about "elementary mental processes" (cf. ibid., p. 46).

55   Properly: "Resolution of the Central Committee of the All-Union Communist Party (Bolsheviks) on the pedological distortions in the system of the People's Commissariats of Education."

56   In the secondary literature this conference is repeatedly referred to as having taken place "shortly after the release of the decree" (cf. e.g. Rückriem 2001, p. 412) or "immediately after the decree was issued" (A.A. Leontiev 2005, p. 60), which is *evidently wrong*. In fact, we can read at the end of G.F.'s report: "This is a short survey of the conference which took place at the editorial board of the journal. How much the time was ripe for that is testified by the fact that *after the conference events of outstanding significance came to pass on the pedagogical front.* We have in mind the historical resolution of the Central Committee from the 4th of June on the 'pedological distortions in the system of the People's Commissariat of Education'" (G.F. 1936, p. 98; transl. and italics by P. Keiler. – N.B.: the correct date of the resolution was the 4th of *July*).

57   The "sacred" status of this posthumously (and under dubious circumstances) compiled opus, commonly celebrated as Vygotsky's "legacy," has been challenged elsewhere in detail by the present author (cf. Keiler 2002, p. 177 f., pp. 339–342; resp. Keiler 2015, p. 154, pp. 301–306).

58   N.B.: In 1935 (i.e. *after* Razmyslov's criticism of Vygotsky but *before* G.F.'s report), S.L. Rubinshtein wrote in his *Osnovy psikhologii [Fundamentals of psychology]*: "An important place in Soviet psychology belongs to Vygotsky, who, together with Lurie [Lur'e], Leontiev and others, elaborated *the theory of the cultural development* of the higher psychological functions [teoriiu kulturnogo razvitiia vysshikh psikhologicheskikh funktsii], the erroneousness of which has been repeatedly disclosed in the press" (ibid., p. 37; transl. and insertions in brackets by P. Keiler).

59   See also V.N. Kolbanovsky's supporting article "On the psychological views of L.S. Vygotsky (on occasion of his 60th birthday)," published in October 1956 in *Voprosy psikhologii.*

60   This is marking the second phase, so to speak, of the symptom-formation, whereas the virtual "identification with the aggressor" had already been realized by Leontiev in 1936 in his "Materials about consciousness", and was confirmed four years later in Luria's and Leontiev's catchword article "Psychology" in the *Great Soviet Encyclopedia* (cf. below, footnote 63).

61   The use of italics here indicates a deviation from the authentic terminology of Vygotsky, which, strictly speaking, is also a conceptual deviation (cf. above, footnote 54).

62   N.B.: Brushlinsky knew very well that it should be "properly psych o l o g i c a l [tochnee, psikhologicheskikh] functions" (ibid., p. 5; transl. and spaced type by P. Keiler), but declared that "in the given context" (i.e. the critical discussion of Vygotsky's theory of thinking) this could "be neglected" (cf. ibid., footnote; transl. by P. Keiler).

63   See above all, the *Fundamentals of general psychology [Osnovy obshchei psikhologii]*, published first in 1940, and in a revised edition in 1946 (in German in 1958 ff.). Here, in the first edition's author index, Vygotsky *among the Russian authors*, together with Pavlov, *ranks second in the number of mentions* (both with 16 mentions), only "beaten" by Lenin (with 25 mentions) (cf. Rubinshtein 1940, p. 589, p. 591). Indeed, in the author index of the

second edition (German version, Rubinstein [9]1977, pp. 860–865), he is ranked with "only" 13 mentions, far behind Pavlov (23 mentions) and Lenin (now only 19 mentions), and even losing third place to I.M. Sechenov (15 mentions), who in the first edition had only 6 mentions. *However, among colleagues in the more strict sense he is still ranked first* (the second being P.P. Blonskii with 7 mentions). It has to be stated that Rubinshtein in most cases is not merely mentioning Vygotsky but is really presenting his conceptions, often discussing them in detail, partly criticizing, partly approving of them. It is no surprise then to find Vygotsky also included in the (thematically organized) bibliography. It is of special interest to us that Rubinshtein, in the chapter on the history of Soviet psychology, first mentions "Vygotsky's theory of cultural development" (cf. Rubinshtein 1940, p. 67; Rubinshtein 1946, p. 101) and then, only a little bit later, dedicates a quite extensive discussion to "the 'theory of the cultural development of the higher psychical functions [teoriia kul'turnogo razvitiia vysshikh psikhicheskikh funcii]', elaborated by L.S. Vygotsky and a group of collaborators" (Rubinshtein 1940, pp. 69 f.; Rubinshtein 1946, pp. 102 f.; transl. by P. Keiler). Indeed, in the second edition this discussion is not as exhaustive as in the first (only 18 lines compared to 30 lines by 75 signs each), but it is still the same length as the paragraph dedicated to "Vygotsky and his collaborators," within the catchword article "Psychology," elaborated by Luria and Leontiev for volume 47 of the *Great Soviet Encyclopedia [Bol'shaia Sovetskaia Èntsiklopediia]* (cf. Luriia & Leont'ev 1940, column 525). Looked at as a whole, even Rubinshtein's 1946 version is more positive than that given by Vygotsky's former, most "intimate" colleagues. Certainly, Rubinshtein reproduces the objection, already offered in the early 1930s, that the "theory of cultural development" starts from "wrong methodological preconditions" by opposing "dualistically the 'cultural' development to the 'natural'" and conceives "development as genetic sociologism", but at the same time he concedes a "certain positive meaning" to its "basic tendency to introduce the idea of development and the historical principle into psychology," and refers to the "genetic and historical tendencies of the theory of the cultural development of the higher psychical functions" as "progress" (cf. Rubinshtein 1946, p. 102; transl. by P. Keiler). Not so Luria and Leontiev. After having reported, in 20 column lines, on the most important fields of research of "L.S. Vygotsky (1896–1934) and his collaborators" (whereby they too do not use the authentic terminology of Vygotsky but speak of "higher psych*ical* processes in man [vysshie psikhicheskie protsessy cheloveka]" and the "decomposition of the higher psych*ical* functions [raspada vysshikh psikhicheskikh funktsii]"), they dedicate the remaining 10 lines (i.e. one-third of the paragraph) to a fundamental critique, with no mitigation whatsoever: "However, in these studies [rabotakh] the process of psychical development [protsess psikhicheskogo razvitiia] was conceived beyond the connection with the development of practical activity and was deduced directly from the fact of man's assimilation [ovladeniia] of ideal [ideal'nymi, in the sense of 'spiritual'] products (speech, concepts), created by human society. At the same time these studies adopted uncritically a number of erroneous idealist and mechanistic principles from bourgeois psychology" (Luriia & Leont'ev 1940, column 525; transl. and insertions in brackets by P. Keiler). After all, it is a gruesome myth that in the aftermath of the "pedology decree" from July 1936 "for all of two decades, Lev Semenovich and his works were under a writ of silence," that "they could not be mentioned or referred to for 20 long years," as Gita Vygodskaia, Vygotsky's daughter, writes (cf. Vygodskaia & Lifanova 1999d, p. 33), or that "Vygotsky's name was forbidden up until 1956," as it has been asserted for a long time by Leontiev's son A.A. Leontiev, who retracted this false testimony only in 2003 (cf. A.A. Leontiev 2005, p. 65). Characteristically, he did not refer to Rubinshtein and his pertinent assessments in 1940 and 1946 (which were balanced if not all positive) but only admitted that there had been criticisms also from within their "own ranks," trying to palliate this in the case of Luria and Leontiev (cf. ibid., p. 66), suppressing the fact that their criticism was close to that uttered by former critics (cf. e.g. G. F.), and that they distorted Vygotsky's views in the same way as the critics of the 1930s had done. Apparently, it was almost heresy to allude to the fact that only Rubinshtein had been able to do what other, much more authoritative (and obliged to keep alive a positive remembrance of Vygotsky in front of the public) colleagues either did not have the courage or the will to do. Ironically, for the first edition of his *Fundamentals of general psychology* Rubinshtein was awarded the Stalin Prize.

64   The imprint of this volume indicates L.S. Slavina as the reviewer, T.A. Vlasova, È.S. Bein, R.E. Levina, N.G. Morozova, and J.I. Shif as responsible for the compilation of the texts, and È.S. Bein, R.E. Levina, and N.G. Morozova as authors of the commentaries – all of them, like Luria and Èl'konin, former Vygotsky collaborators.

65   It was six years after the release of *Thought and language*, that Leontiev and Luria contributed a paper to the omnibus volume *Historical roots of contemporary psychology*, edited by B.B. Wolman, entitled "The psychological ideas of L.S. Vygotskii" which, as the respective editorial footnote says, should appear as "an Introduction to *Selected Papers* of L.S. Vygotskii to be published by Pergamon Press London" (cf. Leontiev & Luria 1968, p. 338, footnote 1). Although identical in its title with the 1956 introduction to the *Selected psychological investigations*, the paper is no completely identical reproduction. However, in regard to the passage of most interest to us, i.e. the assertion that Vygotsky *himself* had invented the denomination "cultural-historical theory," there is perfect congruency: "That is why Vygotskii originally called his psychological conception the *cultural-historical theory of the psyche*, contrasting it with the idealistic interpretation of mental processes viewed as intrinsic primordial properties of the spirit and with the naturalistic concepts that saw no difference between the behavior of an animal and the mental activity of man." (ibid., pp. 341 f.; italics in the original). One year before, Leontiev had already tried to justify the label "cultural-historical theory" as grounded in the very character of the conception itself, not noticing the evident solecism: "In the foreground there was the problem of the historicity of the psyche [istorizma psichiki], the problem of the reorganization [perestroiki] of the psyche under the influence of the creations of human culture ('the cultural-historical theory of the development of the psyche [kul'-turno-istoricheskaia teoriia razvitiia psikhiki]')" (Leont'ev 1967, p. 18; transl. by P. Keiler).

66   To give an idea of how the deviation from Vygotsky's original terminology had taken hold, it has to be mentioned here that Luria was "corrected" by Cole in his "Portrait of Luria" (i.e. the epilogue to Luria's autobiography). Referring to Frankel's 1930 criticism of the *Studies in the history of behavior*, Cole first speaks of the "sociohistorical theory" and the "sociohistorical approach to the study of psychological processes" (cf. Cole 1979, p. 209), then later mentions the "first standard experimental techniques devised by the sociohistorical school" (ibid., p. 210), which he later refers to as the "hitherto [around 1929/1930] unnoticed Vygotskian school" (ibid., p. 211). In the context of the report on Luria's expedition to Central Asia, Cole advances to the "cultural-historical school" (ibid., p. 214). On page 212 Cole had mentioned the "implications of the cultural-historical theory," followed later by a mention of the "criticism of the cultural-historical theory" (ibid., p. 215). At page 216 we find *Luria's* "cultural-historical theory," and one page later, quoting from the report by G.F., Luria is referred to "as one of the representatives of the cultural-historical theory" (cf. ibid., p. 217). Finally, with reference to Luria's "conversion into a neuropsychologist" (taking place in the second half of the 1930s in the aftermath of G.F.'s report on Luria's "uncooperative" behavior at the "conference of psychologists"), Cole states: "There is no doubt that from the beginning he viewed this activity as yet another extension of the cultural-historical theory into a new empirical domain" (ibid., p. 218). As we can see, G.F. is considered a more authoritative source of reference than Alexander Romanovich Luria himself.

67   Cf. the most instructive foreword to the 2nd edition (Leont'ev 1965, p. 4).

68   N.B.: Luria, in "charming exaggeration," is indeed referring to the (early) 1930s, glorifying the real state of affairs which was quite different (cf. van der Veer & Valsiner 1991). But taken as a quasi-quotation, this characterization would be absolutely adequate in regard to the late 1960s and the 1970s, when the Leontiev-Luria group doubtless had established its hegemony in Soviet psychology. (Leontiev had been honored for his *Problems of the development of the psyche* in 1963 with the Lenin Prize, and Luria was

awarded the Lomonossov Prize, first class, in 1967). This also had long lasting effects on how the discussion about Vygotsky was organized on the international stage.

69 Cf. the introduction to this paper.

70 As an example of this tendency, see the bibliographical registration of a 40-page paper entitled "The problem of dementia in Pick's disease [K voprosu o dementsii pri bolezni Pika]," which was published in June 1934 in the medical journal *Sovetskaia nevropatologiia, psikhiatriia, psikhogigiena [Soviet Neuropathology, Psychiatry, Psychohygiene]*, the authors of which, according to the title page, were N.V. Samukhin, G.V. Birenbaum, and L.S. Vygotsky (cf. Samukhin, Birenbaum & Vygotskii 1934, p. 97). Even if we accept that the name Vygotsky appeared not only for tactical reasons (i.e. to facilitate or accelerate the publication) but that he really did co-author this paper (which throughout tends towards the theoretical approach of K. Lewin), it is not correct to list it in the pertinent bibliographies as a work of *Vygotsky*. But all the Vygotsky bibliographies checked by the present author, beginning with the one at the end of the original version of *Thinking and speech* (cf. Vygotskii 1934b, p. 322) and ending with that of Vygodskaia & Lifanova [Shakhlevich] (2000, German version), do exactly this. But more than that, in the "collaborator's" rubric, in five out of seven times, we don't find Nikolai Samukhin mentioned first but Gita Birenbaum (cf. Shakhlevich 1974, p. 159; *Sobr. soch.*, tom 6, p. 375; Vygodskaia & Lifanova 1996, p. 407; Vygodskaia & Lifanova 1999d, p. 94; Vygodskaja & Lifanova 2000, p. 373), at that predominantly "Germanized" to "Birnbaum" (the German word for "pear-tree"). This makes at least some sense and even seems understandable in the case of the German version of the Vygotsky bibliography. But what about the transmogrification to "Berinbaum" (cf. *Sobr. soch.*, Vol. 6, p. 375) or the banishment into non-existence (cf. *Coll. works*, vol. 6, p. 298)?

71 For a more detailed discussion of the history of that network and the respective intergroup dynamics see Yasnitsky 2011b.

References

Abel'skaia, R. & Neopikhonova, Ia.S. (1932). Problema razvitiia v nemetskoi psikhologii i ee vliianie na sovetskuiu pedologiiu i psikhologiiu. *Pedologiia*, 4, pp. 27–36.

Abel'skaia, R. & Neopikhonova, Ia.S. (2000). The problem of development in German psychology and its influence on Soviet pedology and psychology. In R. van der Veer (Ed.), Criticizing Vygotsky, pp. 31–44.

Bejn, E.S., Vlasova, T.A., Levina, R.E., Morozova, N.G. & Shif, J.I. (1983). Posleslovie (Afterword). In L.S. Vygotskii, Sobranie sochinenii, Vol. 5.

Bruschlinski, A.W. (1967). Die „kulturhistorische Theorie" des Denkens [The "cultural-historical theory" of thinking]. In J.A. Budilowa et al., *Untersuchungen des Denkens in der soujetischen Psychologie* [Investigations of thinking in Soviet psychology]. Berlin (GDR): Volk und Wissen.

Brushlinskii, A.V. (1968). *Kul'turno-istoricheskaia teoriia myshleniia (filosoficheskie problemy psikhologii)* [The cultural-historical theory of thinking (philosophical problems of psychology)]. Moscow: Vysshaia Shkola.

Budilova, E.A. (1972). *Filosofskie problemy v sovetskoi psikhologii* [Philosophical problems in Soviet psychology]. Moscow: Idatel'stvo „Nauka".

Bühler, K. (⁴1924). *Die geistige Entwicklung des Kindes* [The mental development of the child]. Jena: Verlag von Gustav Fischer.

Cole, M. (1979). Epilogue. A Portrait of Luria. In A.R. Luria, *The making of mind. A personal account of Soviet psychology*. Cambridge, MA: Harvard University Press.

Davydov, V.V. & Radzikhovskii, L.A. (1980a). Metodologicheskii analiz kategorii deiatel'nosti [Methodological analysis of the category of activity]. *Voprosy psikhologii*, 4, pp. 167–170.

Davydov, V.V. & Radzikhovskii, L.A. (1980b). Teoriia L.S. Vygotskogo i deiatel'nostnyi podkhod v psikhologii (1) [The theory of L.S. Vygotsky and the activity approach in psychology (1)]. *Voprosy psikhologii*, 6, pp. 48–59.

Davydov, V.V. & Radzikhovskii, L.A. (1985). Vygotsky's theory and the activity-oriented-approach in psychology. In J.V. Wertsch (Ed.), *Culture, communication, and cognition: Vygotskian perspectives.*

Dobkin, S. (1982). Ages and days. In K. Levitin, *One is not born a personality*. Moscow: Progress Publishers.

Él'konin, D.B. (1984). Posleslovie [Afterword]. In L.S. Vygotskii, Sobr. soch., Vol. 4.

Engeström, Y. (1988). On the reception and development of activity theory in Scandinavia. In M. Hildebrand-Nilshon & G. Rückriem (Eds.), Proceedings of the 1st International Congress on Activity Theory. Vol. 4, Part 2: State of the art lectures. Berlin (West): System Druck.

Feofanov, M.P. (1932). Teoriia kul'turnogo razvitiia v pedologii kak elektricheskaia [sic] kontseptsiia, imeiushchaia vosnovnom idealisticheskie korni. *Pedologiia*, (1–2), pp. 221–234.

Feofanov, M.P. (2000). The theory of cultural development in pedology as an eclectic conception with basically idealist roots. In R. van der Veer (Ed.), *Criticizing Vygotsky*, pp. 12–30.

Feuerbach, L. (1854/1957). *The essence of Christianity*. Translated from the German by G. Eliot (M. Evans). New York/Evanston/London: Harper & Row.

Feuerbach, L. (1967 ff.). *Gesammelte Werke* [Collected Works] (grammalogue: FGW). W. Schuffenhauer. Berlin: Akademie Verlag.

Frankel, A. (1930). [Against eclecticism in psychology and pedology]. *Povesteniia natsional'nostei*, 7–8. [Wording of the original Russian title and complete dates unknown; sources of reference: Cole 1979; van der Veer & Valsiner 1991.]

G.F. (1936). O sostoianii i zadachakh psikhologicheskoi nauki v CCCR (otchet o soveshchanii psikhologov pri redaktsii jurnala "Pod znamenem marksizma") [About the actual state of affairs and the tasks of the psychological science in the USSR (Report on a conference of psychologists at the editorial office of the journal "Under the banner of Marxism")]. *Pod znamenem marksizma*, 9, pp. 87–99.

Guillaume, P. & Meyerson, I. (1930). Recherches sur l'usage de l'instrument chez les singes. I: Le problème du détour. *Journal de Psychologie normale et pathologique*, 27, pp. 177–236.

Holzkamp, K. & Schurig, V. (1973). Zur Einführung [Introduction]. In A.N. Leontjew, *Probleme der Entwicklung des Psychischen* [Problems of the development of the psychical]. Frankfurt a.M.: Athenäum.

Iaroshevskii, M.G. & Gurgenidze, G.S. (1982). Posleslovie [Afterword]. In L.S. Vygotskii, Sobr. Soch., Vol. 1.

Itogi diskussii po reaktologicheskoi psikhologii [Results of the discussion about reactological psychology] (1931). *Psikhotekhnika i psikhofiziologiia truda*, 4–6, pp. 387–391.

Iudin, E.G. (1978). *Sistemnyi podkhod i printsip deiatel'nosti* [System approach and the principle of activity]. Moscow: Nauka.

Keiler, P. (1976). Die entwicklungspsychologische Konzeption A.N. Leontjews als Gegenstand marxistischer und bürgerlicher Interpretation [The developmental-psychological conception of A.N. Leontiev as subject of Marxist and bourgeois interpretation]. *Sozialistische Politik*, 34/35, pp. 51–94.

Keiler, P. (1981a). Natural history and psychology: perspectives and problems. In U.J. Jensen & R. Harré (Eds.), *The philosophy of evolution*. Brighton: Harvester Press.

Keiler, P. (1981b). Isomorphie-Konzept und Wertheimer-Problem. Beiträge zu einer historisch-methodologischen Analyse des Köhlerschen Gestaltansatzes. Teil II: Anspruch und Wirklichkeit der Theorie der „psychophysischen Gestalten" – Funktionale Systeme und

Wertheimer-Problem [The concept of isomorphism and Wertheimer's problem. Contributions to a historical-methodological analysis of Köhler's Gestalt approach. Part II: Ambition and reality of the theory of "psycho-physical Gestalten." Functional systems and Wertheimer's problem]. *Gestalt Theory*, 3, pp. 93–128.

Keiler, P. (1988a). Von der Schwierigkeit, in der Psychologie Marxist zu sein [On the difficulties to be a Marxist in psychology]. In N. Kruse & M. Ramme (Eds.), *Hamburger Ringvorlesung Kritische Psychologie. Wissenschaftskritik, Kategorien, Anwendungsgebiete* [Hamburg cycle of lectures on Critical Psychology: science-critique, categories, fields of application]. Hamburg: ergebnisse VERLAG.

Keiler, P. (1988b). Betrifft: „Aneignung" [Re: "Appropriation"]. *Forum Kritische Psychologie*, 22, pp. 102–122.

Keiler, P. (1991). Gegenständlichkeit, Sozialität, Historizität: Versuch einer Rekonstruktion der Feuerbach-Wygotski-Linie in der Psychologie [Objectness, sociality, historicity: attempt at a reconstruction of the Feuerbach-Vygotsky-line in psychology]. *Forum Kritische Psychologie*, 27, pp. 89–168.

Keiler, P. (1996). Was bedeutet „Vergegenständlichung" bei Feuerbach und Marx? [What is the meaning of "objectivisation" in the writings of Feuerbach and Marx?]. *Beiträge zur Marx-Engels-Forschung, Neue Folge*, 1996, pp. 111–133.

Keiler, P. (1997/31999). *Feuerbach, Wygotski & Co.: Studien zur Grundlegung einer Psychologie des gesellschaftlichen Menschen* [Feuerbach, Vygotsky & Co.: Studies toward the foundation of a psychology of societal man]. Hamburg/Berlin: Argument Verlag.

Keiler, P. (2002). *Lev Vygotskij – ein Leben für die Psychologie* [Lev Vygotsky – a life for psychology]. Weinheim/Basel: Beltz Taschenbuch.

Keiler, P. (2008). Das Verhältnis A.N. Leont'evs zu Ludwig Noiré. Wissenschaftshistorische und politische Hintergründe der Entstehung der Tätigkeitstheorie [A.N. Leontiev's relationship to Ludwig Noiré. The science-historical and political background of the genesis of activity-theory]. *Forum Kritische Psychologie*, 52, pp. 106–130.

Keiler, P. (2010a). „Beinahe eine Apologie"? – Anmerkungen zur Vygotskij-Kritik A.N. Leont'evs ["Almost an apology"? – annotations on A.N. Leontiev's criticism of Vygotsky] *Tätigkeitstheorie – Journal für tätigkeitstheoretische Forschung in Deutschland*, 2/2010, pp. 7–41.

Keiler, P. (2010b). A.N. Leont'evs „Materialien über das Bewusstsein" (1936) als Schlüsseltext [A.N. Leontiev's „Materials about consciousness" (1936) as key text]. *Tätigkeitstheorie – Journal für tätigkeitstheoretische Forschung in Deutschland*, 2/2010, pp. 67–98.

Keiler, P. (2015). *Lev Vygotsky – ein Leben für die Psychologie. Überarbeitete, aktualisierte, neu formatierte und mit einem Vorwort versehene Version der Originalausgabe von 2002* [Lev Vygotsky – a life for psychology. Revised, actualized, and reformatted version of the original edition from 2002, complemented by a foreword]. Weinheim/Basel: Beltz E-Book.

Keiler, P. (2017). "What is absolutely impossible for *one* person, is possible for two" – a historical-methodological study concerning Feuerbachian elements in the later works of L.S. Vygotsky. *Istoriia rossiiskoi psikhologii v litsakh: Daidjest*, No. 3, pp. 179–211.

Kellog, D. (2011). Untangling a genetic root of Thinking and Speech: Towards a textology of Tool and Sign in Child Development. *PsyAnima, Dubna Psychological Journal*, 4(4), pp. 85–97.

Kellog, D. & Yasnitsky, A. (2011). The differences between the Russian and English texts of Tool and Symbol in Child Development. Supplementary and analytic materials. *PsyAnima, Dubna Psychological Journal*, 4(4), pp. 98–158.

Koffka, K. (²1925). *Die Grundlagen der psychischen Entwicklung. Eine Einführung in die Kinderpsychologie.* [The fundamentals of psychical development. An introduction to child psychology]. Osterwieck am Harz: A.W. Zickfeldt.

Kolbanovskii, V.N. (1956). O psikhologicheskikh vzgliadakh L.S. Vygotskogo. (K shestide-siatiletiiu so dnia rojdeniia) [On the psychological views of L.S. Vygotsky (on occasion of his 60th birthday)]. *Voprosy psikhologii*, 5, pp. 104–113.

Leontiev, A.A. (2005). The life and creative path of A.N. Leontiev. *Journal of Russian and East European Psychology*, 43(3), pp. 8–69.

Leont'ev, A.N. (1930). Razvitie vnutrennei struktury vysshego povedeniia [Development of the inner structure of higher behavior]. In *Psikhonevrologicheskie Nauki v SSSR*. Moscow/Leningrad: Medgiz.

Leontiev, A.N. (1932). The development of voluntary attention in the child. *Journal of Genetic Psychology*, 40, pp. 52–81. (Reprinted in L.S. Vygotsky (1994). *The Vygotsky reader*).

Leont'ev, A.N. (1934). L.S. Vygotskii. *Sovetskaia psikhonevrologiia*, X(6), pp. 188–190.

Leont'ev, A.N. (1959). *Problemy razvitiia psikhiki* [Problems of the development of the psyche]. Moscow: Izdatel'stvo Akademii pedagogicheskikh nauk RSFSR.

Leont'ev, A.N. (1965). *Problemy razvitiia psikhiki* [Problems of the development of the psyche]. Second edition. Moscow: Mysl'.

Leont'ev, A.N. (1967). Bor'ba za problemu soznaniia v stanovlenii sovetskoi psikhologii [The struggle about the problem of consciousness in the rise of Soviet psychology]. *Voprosy psikhologii*, 2, pp. 14–22.

Leont'ev, A.N. (1982). Vstupitel'naia stat'ia: O tvorcheskom puti L.S. Vygotskogo [Introductory chapter: About the creative path of L.S. Vygotsky]. In L.S. Vygotskii, Sobr. soch., Vol. 1.

Leont'ev, A.N. (1983). *Izbrannye psikhologicheskie proizvedeniia: B 2-x T* [Selected psychological works in 2 volumes]. Moscow: Pedagogika.

Leont'ev, A.N. (1998). Uchenie o srede v pedologicheskikh rabotakh L.S. Vygotskogo (kriticheskoe issledovanie) [Teaching about the environment in the pedological works of L.S. Vygotsky (a critical study)]. *Voprosy psikhologii*, 1, pp. 108–124.

Leont'ev, A.N. (2001). *Frühschriften* [Early writings]. Edited by G. Rückriem. Berlin: Pro BUSINESS.

Leont'ev, A.N. (2003a). *Stanovlenie psikhologii deiatel'nosti. Rannie raboty* [The rise of the psychology of activity. Early works]. Edited by A.A. Leont'eva, D.A. Leont'eva & E.E. Sokolovoi. Moscow: Smysl.

Leont'ev, A.N. (2003b). Razvitie pamiati [The development of memory]. In A.N. Leont'ev, *Stanovlenie psikhologii deiatel'nosti. Rannie raboty*.

Leont'ev, A.N. (2003c). K voprosy o razvitii arifmeticheskogo myshleniia rebenka [On the problem of the development of the arithmetical thinking of the child]. In A.N. Leont'ev, *Stanovlenie psikhologii deiatel'nosti. Rannie raboty*.

Leont'ev, A.N. (2003d). L.S. Vygotskii. In A.N. Leont'ev, *Stanovlenie psikhologii deiatel'nosti. Rannie raboty*.

Leont'ev, A.N. (2003e). Materialy o soznanii [Materials about consciousness]. In A.N. Leont'ev, *Stanovlenie psikhologii deiatel'nosti. Rannie raboty*.

Leont'ev, A.N. (2003f). A.N. Leont'ev – L.S. Vygotskomu [A.N. Leontiev to L.S. Vygotsky]. In A.N. Leont'ev, *Stanovlenie psikhologii deiatel'nosti. Rannie raboty*.

Leont'ev, A.N. (2006). *Frühe Schriften. Bd. II* [Early writings, Vol. II]. Edited by G. Rückriem. Berlin: Lehmanns Media.

Leont'ev, A.N. & Luriia, A.R. (1956). Psikhologicheskie vozzreniia L.S. Vygotskogo [The psychological views of L.S. Vygotsky]. In L.S. Vygotskii, *Izbrannye psikhologicheskie issledovaniia* [Selected psychological investigations].

Leont'ev, A.N., Luriia, A.R. & Teplov, B.M. (1960). Predislovie [Foreword]. In L.S. Vygotskii, *Razvitie vysshikh psikhicheskikh funktsii. Iz neopublikovannykh trudov* [Development of the higher psychical functions. From non-published works].

Leontiev, A.N. & Luria, A.R. (1968). The psychological ideas of L.S. Vygotskii. In B.B. Wolman (Ed.), *Historical roots of contemporary psychology*. New York: Harper and Row.

Leontjew, A.N. (1973). *Probleme der Entwicklung des Psychischen* [Problems of the development of the psychical]. Frankfurt a.M.: Athenäum.

Levitin, K.E. (1998). A dissolving pattern. Reflections on the life and work of A.R. Luria (Part 1). *Journal of Russian and East European Psychology*, 36(5).

Luria, A.R. (1928). The problem of the cultural behavior of the child. *Journal of Genetic Psychology*, 35, pp. 493–506.

Luria, A.R. (1934/1935). L.S. Vygotsky. *Character and Personality*, 3, pp. 238–240.

Luria, A.R. (1935). Professor L. S. Vygotsky (1896–1934). *Journal of Genetic Psychology*, XLVI (1), pp. 224–226.

Luria, A.R. (1936/1937). The development of mental functions in twins. *Character and Personality*, 5, pp. 35–47.

Luria, A.R. (1979). *The making of mind. A personal account of Soviet psychology*. Edited by M. Cole & S. Cole. Cambridge, MA: Harvard University Press.

Luria, A.R. & Vygotsky, L.S. (1992). *Ape, primitive man, and child. Essays in the history of behavior*. New York/London/Toronto: Harvester Wheatsheaf.

Luriia, A.R. (1930). Funktsiia znaka v razvitii povedeniia rebenka [The function of the sign in the development of the child's behavior]. In *Psikhonevrologicheskie Nauki v SSSR*. Moscow/Leningrad: Medgiz.

Luriia, A.R. (1982). Poleslovie [Afterword]. In L.S. Vygotskii, Sobr. soch., Vol. 2.

Luriia, A. & Leont'ev, A. (1940). Psikhologiia [Psychology]. In *Bolshaia sovetskaia Entsiklopediia* [Great Soviet encyclopedia], Vol. 47. Moscow: Gosudarstvennyi institut "Sovestkaia entsiklopediia".

Mecacci, L. & Yasnitsky, A. (2011). Editorial changes in the three Russian editions of Vygotsky's "Thinking and Speech" (1934, 1956, 1982): Towards [an] authoritative and ultimate English translation of the book. *PsyAnima, Dubna Psychological Journal*, 4(4), pp. 159–187.

Petrovskii, A.V. (1967a). *Istoriia sovetskoi psikhologii. Formirovanie osnov psikhologicheskoi nauki* [History of Soviet psychology. Formation of the fundamentals of psychological science]. Moscow: Izdatel'stvo prosveshchenie.

Petrovskii, A.V. (1967b). Sovetskaia psikhologicheskaia nauka na pod'eme [Soviet psychological science in the rise]. *Sovetskaia pedagogika*, XXXI(11), pp. 48–60.

Puzyrei, A.A. (1986a). Neopublikovannaia rukopis' L.S. Vygotskogo [An unpublished manuscript of L.S. Vygotsky]. *Vestnik Moskovskogo Universiteta, Seriia 14, Psikhologiia*, 1, pp. 51–52.

Puzyrei, A.A. (1986b). Primechaniia [Annotations]. *Vestnik Moskovskogo Universiteta, Seriia 14, Psikhologiia*, 1, pp. 63–65.

Puzyrei, A.A. (1989a). An unpublished manuscript by Vygotsky. *Soviet Psychology*, 27(2), pp. 53–54.

Puzyrei, A.A. (1989b). Notes. *Soviet Psychology*, 27(2), pp. 73–77.

Puzyrei, A.A. & Vygotsky, L.S. (2007). In memory of L.S. Vygotsky (1896–1934). L.S. Vygotsky: Letters to students and colleagues. *Journal of Russian and East European Psychology*, 45(2), pp. 11–60.

Razmyslov, P. (1934). O 'kul'turno-istoricheskoi psikhologii' Vygotskogo i Luria. *Kniga i proletarskaia revoliutsiia*, 4, pp. 78–86.

Razmyslov, P. (2000). On Vygotsky's and Luria's "cultural-historical theory of psychology". In R. van der Veer (Ed.), *Criticizing Vygotsky*, pp. 45–58.

Rubinshtein, S.L. (1935). *Osnovy psikhologii* [Fundamentals of psychology]. Moscow: Gosudarstvennoe uchebno-pedagogicheskoe izdatel'stvo.

Rubinshtein, S.L. (1940). *Osnovy obshchei psikhologii* [Fundamentals of general psychology]. Moscow: Gosudarstvennoe uchebno-pedagogicheskoe izdatel'stvo NARKOMPROSA RSFSR.

Rubinshtein, S.L. (1946). *Osnovy obshchei psikhologii. Izdanie vtoroe* [Fundamentals of general psychology. Second edition]. Moscow: Gosudarstvennoe uchebno-pedagogicheskoe izdatel'stvo Ministerstva prosveshcheniia RSFSR.

Rubinstein, S.L. (^{9}1977). *Grundlagen der Allgemeinen Psychologie* [Fundamentals of general psychology]. Berlin (GDR): Volk und Wissen.

Rudneva, E.I. (1937). *Pedologicheskie izvrashcheniia Vygotskogo*. Mocow: Gosudarstvennoe uchebno-pedagogicheskoe izdatel'stvo.

Rudneva, E.I. (2000). Vygotsky's pedological distortions. In R. van der Veer (Ed.), *Criticizing Vygotsky*, pp. 75–96.

Rückriem, G. (2001). Nachwort. Daten zur Biographie A.N. Leont'evs (1903–1979) im Zeitraum bis 1940 [Afterword. Dates concerning the biography of A.N. Leontiev (1903–1979) in the period until 1940]. In A.N. Leont'ev, *Frühschriften* [Early writings]..

Samukhin, N.V., Birenbaum, G.V. & Vygotskii, L.S. (1934). K voprosu o dementsii pri bolezni Pika [About the problem of dementia in Pick's disease]. *Sovetskaia nevropatologiia, psikhiatriia, psikhogigiena*, III(6), pp. 97–136.

Shakhlevich, T.M. (1974). Bibliografiia trudov L.S. Vygotskogo (k 40-letiiu so dnia smerti) [Bibliography of the works of L.S. Vygotsky (at the 40th anniversary of his death)]. *Voprosy psikhologii*, 3, pp. 152–160.

Talankin, A.A. (1931). Po polojenii na psikhologicheskom fronte [On the turnaround at the psychological front]. *Sovetskaia psikhonevrologiia*, 2–3, pp. 8–23.

Talankin, A.A. (2000). On the Vygotsky and Luria group. In R. van der Veer (Ed.), *Criticizing Vygotsky*, pp. 10–11.

Van der Veer, R. (1997a). Some major themes in Vygotsky's theoretical work. An introduction. In L.S. Vygotsky, Coll. works, Vol. 3.

Van der Veer, R. (1997b). Notes to the English edition. In L.S. Vygotsky, Coll. works, Vol. 3.

Van der Veer, R. (Ed.) (2000). *Criticizing Vygotsky. Journal of Russian and East European Psychology*, 38(6).

Van der Veer, R. (2000a). Editor's introduction. In R. van der Veer (Ed.), *Criticizing Vygotsky*, pp. 3–9.

Van der Veer, R. & Valsiner, J. (1991). *Understanding Vygotsky: A quest for synthesis*. Oxford/ Cambridge, MA: Blackwell.

Van der Veer, R. & Yasnitsky, A. (2011). Vygotsky in English: What still needs to be done. *Integrative Psychological and Behavioral Science*, 45(4), pp. 475–493.

Vygodskaia, G.L. & Lifanova, T.M. (1996). *Lev Semenovich Vygotskii. jisn' – deiatel'nost' – shtrikhi k portretu* [Lev Semenovich Vygotsky. Life – activiy – sketches for a portrait]. Moscow: Smysl.

VygodskaiaG.L. & Lifanova, T.M. (1999a, 1999b, 1999c, 1999d). Lev Semenovich Vygotsky. *Journal of Russian and East European Psychology*, 37(2, 3, 4, 5).

Vygodskaja, G.L. & Lifanova, T.M. (2000). *Lev Semjonovič Vygotskij: Leben – Tätigkeit – Persönlichkeit* [Lev Semionovich Vygotsky: Life – Activity – Personality]. Hamburg: Verlag Dr. Kovač.

Vygotski, L.S. (1929). The problem of the cultural development of the child. *Journal of Genetic Psychology*, 36, pp. 415–434.

Vygotskii, L.S. (1924). K psikhologii i pedagogike detskoi defektivnosti [About the psychology and pedagogy of children's defectivity]. In L.S. Vygotskii (Ed.), *Voprosy vospitaniia slepykh, glukhonemykh i umstvenno ostalykh detei* [Questions of the education of blind, deaf-mute, and mentally retarded children]. Moscow: Izdatel'stvo SPON NKP.

Vygotskii, L.S. (1925). Soznanie kak problema psikhologii povedeniia [Consciousness as a problem of the psychology of behavior]. In *Psikhologiia i marksizm*. Leningrad: Gosudarstvennoe Izdatel'stvo.

Vygotskii, L.S. (1928). Problema kul'turnogo razvitiia rebenka [The problem of the cultural development of the child]. *Pedologiia*, 1, pp. 58–77.

Vygotskii, L.S. (1930). Razvitie vysshikh form povedeniia v detskom vozraste [Development of higher forms of behavior in childhood]. In *Psikhonevrologicheskie Nauki v SSSR*. Moscow/Leningrad: Medgiz.

Vygotskii, L.S. (1931). *Pedologiia podrostka. Zadaniia 9–16* [Pedology of the adolescent. Assignments 9–16]. Moscow: Izdatel'stvo BZO.

Vygotskii, L.S. (1932). Problema rechi i myshleniia rebenka v uchenii J. Piaje. Kriticheskoe issledovanie [The problem of thinking and speech in the teaching of J. Piaget. A critical investigation]. In *J. Piaje, Rech' i myshlenie rebenka*. Moscow/Leningrad: Uchpedgiz.

Vygotskii, L.S. (1934a). Psikhologiia i uchenie o lokalizatsii [Psychology and the teaching of localization]. In Pervyi Vseukrainskii s'ezd nevropatologov i psikhiatrov. Tezisy dokladov [First All-Ukrain Congress of Neuropathologists and Psychiatrists. Abstracts of reports]. Char'kov.

Vygotskii, L.S. (1934b). *Myshlenie i rech'. Psikhologicheskie issledovaniia* [Thinking and speech. Psychological investigations]. Moscow/Leningrad: Socekgiz.

Vygotskii, L.S. (1956). *Izbrannye psikhologicheskie issledovaniia* [Selected psychological investigations]. Edited by A.N. Leont'eva & A.R Luriia. Moscow. Izdatel'stvo Akademii pedagogicheskikh nauk RSFSR.

Vygotskii, L.S. (1960). *Razvitie vysshikh psikhicheskikh funktsii. Iz neopublikovannykh trudov* [Development of the higher psychical functions. From non-published works]. Edited by A.N. Leont'eva, A.R. Luriia, & B.M. Teplova. Moscow: Izdatel'stvo akademii pedagogicheskikh nauk.

Vygotskii, L.S. (1982–1984). Sobranie sochinenii (grammalogue: *Sobr. soch.) v 6-ti tt.* [Collected works (grammalogue: Sobr. soch.) in 6 vols.]. Moscow: Pedagogika.

Vygotskii, L.S. (1986). Konkretnaia psikhologiia cheloveka. *Vestnik Moskovskogo Universiteta, Seriia 14, Psikhologiia*, 1, pp. 52–63.

Vygotskii, L.S. (2003). Predislovie k knige A.N. Leont'eva "Razvitie pamiati" [Foreword to A.N. Leont'ev's book "The development of memory"]. In A.N. Leont'ev, *Stanovlenie psikhologii deiatel'nosti. Rannie raboty* [The rise of the psychology of activity. Early works]. Moscow: Smysl.

Vygotskii, L.S. & Leont'ev, A.N. (2003). Predislovie k knige A.N. Leont'eva "Razvitie pamiati" [Foreword to A.N. Leont'ev's book "The development of memory"]. In A.N. Leont'ev, *Stanovlenie psikhologii deiatel'nosti. Rannie raboty*.

Vygotskii, L.S. & Luriia, A.R. (1930). *Etiudi po istorii povedeniia. Obez'iana – Primitiv – Rebenok* [Studies in the history of behavior. Ape, primitive man, child]. Moscow/Leningrad: Gosudarstvennoe idatel'stvo.

Vygotsky, L.S. (1987–1999). *Collected Works* (grammalogue: Coll. works), Vols. 1–6. Edited by R.W. Rieber et al. New York: Plenum.

Vygotsky, L.S. (1989). Concrete human psychology. *Soviet Psychology*, 27(2), pp. 54–73.

Vygotsky, L.S. (1994). *The Vygotsky reader*. Edited by R. van der Veer & J. Valsiner. Oxford/Cambridge, MA: Blackwell.

Vygotsky, L.S. (1997). *Educational psychology*. Boca Raton, FL: St. Lucie Press.

Vygotsky, L. & Luria, A. (1994). Tool and symbol in child development. In *The Vygotsky reader*.

Wertsch, J. (Ed.) (1985). *Culture, communication and cognition: Vygotskian perspectives*. Cambridge, MA/London/New York: Cambridge University Press.

Wygotski, L. (1985/1987) *Ausgewählte Schriften, 2 Bände* [Selected Works, 2 volumes; grammalogue: ASch]. In deutscher Sprache herausgegeben von J. Lompscher [Edited in German by J. Lompscher]. Berlin (GDR): Volk und Wissen. (Reprographical reprint 2003, Berlin: Lehmanns Media).

Yaroshevsky, M.G. (1999). Epilogue. In L.S. Vygotsky, *Collected Works, Vol. 6*.

Yasnitsky, A. (2010). Guest editor's introduction. "Archival revolution" in Vygotskian studies? Uncovering Vygotsky's archives. *Journal of Russian and East European Psychology*, 48(1), pp. 3–13.

Yasnitsky, A. (2011a). The Vygotsky that we (do not) know: Vygotsky's main works and the chronology of their composition. *PsyAnima, Dubna Psychological Journal*, 4(4), pp. 53–61.

Yasnitsky, A. (2011b). Vygotsky Circle as a personal network of scholars: Restoring connections between people and ideas. *Integrative Psychological and Behavioral Science*, 45(4), pp. 422–457.

Zaporojets, A.V. (1959/1965). Primechaniia [Annotations]. In A.N. Leont'ev, *Problemy razvitiia psikhiki* [Problems of the development of the psyche].

Zavershneva, E.Iu. (2009). Issledovanie rukopisi L.S. Vygotskogo "Istoricheskii smysl psikhologicheskogo krizisa" [Investigation of the manuscript of L.S. Vygotsky's "The historical meaning of the psychological crisis"]. *Voprosy psikhologii*, 6, pp. 119–137.

Zavershneva, E.Iu. (2010a). The Vygotsky family archive (1912–1934). *Journal of Russian and East European Psychology*, 48(1), pp. 14–33.

Zavershneva, E.Iu. (2010b). The Vygotsky family archive: New findings. Notebooks, notes, and scientific journals of L.S. Vygotsky (1912–1934). *Journal of Russian and East European Psychology*, 48(1), pp. 34–60.

Zavershneva, E.Iu. (2010c). "The way to freedom" (On the publication of documents from the family archive of Lev Vygotsky). *Journal of Russian and East European Psychology*, 48(1), pp. 61–90.

Zavershneva, E.Iu. (2012a). "The key to human psychology." Commentary on L.S. Vygotsky's notebook from the Zakharino hospital (1926). *Journal of Russian and East European Psychology*, 50(4), pp. 16–41.

Zavershneva, E.Iu. (2012b). Investigating L.S. Vygotsky's manuscript "The historical meaning of the crisis in psychology." *Journal of Russian and East European Psychology*, 50(4), pp. 42–63.

Zavershneva, E.Iu. & Osipov, M.E. (2012). Primary changes to the version of "The historical meaning of the crisis in psychology". published in the Collected works of L.S. Vygotsky. *Journal of Russian and East European Psychology*, 50(4), pp. 64–84.

Zavershneva, E.Iu. & van der Veer, R. (Eds.) (2018). *Vygotsky's notebooks. A selection*. New York: Springer.

Zinchenko, V.P. (1985). Vygotsky's ideas about units for the analysis of mind. In J.V. Wertsch (Ed.), *Culture, communication, and cognition: Vygotskian perspectives*.

6

FROM SUPERHUMANS TO SUPERMEDIATORS

Locating the extraordinary in CHAT

Clay Spinuzzi

Cultural-historical activity theory (CHAT)[1] emerged from the Vygotskian tradition in Soviet psychology, a tradition that grounds its understanding of consciousness and personality in materialist, monist Marxist theory. Engeström (2014) describes three "generations" of CHAT. First was Vygotsky's[2] work, which was centered around the concept of mediation, but limited to individuals or dyads. Second was Leontiev's development of the theory, which introduced the unit of analysis (labor activity) and expanded it to apply to groups. Third was the work of Engeström and others in the West, who expanded the theory to address multiple interacting activity systems. The story is that of linear development and expansion[3] of Vygotsky's fundamental psychological insights to address broader social systems.

That development has gone on for about 90 years, and the project has transformed significantly during that time. To understand how much, let's examine two quotes.

The first quote is from Lev Vygotsky's (1930) "The Socialist alteration of man." After invoking Nietzsche's notion of a superman [sic], Vygotsky quotes Marx and Engels to argue that humanity will be extraordinarily transformed through socialism:

> In this sense Engels, who had examined the process of evolution from the ape to man, said that it is labour which created man. Proceeding from this, one could say that new forms of labour will create the new man and that this new man will resemble the old kind of man, "the old Adam", in name only, in the same way as, according to Spinoza's great statement, a dog, the barking animal, resembles the heavenly constellation Dog.
>
> *Vygotski 1930/1994*

The second quote is from Yrjö Engeström's forthcoming *Expertise in Transition: Expansive Learning in Medical Work*. In discussing his studies of organized medical work, Engeström states:

These factors create situations in which employees at all levels of the hierarchy, and increasingly also their clients, face tasks that they find impossible to solve. There is something curious about this impossibility. Each individual, including highly educated professionals and managers, may testify that the situation was clearly beyond his or her control. Yet, most of these situations are somehow resolved and work goes on. Moreover, often none of the persons involved can quite reconstruct or fully understand what actually happened and how the solution was found. In other words, *people at work somehow go beyond their own limitations* all the time.

Engeström 2018, in press, my emphasis

The contrast between the two quotes is startling. Yes, both describe an extraordinary expansion of abilities. But they locate the extraordinary in different places.

In "The Socialist Alteration of Man," Vygotsky locates the abilities in the individual. The mechanism of this transformation, as Vygotsky discusses elsewhere (Vygotsky & Luria 1930/1993; Vygotsky & Luria 1930/1994; Vygotsky 1934/2012), was internalized symbolic or psychological tools, especially speech. These internalized tools, Vygotsky argued, allowed people to dramatically develop beyond their former limitations. They are *superhumans*, developing individual capabilities that previous generations could not.

Engeström, however, locates the abilities in the activity in which the individual is situated: "people at work somehow go beyond their own limitations all the time," but "often none of the persons involved can quite reconstruct or fully understand what actually happened and how the solution was found." Although the individual does develop, s/he does not develop dramatically. Instead, what develops dramatically are the mediators – the external physical and symbolic tools as well as the rules and division of labor of an activity. These are *supermediators*, providing capabilities that enhance the work of relatively unchanged collections of individuals.

When looking at such stark differences, we might be tempted to think that these "generations" of activity theory are not related at all – critics have argued that Vygotsky's cultural-historical theory is fundamentally different from Leontiev's activity theory (e.g. Kozulin 1999; Miller 2011), and that Leontiev's activity theory is also different from Westernized cultural-historical activity theory (CHAT or 3GAT) (e.g. Avis 2009; Peim 2009; Miller 2011). Nevertheless, we can trace the historical development of CHAT from Vygotsky to the present. This development has twists and turns – as Latour (1996) says, there is no translation without betrayal – but the genealogy is there. And understanding it can help us to better understand the applications of both of these "generations." In this chapter, I examine the development of the extraordinary across the three generations of activity theory, identifying key inflection points in this development. I conclude by discussing implications for developing CHAT further.

The three generations of activity theory

As noted, Yrjö Engeström tells this story of how activity theory evolved in three generations, which I'll designate below as 1GAT, 2GAT, and 3GAT. This account is not universally accepted. Nevertheless, Engeström's story ascribes coherence across the three generations or traditions, demonstrating how each generation is built on (an interpretation of) a previous generation. It thus provides a ready template for analyzing transformations across the three generations. Engeström's three generations are:

1GAT: This generation was centered around Vygotsky's insight into mediation, illustrated in Vygotsky's triangular model of subject, object, and mediating artifact. Inserting a cultural artifact into the subject-object relationship "was revolutionary in that the basic unit of analysis now overcame the split between the Cartesian individual and the untouchable societal structure. ... Objects became cultural entities and the object orientedness of action became the key to understanding human psyche" (Engeström 2014, p. xiv). Yet, Engeström adds, the focus was limited to the individual.

2GAT: That limitation was "overcome by the second generation, led and inspired by Leont'ev's work" (Engeström 2014, p. xiv). Leontiev "showed how historically evolving division of labor had brought about the crucial differentiation between an individual action and a collective activity" (ibid., pp. xiv–xv). Yet, Engeström says, "the relationship between object-oriented production and communicative exchange between people remained somewhat unclear in Leont'ev's work" and Vygotsky's triangle diagram was never graphically expanded in this work (ibid., p. xv). Beyond that, in the Soviet Union, activity theorists mostly restricted their studies to "play and learning among children" (as well as rehabilitation and "defectology" or special needs education) and "Contradictions of activity remained an extremely touchy issue" (ibid., p. xv). In the 1970s, he recounts, radical researchers in the West picked up the concept and applied it to other domains, including work, and Ilyenkov's writings on contradictions became incorporated (ibid., p. xv).

3GAT (also known as CHAT): Here, Engeström drops the human actors in his sentences, but the described agenda is the one that he himself defined.

> The third generation of activity theory is developing conceptual tools to understand networks of interacting activity systems, dialogue, and multiple perspectives and voices. In this mode of research, the basic model is expanded to include minimally two interacting activity systems. This move toward networks of activities, while still in an embryonic form, was anticipated in the original text of *Learning by Expanding*.
>
> *Engeström 2014, p. xv*

For Engeström – and for other commentators on the development of activity theory (e.g. Kaptelinin & Nardi 2006; Spinuzzi 2011; Yamazumi 2007) – the key spokespeople of this tradition are Vygotsky (1GAT) and Leontiev (2GAT). For the third generation, we can point to Engeström himself as a key spokesperson.

Also, as noted, Engeström presents this story as describing linear development. Yet these different generations locate their focal phenomena in different places. Put another way, each generation seeks to explore and explain *extraordinary* abilities. But the generations focus on different extraordinary abilities located in different places. Here I ask: Why? How did the focus change, why, and what does it mean for a coherent AT?

1GAT: Vygotsky and the superhuman

Soviet psychology was a chaotic field in the 1920s. Some psychologists – such as Georgii Chelpanov, who founded the Moscow Institute of Psychology – believed that psychology should be separate from ideology. Others – such as Chelpanov's graduate student, Konstantin Kornilov – argued that a specifically Marxist, materialist psychology had to be developed. This disagreement came to a head at the 1923 psychoneurological congress, where Kornilov appealed for a Marxist psychology and Chelpanov objected in print. In the fallout, Chelpanov was dismissed from the directorship, replaced by Kornilov (Joravsky 1989, p. 224; cf. Krementsov 1996; Petrovsky 1990).

Kornilov pursued a "materialist," "Marxist" line of psychology called reactology, which focused strictly on reactions and avoided issues of consciousness. Nevertheless, Kornilov allowed differing perspectives under his directorship. When Vygotsky presented a paper at the second neuropsychological congress in 1924, arguing that psychological reductionism was not required by Marxism (Joravsky 1989, p. 259), Kornilov was persuaded to hire him.

Beyond consciousness, Vygotsky was intrigued by Trotsky's assertion that under socialism, "The average human type will rise to the heights of an Aristotle, a Goethe, or a Marx" (Trotsky 1923/2005, pp. 206–207). After Trotsky was ousted from the Party in 1927, Vygotsky stopped citing him. Yet Vygotsky remained focused on the task of raising humankind to a new plane – that is, realizing the New Man [sic] (van der Veer & Valsiner 1991). The mechanism for this improvement was humans' ability to mediate their own actions through semiotic tools, controlling themselves from the outside.

The case of the extraordinary: Children's memory

In their 1930 book *Studies on the history of behavior: Ape, primitive, and child*, Vygotsky and Luria described memory experiments conducted by themselves and their associates. Children past a certain age were first tested in terms of natural (unmediated) memory, then given mediators (cards with colors on one side) and tested again. The children tended to do better in mediated tasks, not because their natural memory improved, but because they could substitute the mediator for their own memory (Vygotsky & Luria 1930/1993, p. 180). Yet, as the authors demonstrated with a discussion of Leontiev's forbidden colors experiment (ibid., pp. 190–192), these mediators could be internalized: "the process of attention still remained indirect; although instead of externally indirect, it became internally indirect" (ibid., p. 192). That is, children's *natural* memory did not improve; instead, they developed a *cultural* memory by internalizing psychological tools that changed and systematized the task. Thus, for older children, the cards played little role in their memory. As Vygotsky summarized elsewhere, for a child, to think is to remember; for an adolescent, to remember is to think (Vygotsky 1934/1997a, p. 99).

Vygotsky and Luria concluded that the difference between natural (biological, evolutionary, organic) ability and cultural ability was crucial (e.g. Vygotsky and Luria 1930/1993, p. 230; Vygotsky 1934/1997a, p. 96; Vygotsky 1931/1997b, p. 16; Vygotsky 1929/1994, p. 57). Indeed, although Vygotsky in *The psychology of art* (1925/1974) echoed Trotsky by claiming that tool use yields both biological adaptation *and* psychological development, by 1934/1997a he claimed that "the biological evolution of man was finished *before* the beginning of his historical development" (Vygotsky 1934/1997a, p. 97, my emphasis).

Thus their study of memory (and other executive functions) located extraordinary abilities within the socialized human mind – specifically, in the psychological tools that individuals develop or assimilate as they learn from culturally more advanced partners. This orientation reflected the cases that were investigated by Vygotsky and colleagues during this period: pedagogy, defectology (i.e. special needs education), rehabilitation, and an abortive fourth branch of cross-cultural psychology represented by Luria's Uzbek expedition (Luria 1976; cf. Lamdan & Yasnitsky 2016).

This conception of the extraordinary reflected Vygotsky's enduring interest in the Nietzschean superman reinterpreted as the New Soviet Man – an interest that was most obvious in his 1930 "The Socialist alteration of man," but that also appeared as early as his dissertation *The psychology of art* (1925/1974), which referenced Trotsky's use of the Nietzschean superman in *Literature and revolution* (1923/2005; see Rosenthal 2002 for a study of how the superman trope was taken up as the New Man in Soviet culture). Read together, *Studies on the history of behavior* Chapter 1, "The Socialist alteration of man," and "Tool and symbol in child development" provide a coherent argument: that psychological tools *made* Man and could *perfect* Man. Vygotsky's work, therefore, was positioned as a Marxist psychology poised to reach the Soviet goal of the New Man (Yasnitsky, 2018).

To understand how this concept of the extraordinary interacted with Vygotskian theory, below we'll discuss the unit of analysis; subject and object; and mediators.

Unit of analysis; agency

The *unit of analysis* bounds the investigated phenomenon, where extraordinary abilities can emerge. In the studies of the Vygotsky Circle, extraordinary abilities manifested in a dyad of less and more culturally advanced participants: teacher and student; older and younger student; literate and preliterate; rehabilitator and rehabilitated. It was in this dyad that the extraordinary could be investigated and developed.

In this dyad, agency was assumed to be an individual's. But, in keeping with Vygotsky's optimistic view of the socialist alteration of man, the individual was portrayed as desiring to become more culturally advanced – that is, in alignment with the more culturally advanced participant. This individual progressively learned mental functions (foremost among these, speech), and in doing so, mastered herself or himself more fully, building higher mental functions on lower ones.

Since he focused on individuals' cultural development, Vygotsky took as his unit of analysis *word meaning* or, more generally, sense (Vygotsky 1927; Vygotsky 1934/2012; cf. Blunden 2010; Miller 2011). As Vygotsky argued in his last book, "Psychology, which aims at a study of complex holistic systems, must replace the method of analysis into elements with the method of analysis into units. What is the unit of verbal thought that is further unanalyzable and yet retains the properties of the whole? We believe that such a unit can be found in the internal aspect of the word, in *word meaning*" (Vygotsky 1934/2012, p. 5).

Subject and object; mastery

The *subject-object distinction* identifies a transformation in which the extraordinary can make a difference.

Across Vygotsky's different phases of thought, one consistent theme was *self-mastery*: the individual's ability to exert control over herself or himself (Vygotsky & Luria 1930/1993; Vygotsky 1934/1997a, Ch. 5; Vygotsky 1931/1997b; Vygotsky 1930/1997c, Ch. 5; Vygotsky 1934/1997d). His conceptualization of higher mental functions changed over time, but his focus on self-mastery was consistent.

In fact, self-mastery underpinned his distinction between psychological and physical tools: psychological tools (signs) allowed humans to master or control their own behavior, while physical tools allowed them to control or subjugate nature (Vygotsky 1931/1997b, pp. 61–62). That is, psychological tools were used when the *self* was the object of one's activity; physical tools were used when external *nature* was the object.

Vygotsky and Luria thus took up Engels' (1971) dictum that "labor created man," routing it through this theme of self-mastery: *In this sense*:

> "labour created man himself," i.e. created the higher psychological functions which distinguish man as man. Primitive man, using his stick, by means of outer sign masters the processes of his own behaviour and subordinates his activity to the aim which he forces external objects to serve: tool, soil, rice.
>
> *Vygotsky & Luria 1930/1994, p. 165; cf. Vygotski 1930/1994*

That is, it was not simply the instrumental domination of nature that transformed animals into humans – it was how this focus led humans to organize higher mental functions, enabling self-mastery, mediated through signs. This self-mediatory aspect, in Vygotsky's view, had created humans and could develop them further still, so much further that they would eventually far surpass the abilities of modern humans. The conditions for that extraordinary development could be found in socialism. In the USSR, the proletariat had risen up to rule over the bourgeoisie, as Lenin had predicted in *The State and Revolution* (Lenin 1987, drawing from Marx's 1922 *Critique of the Gotha Program*), leading to a classless society. In this society, the *withering away of the state* could occur (Lenin 1987, p. 280): the functions of the government would eventually be minimized and taken over by a rotation of volunteers (Lenin 1987, p. 307). External state control would be replaced by internal mastery.

Echoing the concept of the withering away of the state, some educators claimed that education should be based on spontaneous processes within beneficial environments – a "withering away" of school. This notion sometimes entailed the extreme decentering of the teacher (Bauer 1952, p.44). Vygotsky did not endorse this view, but some Stalinist critics would later associate him with it – a dangerous view to hold by that point. After Lenin's death, Stalin had made it clear that the state would not be withering away anytime soon (Stalin 1924/1939).

Mediators

The *mediators* represent the method of the transformation – how the extraordinary is applied.

As mentioned above, Vygotsky distinguished between two sorts of mediators: psychological and physical tools. Vygotsky warned that although we can speak of signs as tools, this analogy could not be carried through to the bitter end, and "we must not anticipate finding much similarity to working tools in these devices that we call signs" (Vygotsky 1931/1997b, p. 60; cf. Vygotsky 1930/1997c). What he called the "instrumental function of the sign" was "the function of stimulus-device fulfilled by the sign with respect to any psychological operation, that it is a tool of human activity" (Vygotsky 1931/1997b, p. 60). We cannot collapse the distinction between tool and sign: "tools as devices for work, devices for mastering the processes of nature, and language as a device for social contact and communication, dissolve in the general concept of artifacts of artificial devices" (ibid., p. 61). Rather, Vygotsky argued that we should understand the difference in this way the use of *signs* was a mediating activity in which humans regulate their own behavior (inward), while the use of *tools* was a mediating activity in which humans subjugate nature (outward) (ibid., pp. 61–62). These were "diverging lines of mediating activity" (ibid., p. 62; cf. Miller 2011).

Similarly, in "The instrumental method in psychology" (Vygotsky 1930/1997c), Vygotsky stated that psychological tools – "artificial devices for mastering [an individual's] own mental processes" – could be considered in analogy to physical tools. But it was only an analogy and "cannot be carried through to the very end until all features of both concepts coincide." The point of analogical comparison was "the role these devices play in behavior, which is analogous to the role of a tool in labor." Such psychological tools were "artificial formations" – social and "directed toward the mastery of [mental] processes" (ibid., p. 85). And "by being included in the process of behavior, the psychological tool modifies the entire course and structure of mental functions by determining the structure of the new instrumental act, just as the technical tool modifies the process of natural adaptation by determining the form of labor operations" (ibid., p.85). That is, for Vygotsky, labor was the domain of physical tools and behavior was the domain of psychological tools.

The higher mental functions, for Vygotsky, were constructed abilities – although they were *built* on natural abilities (lower mental functions), the higher mental functions were thoroughly cultural, symbolic tools. For instance, logical memory was built on natural memory, but exceeded it. By learning the cultural heritage of symbolic mediators, a less culturally advanced participant could build her abilities:

> a human being evolves and develops as a historical, social being. Only a raising of all of humanity to a higher level in social life, the liberation of all of humanity, can lead to the formation of a new type of man.
>
> *Vygotsky 1930/1994b, p. 181*

Through education, human beings could acquire more cultural tools and relate them more effectively, acquiring superhuman abilities, ascending to the New Man.

Summary: The extraordinary in 1GAT

For Vygotsky, then, extraordinary abilities were located in the individual's attainment of cultural tools and her or his cultural evolution. Although he understood the individual mind as thoroughly social, his focus was not on social interactions so much as how cultural tools enabled new abilities within the individual's psyche. We can see Vygotsky's viewpoint on such abilities in two cases that Luria took up during Vygotsky's lifetime and shortly after his death.

One case involved a truly extraordinary ability. Luria and Vygotsky had begun interviewing a mnemonist, who had an eidetic memory, and Vygotsky's notes suggested that he planned to write a book about the case (Zavershneva 2016). After Vygotsky's death, Luria continued to keep contact with the mnemonist, eventually writing a book (Luria 1968) that not only described how the man's extraordinary memory worked but also how it had shaped his personality.

The other case involved an extraordinary development of ability. Vygotsky had proposed understanding the seams between biological and cultural systems of activity by examining "deviations from the normal type," including "the so-called defective," in which natural-cultural merging does not occur normally (Vygotsky 1931/1997b, p. 23). In the 1930s, Luria took up such a challenge when uniovular twins entered his clinic at the age of four due to their severe lack of social development. Initially "their speech consisted only in a small number of barely differentiated sounds which they used in play and communication" (Luria & Yudovich 1959, p. 39), barely understood others' speech (ibid., p. 40), and did not understand symbolic play (ibid., p. 41). Applying the theories that he and Vygotsky had developed, Luria separated the twins. He identified the weaker twin – the one who lagged developmentally – and gave that twin special activities that amounted to what we would now call speech therapy. The other twin was the "control," receiving no additional intervention. For the trained Twin A, abstractions, functional categories, and logical deductions all became easier because they all depended on the mediation of speech (ibid., p. 99). When, after ten months, "both twins were set problems involving a set of operations with the aid of their own speech, it was demonstrated that an elementary special operation with the aid of speech was accessible to the trained Twin A but remained inaccessible to Twin B who had not undergone special speech training" (ibid., pp. 100–101). Neither twin would reach normal abilities, but both had improved, and Twin A had improved extraordinarily, manifesting abilities that Twin B could not.

Unfortunately, Luria does not report whether Twin B ever received similar interventions.

2GAT: Leontiev and the supervision of labor

Vygotsky died in 1934. By 1937 his school had been denounced for its association with pedology[4] and his associates had to reposition themselves to survive within the Stalinist milieu. Arguably in response to trends in Stalinist science (Krementsov 1996), these associates took the ideas of Vygotsky's instrumental period and transformed them to meet the requirements of *partiinost'* (partisanship/party nature), Marxism, and practicality. Their efforts were relatively successful, allowing many of Vygotsky's associates to survive and sometimes thrive under Stalinism.

For instance, in 1943, A.N. Leontiev and A.R. Luria were put in charge of rehabilitation hospitals, where they served the practical aim of rehabilitating injured soldiers. Luria's hospital focused on brain injuries, allowing him to develop the field of neuropsychology that he and Vygotsky had begun studying before the latter's death (cf. Luria 1962/1966a; Luria 1963/1966b; Luria 1972). Leontiev's hospital focused on hand and arm injuries, leading him to study how body trauma reorganizes body functions and perceptions.

Even before Vygotsky's death, Leontiev had collapsed the distinction between physical and psychological tools, insisting that labor had to be the unit of analysis in a Marxist psychology. Given the orthodoxies of Stalinist science, this conception was more politically viable, and it fit closely with the ideology of the bureaucratic state: a state that took a managerial viewpoint, promoting a single correct view and a narrow state-centered range of acceptable motivations for its citizens. Leontiev, the administrator, in effect located the extraordinary within supervision.

The case of the extraordinary: Rehabilitation of amputees

In their book *Rehabilitation of hand function* (Leont'ev & Zaporozhets 1945/1960), published at the end of World War II and reviewing their work at the rehabilitation hospital, Leontiev & Zaporozhets recounted experiments in hand rehabilitation from the perspective of Soviet psychology. In the process, they lay down markers for what would eventually become the dominant framework for Soviet psychology, activity theory.

In one chapter, Leontiev reported on rehabilitation after Krukenberg's operation – an operation for someone whose hand has to be amputated. Essentially, the radius and ulna are separated and the pronator teres muscle is wrapped around both, allowing the patient to use the two bones as an elongated pincer. Obviously, this operation requires the patient to substantially reconstruct both motor and sensory impulses. In their experiments, the research team concluded that this reconstruction does not simply involve elementary sensation: untrained patients couldn't tell if they were feeling a cube or a cylinder. But they could be trained to interpret these sensations (ibid.).

Leontiev argued that in cases of such trauma, the motor experience is disorganized: "even when there is complete anatomical preservation of the central and peripheral system, the co-ordination of the movement may be disturbed to some degree" (ibid. p. 18). Thus, he argued, rehabilitation should first focus on restoring coordination. To improve coordination, the researchers developed feedback loops for patients, reorganizing the task around different stimuli. For instance, in one experiment, they used a kymograph – crediting Luria's (1937/1960) work with the combined motor method – to provide feedback to patients as they undertook tasks with the uninjured and injured limbs (Leont'ev & Zaporozhets 1945/1960, p. 19). When patients had this visual feedback, they were able to smooth out their movements in mere moments (ibid., p. 21). The task had been reorganized around different stimuli.

Leontiev's co-author Zaporozhets noted that the motivation of activity had a large impact on outcomes – "casual and meaningless orders" could have a "chilling effect" on recovery, while "more consequential and complicated tasks" could accelerate it (ibid., p. 149). He even gave the example of dispirited patients reviving when they were given the meaningful task of manufacturing "window frames and furniture to replace that destroyed by the Germans at Stalingrad" (ibid., p. 150). Overall, Zaporozhets lauded "the general tonic and encouraging power of rational work activity" (ibid., p. 146), an untrammeled good providing a meaningful frame for rehabilitation. Labor, which had created humanity (Engels 1971; Leontyev 1959/2009b), could also rehabilitate it.

Importantly, throughout the book, rehabilitation was framed in managerial terms: How could injured soldiers be rehabilitated enough to rejoin the war effort or to join the labor force? The common orientation to national motives was simply assumed: beat the Nazis, build the Soviet nation. Thus, their study located the extraordinary in common labor and cultural heritage – supervised by the State.

Unit of analysis; agency

The *unit of analysis* bounds the investigated phenomenon, where the extraordinary can be seen or can emerge. In Leontiev's case, the unit of analysis was founded on labor activity from a managerial viewpoint.

As mentioned, in the early 1930s, Leontiev differed from Vygotsky. Vygotsky had drawn a distinction between psychological tools (which allowed internal mediation or self-mediation) and physical tools (which allowed external mediation or mediation of nature); he saw these as "diverging lines of mediated activity" (Vygotsky 1931/1997b, p. 62) and focused on self-mediation as the central phenomenon. But by 1931 Leontiev had turned to labor activity itself as the central phenomenon, and in so doing, had collapsed the two kinds of tools into the general category of mediation. So did the rest of the Kharkov School, which "dismissed Vygotsky's neglect of external practical activity" (Haenen 1996, p. 26). Haenen adds that "Leontiev complained that 'it is impossible to find the cause of the development of meaning within social interaction itself' and dedicated himself to discovering 'what lies behind social interaction'" (ibid., p. 79), concluding that "the origin of consciousness had to be found in external activity" (ibid., p. 80).

Vygotsky disapproved of this collapse of physical and psychological mediators, but he died of tuberculosis in 1934. In 1936, the Central Committee of the Communist Party of the Soviet Union banned pedology, specifically charging it with the pseudoscientific, anti-Marxist belief that children's progress depended entirely on the two factors of heredity and environment (A.A. Leontiev 2005, p. 58). The Decree called for severe criticism of pedologists and their books. It came, most disastrously in Rudneva's January 1937 article "Vygotsky's pedological distortions," a blistering Stalinist critique of Vygotsky's school (Rudneva 1937/2000). Like an earlier critic (Razmyslov 1934/2000), Rudneva tied Vygotsky to positions attributed to pedology: mechanism, the overemphasis of the environment, and the so-called withering away of school – a position that had been decisively repudiated in the Decree. She also attacked Vygotsky for not grounding his work in Lenin's theory of reflection, for rooting it in word meaning rather than productive activity or labor, and for relying on bourgeois "sociologizing;"[5] and separating natural and cultural development. This denunciation included the entire Vygotsky Circle and specifically named Leontiev and Luria.

In response, in 1937, Leontiev delivered a lecture critiquing Vygotsky and reframing his own work. This lecture (Leontiev 1937/2005c) and contemporaneous works (Leontiev & Luria 1937/2005; Leontiev 1940/2005a, Leontiev 1940/2005b) read as if they had used Rudneva's criticism as a checklist: the authors condemned fatalistic determination; criticized Vygotsky's use of Durkheim; rejected his focus on word meaning in favor of object-mediated labor activity; and embraced Lenin's reflection theory (reframed in terms of internalization). Of Rudneva's grievances, only one was not directly addressed: the separation of natural and cultural development. This issue was indirectly addressed through mediation: human activity was mediated, unlike animal activity (Leontiev 1940/2005a). Leontiev eventually formulated this characterization pithily, by quoting Engels: "'Labour,' Engels wrote, 'created man himself'. Labour also created man's consciousness" (Leontyev 1959/2009b, p. 181).

Leontiev's focus on labor activity offered a *rhetorical* solution, one that arguably allowed the cultural-historical school to survive and sometimes thrive as a Stalinist science. Yet it introduced a *methodological* problem, since it made activity both the phenomenon under investigation and the explanatory principle – a problem about which Vygotsky had warned in his unpublished 1927 methodological manuscript (Kozulin 1984; Kozulin 1999).

Within this approach, Leontiev, like Vygotsky, still investigated dyads of less and more culturally advanced participants within cases such as pedagogy, defectology, and rehabilitation. And again like Vygotsky, Leontiev assumed that the less culturally advanced participant generally shared the motivations of the more culturally advanced one. Leontiev did acknowledge that the less culturally advanced participant may have their own motivations as well, and in fact are polymotivated (Leontyev 1978/2005). For instance, a student might be motivated by an examination mark rather than by gaining productive knowledge (Leontyev 1959/2009b). But for Leontiev, this dyadic relationship occurred within a more expansive set of structured social relations bounded by labor activity. The more culturally advanced participant represented the State; that participant's task was to lead the individual into the State's service.

We can see this orientation in the hand rehabilitation study, in which the individuals are portrayed as disorganized people who must be reorganized so that they could serve the State in other ways – if they could not fight the Nazis directly, they could manufacture goods for the war effort, rehabilitating themselves through labor (Leont'ev & Zaporozhets 1945/1960, p. 150). Other examples include training paratroopers (Leontyev 1978/2005) and students (Leontyev 1959/2009b, pp. 413–414). In a 1949 piece – written just after Lysenko's triumphant speech at the August VASKhNIL meeting (Krementsov 1996, pp. 158–159) – Leontiev emphasized the State's role in shaping students to become ideal Soviet citizens:

> But life itself, the child's activity which determines in its course his mental development, is not spontaneous – it is under the influence of education and instruction. In a Socialist society, which does not develop spontaneously but is directed by men, education is the decisive force which forms man intellectually. It must correspond to the aims and the needs of the entire society, of the entire people or, in other words, it must fully agree with real human needs, and also with those of individual man.
>
> *Leontiev 1949/1961, pp. 36–37*

The above implies more than Western-style individual psychology, and even more than Vygotsky's dyadic psychology – it implies:

> a historical psychology, a theory of the historical development of the mental factor at different stages of society and in representatives of different social

classes, of the basic changes in human experience produced by the abolition of private property and by the planned transformation of this experience under conditions of gradual transition from socialism to communism.

ibid., p. 37

Along these lines, Rahmani characterizes Leontiev in this period as seeing two major tasks for Soviet psychology: "to define the structure of man's activity through an analysis of the relationships between activity as a whole, actions and operations" and "to clarify the concept of meaning" (Rahmani 1973, p. 47). Both tasks imply not just a psychology but a sociology – a point to which we will return later.

Subject and object; state mastery

The *subject-object distinction* identifies a transformation in which the extraordinary can make a difference. For Leontiev, as we have seen, the subject was an individual who related to, and labored to transform, a common object. This labor occurred within an ensemble of social relationships – and since "a Socialist society ... does not develop spontaneously but is directed by men" (Leontiev 1949/1961, p. 36), the Soviet state played a critical role in guiding and developing individuals through education. In fact, Leontiev portrayed the State as consciously welcoming the child to "the society of men," specifically in how it "actively makes him engage in activities"; but "This does not happen without a conscious setting by society of the aims of education and instruction" (ibid., p. 38). Elsewhere, Leontiev more pithily stated that "one is not born a personality" (quoted in Levitin 1982, p. 183) and stated that "a child, at birth, is a candidate for humanity; it cannot become human in isolation; but has to learn to become a man in contact with other men" (Leontyev 1959/2009b, p. 118).

Put another way, the subject was itself the object of the State, to be transformed through education. This transformation could maximize the individual's cap-abilities: "Investigation of the laws governing the formation of psychic properties serves a great practical aim: the fullest possible development of the capabilities of every individual. Soviet psychologists see this as one of their most important tasks" (Leontiev 1954/1957, p. 232). Here we see echoes of Vygotsky's "peak psychol-ogy" (see Zavershneva 2016). But the route to that peak led through State super-vision, through which the subject could learn to reorganize and self-regulate. By accepting State supervision, the subject – here, the less culturally advanced partner, working in a dyad with the educator or rehabilitationist – became capable of extraordinary things. Soldiers regained use of their limbs; amputees could learn again how to discern shapes (Leont'ev & Zaporozhets 1945/1960). Tone-deaf people could learn pitch (Leont'ev 1969). People could even be trained to do the *impossible*, such as sensing light with their hands (Leontyev 1959/2009b Ch.3, in a study that A.A. Leontiev later acknowledged qualified as parapsychology: Leontiev 2005, p. 65). Such extraordinary feats were accessible to citizens who accepted the appropriate supervision and aligned their motivations with the State's.

Mediators

The *mediators* represent the method of the transformation – how the extraordinary is applied. In Leontiev's formulation, he examined two kinds of mediators: tools and the division of labor. As he puts it in *Problems of the Development of Mind*, labor is from the beginning mediated by (a) tools and (b) social relations, i.e. in joint, collective activity: "Only through a relation with other people does man relate to nature itself, which means that labour appears from the very beginning as a process *mediated by tools* (in the broad sense) and at the same time *mediated socially*" (Leontyev 1959/2009b, p. 185, my emphasis).

Tools

As we have seen, Leontiev transformed Vygotsky's formulation by considering labor activity as the direct origination point for human psychology, thus collapsing the distinction between tool/sign and external nature/self-regulatory behavior that Vygotsky had established.

For Leontiev, physical tools *were* psychological tools: storehouses of cultural knowledge, but only within a framing activity. They represented a cultural heritage every bit as much as Vygotsky's psychological tools. Yes, he conceded, animals also use tools, but not to mediate a community relationship or productive activity. "The difference" is in "the *activity itself in which they are included*" (Leontyev 1959/2009b, p. 185, my emphasis). Animals use tools for immediate action, not social activity (ibid., p. 185); but in human hands, "A tool is ... the product of social practice and of social labour experience" (ibid., p. 193). Indeed, tool mediation gives its user's action "a new structure that reflects the new objective relations: the properties of the tool, the object of labor, and the purpose of labor – its product" (Leontiev 1967/1972, p. 153).

These physical tools could embed cultural knowledge because they functioned as congealed operations or crystallized activity: "Obviously, a tool is a material object in which are crystallized methods and operations, and not actions or goals." (Leontyev 1959/2009b, p. 102). This notion of crystallization was developed further in a later paper (Leont'ev 1969), in which he argued that psychological and physical tools alike were objectifications of embedded human activity, objectifications that could be unlocked in appropriate activity. Specifically, "work is crystallized" in tools; in using tools and instruments, human beings consolidated the gains that they had made through their cultural heritage (ibid., p. 425). For Leontiev, the individual's relations to the world of human objects are mediated via relations with people, including in process of exchange. Through this process, "the individual reproduces abilities which the species *Homo sapiens* acquired in its social and historical evolution" – what animals acquire through biological inheritance, humans acquire through learning (ibid., p. 426). Compare this view with Vygotsky, who focused on the cultural transmission of psychological tools through word meaning (e.g. Vygotsky 1934/2012). Even when he discussed physical tools, Vygotsky emphasized the combination of the tool's impact on nature with the sign's stimulation of behavior (Vygotsky & Luria 1930/1993, p. 138).

Division of labor

Importantly, Leontiev introduced a second, separate mediator: the division of labor, whose emergence was connected to the separation of activity and action. "The appearance of goal-directed processes or actions in activity came about historically as the result of the transition of man to life in society" (Leontyev 1977/ 2009a, p. 99). People in activity, he said, have their own needs satisfied via collective activity (Leontyev 1959/2009b, p. 400). The division of labor is uniquely human (ibid., pp. 176–177) and entails dividing object from motive (ibid., p. 187). He argued that the subject – and specifically consciousness – emerges from this tension between object and motive (ibid., pp. 239–241).

For instance, consider Leontiev's famous illustration of primitive hunters who developed a division of labor to support collective activity:

> It now fell to the lot of some individuals, for example, to main-tain the fire and to cook food on it, and of others to procure the food itself. Some of those taking part in the collective hunt fulfilled the function of pursuing game, others the function of waiting for it in ambush and attacking it
>
> *Leontyev 1959/2009b, p. 186*

Whereas animals' activity responds directly to their biological needs, human beings develop activity "in the conditions of a collective labour process" (ibid., p. 186). For instance, a human being may want to hunt an animal, but his part in the hunt is to beat the bushes and frighten animals toward others in the hunting party. This *action* does not coincide with the individual's *motive* (frightening animals away seems to be the opposite of catching an animal), but it does achieve the individual's *object* (he shares in the spoils of the hunting party) (ibid., p.187). The action does not make sense except in terms of joint labor activity:

> the given individual's relation with the other members of the group, by virtue of which he gets his share of the bag from them, i.e. part of the product of their joint labour activity. This relationship, this connection is realised through the activity of other people, which means that it is the activity of other people that constitutes the objective basis of the specific structure of the human individual's activity, means that historically, i.e. through its genesis, the connection between the motive and the object of an action reflects objective social connections and relations rather than natural ones.
>
> *Leontyev 1959/2009b, pp. 188–189*

Leontiev quotes Engels' root claim: "The cause underlying the humanising of man's animal-like ancestors is the emergence of labour and the formation of human society on its basis. 'Labour,' Engels wrote, 'created man himself'. *Labour also created man's consciousness."* (Leontyev 1959/2009b, p. 181, my emphasis). And in Leontiev's view, changes in labor could also remake human consciousness in fundamental ways – specifically in the shift from capitalist to socialist production, which leads to "a transition to a new, inner structure of consciousness, to a new 'formation' of it, viz. to the consciousness of socialist man" (ibid., p. 237). Like Vygotsky, Leontiev saw socialism as producing a New Man [sic]; but unlike Vygotsky, he saw labor activity as the essential unit of analysis and change, and thus the division of labor as a second essential mediator between the individual and the object.

In developing his views of these two mediators – tools and division of labor – Leontiev provided an explanation that arguably moved away from the *psychological* toward the *sociological*. Whereas Vygotsky described dyads, Leontiev described social formations (Blunden 2010, p. 164). As Leontiev's collaborator Zaporozhets remarked in 1969:

> I think that at one time we confused the psychological with the non-psychological, i.e., with some sort of logical, sociological characterization of activity, of its basic components and the structural interrelations that occur therein, etc.
>
> *Zaporozhets et al. 1969/1995, p. 12*

But more than that, in making labor activity the essential phenomenon of study, Leontiev portrayed human consciousness as an effect that could be managed by properly supervising the activity that produced it.

Summary: The extraordinary in 2GAT

In Leontiev's formulation, the extraordinary was not located in the individual – a superhuman – but rather in the *supervision* of an individual within a social order. Individuals became individual (and, indeed, human) by engaging in collective activity in which object and motive were separated and held in tension. They became capable of extraordinary things by accepting their cultural inheritance (tools, division of labor) and the self-monitoring that went along with their role in a managerial state.

These themes come together in a reminiscence that Leontiev's grandson recorded in 1978 just before Leontiev's death (Leontyev 1978/2005). Here, Leontiev discusses the question of polymotivation, illustrating the question with a study of parachute training before World War II. The seven-story parachute tower was used (a) to train parachutists and (b) "as an amusement ride to the park's visitors" (ibid., p. 84). Leontiev added that "the jumps were absolutely safe. We had only one single accident the whole time we were working there" (ibid., p.86). He and his collaborators tested how different conditions changed the likelihood that people would jump from the tower, then concluded that individuals were responding to both cortical and subcortical commands: cortical commands were rational and in accordance with the training, while subcortical commands were irrational and focused on self-preservation. By changing conditions, they could appeal to the cortical level while bypassing the subcortical – for instance, by obscuring the view with paper, but explaining to the parachutist exactly what would happen – and thereby reach higher levels of compliance (ibid., pp. 85–86). Sensitive supervision could create the conditions for the individual to selflessly accept the State's goals, thereby becoming capable of extraordinary things: confidently jumping from a seven-story building, learning to regain their range of movement, and even miraculously sensing light with their hands.

3GAT: Engeström and supermediators

Leontiev died in 1979, but in the 1980s, his work was picked up by Northern European scholars to help address two specific areas: (a) expertise and (b) human-computer interaction. These areas had both been dominated by information-processing cognitive psychology, which provided powerful insights into individual cognition but proved quite limited when addressing sociocultural issues in inter-ventionist research (e.g. Bannon and Bødker 1991; Engeström 1992). Of most interest to us is how two specific individuals – Yrjö Engeström and Susanne Bødker – separately applied activity theory to research projects that were oriented to improving design. These two strands rapidly merged into the version of CHAT most often seen in studies of expertise and human-computer interaction: a version that has been modified to address *collective subjects* in *multiple connected activities* in order to support *codesigned interventions*. These three modifications effectively relocated the extraordinary in CHAT: from the individuals to the mediators.

Two cases of the extraordinary: A hospital and a computer interface

As mentioned, two strands of research in Northern Europe separately took up activity theory: expertise (in Finland) and human-computer interaction (in Den-mark). In both, multiple participants (that is, collective subjects) engaged in dialo-gue, drawing on different experiences to codesign an emergent object, one that would become a mediator in their collective work. In doing so, they had to con-nect and analyze multiple activities. To understand these strands, we will consider two cases: (a) the redesigning of interactions in a hospital and (b) the designing of an interface.

Codesigning a division of labor: A hospital

Cole and Engeström (1993) describe a project in which investigators worked with Finnish hospital personnel to design a new division of labor. In the old division of labor, doctors rotated patients: when a doctor became available, she or he would take the next patient in line. In the new one, doctors became responsible for patients in their zones, meaning that they repeatedly saw and formed relationships with specific patients. This new division of labor yielded a new understanding of the object – patient care (ibid., pp. 37 39). The redesigned division of labor was a success: "The new model dramatically changed the availability and access of care ... there is no longer a shortage of physicians willing to work in the stations" (ibid., p. 39). Cole and Engeström described this redesign process in terms of Vygotsky's Zone of Proximal Development (ZPD; Vygotsky 1978[6]), but rather than applying the ZPD concept to a dyad, they applied it to an entire collective activity system, yielding an expansive cycle (ibid., p. 41).

Here and in his other work, Engeström took up Leontiev's activity theory as a way to address the question of developing expertise in organizations (Engeström 1987/2014; Engeström 1992; Engeström 1996). He studied adult, able-bodied participants with the assumption that these participants had already developed their own sets of expertise as fully formed agents, typically in peer- or near-peer power relationships such as medical care; the goal was to understand these encounters, work with representative participants to mutually reconfigure them, and thus improve outcomes for a general population. Through these studies, Engeström developed the Developmental Work Research (DWR) approach and the intervention-and-research process called Change Laboratory (Engeström 1999). This strand was also taken up in human-computer interaction as well as in education and affiliated disciplines.

In taking up activity theory, Engeström (1987/2014) added several things. First, he provided a graphical heuristic for picturing Leontiev's activity system (and added a component, rules). Second, he integrated Ilyenkov's (1982) theorization of contradictions, making them crucial to CHAT analysis. Third, he expanded the analysis to activity networks, that is, two or more interacting activity systems. Fourth, he applied analyses of historical changes to work organization and work forms, drawing from Westerners such as Powell, Zuboff, and Castells. And fifth, he supplemented the dialectical base with the dialogics of Bakhtin (1981). It's unclear whether at this point Engeström was aware of Bakhtin's disparaging of dialectics in his unpublished notebooks (Bakhtin 1986).

Codesigning a tool: An interface

Meanwhile, Bødker (1991) took up Leontiev's activity theory as a framework for underpinning her work in participatory design (see Bødker 2009 for a retrospective; see Spinuzzi 2002 and Spinuzzi 2005 for a history). In this approach, computer scientists and workers collaborated in developing new computer systems to better support the workers' labor (e.g. Bødker et al. 1987). To that aim, Bødker developed Leontiev's levels of activity to characterize collective activities, goal-directed actions, and unconscious operations (Bødker 1991). The goal was decidedly *not* to develop individual workers to conform to a new regime; rather, representative participants contributed their considerable expertise to the design of new software tools, tools that could fit into the participants' existing workflows, conceptual schemes, and expertise (in a word, their social relations), supporting the population and allowing them to accomplish their work more effectively. (Significantly, the participants they selected were *political representatives*, empowered to represent the interests of a population of workers, not *functional representatives* chosen because their characteristics were similar to that population; see Spinuzzi 2005.) In fact, this goal of mutually redesigned tools and workflows was motivated in part by regulations that gave unions a say in how work was to be conducted – creating a power dynamic quite different from the top-down, hierarchical relations found in the schooling and rehabilitation settings in which 1GAT and 2GAT developed. This strand was taken up broadly within human-computer interaction and computer-supported cooperative work in the 1990s, especially in the USA (e.g. Nardi 1996).

Later work merged the two traditions: Engeström's articulation of activity systems and activity networks was often combined with Bødker's articulation of the three levels of activity. In both cases, the extraordinary was portrayed as residing in *mediators*: both mediators passed down to participants and mediators consciously developed by those participants. Through the notion of crystallization forwarded by Leontiev, mediators were seen as material instantiations of cognitive operations, a cultural inheritance that could instantiate best practices. But in this third generation of activity theory, mediators were not simply evolved and inherited – they themselves became the objects of design activity, consciously and collectively designed to solve problems in an ongoing activity. And this new relationship to mediators meant that the role of human actors changed as well: rather than mastering a defined object through defined mediators, human actors developed and crystalized expertise as they directed their activity toward an emergent object. Whereas Vygotsky and Leontiev emphasized transforming *individuals* (via self-mastery or state mastery), 3GAT approaches emphasized transforming *mediators* through dialogic negotiation by collective subjects to produce new collective designs and interventions, consequently reforming adjacent activities. Whereas in Vygotsky individuals transformed themselves, and in Leontiev the State transforms individuals, in Engeström and Bødker, individuals transformed activities.

With 3GAT's shift to design research comes the concept of *activity networks*: i.e. constellations of interconnected, not necessarily hierarchically related activities in which one activity's object could function as another activity's mediator. The term was coined in Engeström (1987/2014), but the concept was also implied in Bødker (1987)[7] (see also Bødker 1991), and was necessary for analyzing design within interconnected systems of expertise. Consider a writer, who labors to produce her *object* (a script). The script is then given to a television announcer, who uses the script as a *tool* in a second activity (Bødker 1991, p. 37). Or consider a sick child, who is the *object* of both a general practitioner and a hospital physician, who have different expertise and work within different bureaucratic systems (Engeström 2001). In these cases, the interlocking activities have different objects or attempt to transform the same object differently.

Unit of analysis; agency

The *unit of analysis* bounds the investigated phenomenon, where the extraordinary can be seen or can emerge. In 3GAT, the unit of analysis was the *activity system*, in which collective subjects cyclically labor to transform a common object. The activity system is conceived as dynamic and evolving: all parts of the system might change due to internal or external contradictions, and certainly the composition of the collective subject changes over time as people enter and exit the activity.

In this third generation, activity theory was reoriented from general psychological problems to *design research*. This shift has been underexplored in the literature, yielding confusion at different points. For instance, David Bakhurst complains that third-generation activity theory has strayed from "a fundamental explanatory strategy" to "a method for modelling activity systems with a view to facilitating not just understanding, but practice. Activity theory in [this] sense is, among other things, a way of modelling organizational change" (Bakhurst 2009, p. 205). "What we have is a model or a schema that has minimal predictive power" (ibid., p. 206). This is true, but such a model was necessary to facilitate design research – research that is conducted not *on* participants but *with* participants, oriented toward the interests of those participants, and yielding joint emergent knowledge. In the third generation, then, the point was not to provide a "fundamental explanatory strategy" but to model change and facilitate practice. The model perhaps has "minimal predictive power," but its descriptive power is what anchors its approach, which facilitates researcher-participant deliberation. This deliberation was applied to designing new work organization, new practices, and new tools – that is, better mediators that could revolutionize the activity.

Here, the role of researchers was to facilitate interventionist work by the collective subjects who were involved in the ongoing activity. This new role yielded significant shifts in how 3GAT understood subjects and objects as well as mediators.

Subject and object; mastery

The *subject-object distinction* identifies a transformation in which the extraordinary can make a difference. In 3GAT, the new orientation to interventionist or design research necessitated a shift from individual to collective subjects, which would be necessary for discussing organizational intervention in situations in which a researcher would not have a clear line of authority over the researched. In 1GAT and 2GAT, a less culturally advanced participant would pursue a higher level of mastery with the help of a more culturally advanced one; in 3GAT, the participants were considered equally advanced, but with different sets of expertise, and pursued an emergent design (that is, something that did not yet exist) rather than (re)learning an existing skill or ability. Given this relationship, the collective subjects had to engage in deliberative dialogue with each other.

The collective subject required attention to other details. For instance, although Leontiev acknowledged that an individual subject might have multiple motives, he insisted on a single evaluative perspective (a "forced perspective"; see Spinuzzi 2017). In contrast, Engeström and Bødker assumed that collective subjects had both multiple motives and multiple perspectives. These motives and perspectives were made explicit and deliberated during the design process, typically with participatory exercises. In this interventionist research strand, participants are a subset of the potential users of the resulting intervention; they represent a larger population.

In design research, the object of the activity is the design – in this case, the mediator (tool, rule, or division of labor) being redesigned. That mediator is then incorporated into the existing activity in order to transform it for the better. For instance, the hospital implements a new division of labor (Cole & Engeström 1993) and the newspaper publisher implements a new software tool (Bødker et al. 1987). Thus, the collective subjects relate to two objects: the design object and the object of the ongoing activity in which the design object will serve as a mediator.

Certainly Engeström, Bødker, and others in this 3GAT tradition would not deny that individual development occurs. But unlike in Vygotsky or Leontiev, the individual is not the focus of the transformation – their collective social interaction is. In fact, in Engeström's later work, some objects – "runaway objects" – are understood as too large and enmeshed in too many activities to be apprehended by any single subject (Engeström 2008).

Mediators

The *mediators* represent the method of the transformation – how the extraordinary is applied. As discussed, mediators include tools (which mediate between subject and object), rules (which mediate between the subject and a community), and division of labor (which mediates between a community and its object). These mediators are analytically separate, but they are recognized as interacting in a bounded case. Their relationships are often modeled in an activity system diagram – Engeström's famous triangle heuristic – to identify their interactions. Here, we will specifically examine tool mediation and how it has been conceived differently from previous generations.

As noted, Engeström and Bødker both took Leontiev's work as a starting place for their own. For Leontiev, mediators included tools (understood as crystallized operations passed down as a cultural inheritance) and division of labor (understood as precipitating the split between object and motive, and thus the starting point of human consciousness). Both of these mediators were seen as evolving over time. Leontiev did not explore either as serving as an object in its own right. But Engeström and Bødker both engaged in interventionist research, i.e. in *designing mediators* to improve a shared activity. Thus, the mediator served as the object of a related activity. In the Northern European milieu, this design work was not the purview of State supervisors but rather of the workers who would use the resulting designs. Thus, collective design meant understanding several activities and their relationships: a current activity, a future activity, other activities that might be affected, and finally the design activity being undertaken to design new tools (such as interfaces; Bødker 1991) or divisions of labor (such as work organization; Engeström 1992). Hence Engeström developed the idea of the activity network and drew on Ilyenkov to discuss external as well as internal contradictions.

In this understanding, tools were understood as crystallized labor, but intentionally and dialogically codesigned. Based on relatively thin discussions of crystallization in Leontiev's works, this notion was taken up in 3GAT, especially in the participatory design tradition (Bannon and Bødker 1991; Bertelsen and Bødker 2000; Bødker and Petersen 2000; Bødker & Klokmose 2011; Spasser 2000), where it provided a way to conceptualize how interface elements could both frame actions and embed expertise.

This notion of crystallization ran parallel to the notion of *genre* in writing studies, where 3GAT was soon taken up. Genre was understood as a temporarily stabilized tool-in-use, a recurrent textual solution to a recurrent problem (Schryer 1993). That is, like crystallization, genre both framed actions and embedded expertise. Genre was soon theorized in a 3GAT framework (Artemeva & Freedman 2001; Freedman & Smart 1997; Russell 1997a; Russell 1997b; Spinuzzi 2003), yielding a synthesis that has most frequently been used in workplace studies of writing.

In both of these traditions, investigations have tended to encompass multiple participants in ongoing activities, activities that are mediated not by a single tool but by multiple tools in complex relationships. Consequently, Bødker has gone on to explore complex mediation (Bødker & Andersen 2005) and artifact ecologies (Bødker & Klokmose 2011; Bødker & Klokmose 2012). Similarly, writing studies have examined complexes such as genre ecologies (Freedman & Smart 1997; Spinuzzi 2003). The individual participants may develop and learn a bit, but (especially in the USA) they enter and exit organized activities rapidly (cf. Spinuzzi 2015). Developing individuals, then, has a more limited effect on the ongoing activity than designing mediators, which can become long-term features of the activity. Mediators can be redesigned and redeveloped limitlessly, and the resulting mediated activity takes the center stage in development.

Summary: The extraordinary in 3GAT

The result of this third generation of activity theory was a more focused examination of interpretation; interactions, especially disagreements; and a link to existing hermeneutic theory. These characteristics reoriented it toward *design research* – that is, research into how to redesign mediators – physical tools (instruments), rules (workflow, conventions), and division of labor (roles, responsibilities) – to make activities better for the population engaged in them. The population itself might change, and in workplace contexts, it certainly will, since lifelong employment is essentially dead. But the focus of 3GAT was not on their individual change but rather on how redesigning mediators could change the social system in which they were embedded.

Let's end with one more illustrative case: home care of the elderly in the City of Helsinki (Nummijoki & Engeström 2010). First, the authors illustrated the contradiction in the object of current home care: the home care service saw the object in terms of duties, while the client saw it in terms of their own life (ibid., p. 51). After discussing the problems with the current situation, the authors explained how they used the Developmental Work Research cycle to design a Mobility Agreement: an agreement between the home case service and each client (ibid., p.54). The authors then examined transcripts from pre- and post-agreement visits, noting layered development in home care. The Mobility Agreement was seen as *co-configuration*:

> Co-configuration requires new kinds of agency from both the client and the provider of the service. The client must continually assess his or her own needs and experiences and take initiatives to shape the service accordingly. The service provider must be willing to change the shape of the service and experiment with new patterns of service when a need arises.
>
> *Nummijoki & Engeström 2010, p. 49*

That is, a new interventionist *process* resulted in designing a new *tool* in order to create new *agency* for the collective subject of the activity. And although this new agency developed patient by patient, it was facilitated through the new mediator – a supermediator that solved problems in interchangeable groups of people.

Conclusion and Implications

Just as Vygotsky's focus on the New Man was grounded in post-Revolution expectations, 3GAT's focus on mediators and its de-emphasis on individual human capabilities was grounded in contemporary Western perspectives (Table 6.1). For Vygotsky's USSR of 1930, the nation was united in a march toward a shared, transcendent future; the transformation of individuals happened mainly in schools and rehabilitation settings, where the individuals had little say over their transformation. What was required was a *psychology*. For Leontiev's USSR of 1945, the State promised to perfect its citizens through labor; it was still implemented in schools and rehabilitation settings, and it was still a psychology, but with sociological leanings.

In contrast, for Engeström's Finland and Bødker's Denmark of 1987, no entity – neither State nor employer – had the authority to unilaterally direct individuals; their role was to empower those citizens to reach mutual goals in defined organizations. The individuals could change if they wanted to; but the researchers could work with individuals to codesign mediators. What was required was a *sociology* of organizations.

This pivot to mediators is part of what drives recent attempts to integrate dialogism, multiperspectivity, and multiplicity into CHAT. When individuals are no longer the object of change, but partners for change, their perspectives have to be integrated.

What does this mean for a coherent CHAT, both now and in the future?

On the one hand, I believe we can see a clear line of development from one generation to the next. Although there are significant disagreements (for instance,

TABLE 6.1 Contrasts between Vygotsky and contemporary CHAT.

	Vygotsky ("1GAT")	Leontiev ("2GAT")	Contemporary CHAT ("3GAT")
Theory	Grand	Middle-range	Middle-range
Research focus	Basic	Applied, practical	Applied, practical
Disciplinary orientation (research)	Psychology	Psychology, psycho-physiology, sociology	Sociology
Disciplinary orientation (application)	Pedagogy, defectology, rehabilitation, cross-cultural psychology (dyads of more and less culturally advanced practitioners)	Pedagogy, defectology, rehabilitation (dyads of more and less culturally advanced practitioners)	Management (systems of employees and managers); design (systems of users and symbolic artifacts)
Unit of analysis	Meaning and (later) sense	Labor activity	Organizational activity and (later) activity networks
Empirical focus	Individuals and dyads; individual subjects	Individuals-in-activity and dyads; individual subjects	Groups, organizations, and (later) interconnected social systems; collective subjects
Location of development or change	The individual's capabilities (becoming superhuman)	The individual's capabilities (becoming supervised)	The organization's capabilities (designing supermediators)
Agent	Self	State	Participants

Vygotsky and Leontiev's disagreement about the unit of analysis), these disagreements were built on common understandings and iterated, arguably in interaction with the political milieus in which they were enacted.

Yet, there is no transportation without transformation (Latour 1996). Each generation, in taking up the concepts of the previous generation, had to transform them for new milieus and new uses. And, taken together, these transformations have moved CHAT far indeed: from basic research of individual learners to applied interventionist research of organizations – that is, from 1GAT's psychology to 3GAT's de facto sociology.

And I think this is what explains the shift: in each generation of activity theory, *the extraordinary is that which can be controlled and transformed.*

Toward a 4GAT

What does the above mean for the development of a 4GAT? Engeström sees its development as continuing to follow a sociological path, examining not only distinct organizations but also overlapping social processes such as social production and peer production, processes that "become simultaneous, multidirectional, and often reciprocal" (Engeström 2009, p. 309). I agree, but a 4GAT still faces latent problems that have been left unresolved during the 3GAT pivot to design research. First, the common object of an activity (or network of activities) has inexorably expanded; to ground an empirical analysis, the object must be scoped and stabilized (Spinuzzi 2011). Second, in overlapping, interpenetrating activities, the notion of cyclical development, so key to early 3GAT explanations of the activity system, becomes difficult to empirically distinguish or practically sustain (Spinuzzi 2008); for an activity network to hang together, the cycles of different activities must be not necessarily identical but at least synchronized (Spinuzzi 2017). Finally, the move to collective subjects in each activity, and the overlapping of different activities, necessarily makes the object multiple or fractional (Spinuzzi 2017). That is, as activity theory is applied to larger and broader social groups, it requires further development in order to function well as an interventionist sociology. Whether it can do so while maintaining strong coherence with its predecessors is a question yet to be answered.

Notes

1 Throughout, I will use the designator "CHAT" synonymously with "third-generation activity theory" (3GAT) to draw a distinction between this strand and other strands of activity theory being used in various quarters. CHAT refers to the strand of activity theory that includes developments by Yrjö Engeström, Michael Cole, and others; it has been derided as "Americanized" (Miller 2011) although Engeström himself is Finnish.
2 For consistency, I use the spellings "Vygotsky," "Luria," and "Leontiev" in the text, although these names are sometimes transliterated differently in quotations and citations.
3 During his keynote at ISCAR 2017, Engeström described each generation as a qualitative transformation of the previous generation.
4 An interdisciplinary field that studied the development of the child, promoted by Vygotsky and others. For an overview, see Ewing (2001).
5 The USSR had banned sociology as a bourgeois pseudoscience a few years earlier, in 1929 (Osipov 2009).
6 Valsiner (1991) notes that *Mind in Society* was not a Vygotsky book so much as a collection of different works by Vygotsky and his colleagues, "a potpourri … collected together from different sources and linked in ways judged to fit the 'recipient' culture better than the original" (ibid., p. 155).
7 Bødker's 1991 book was based on her 1987 dissertation, which was completed the same year as Engeström's original publication of *Learning by Expanding* (1987). Bødker and Engeström did not know about each others' work until later (Bødker 2009).

References

Artemeva, N., & Freedman, A. (2001). "Just the boys playing on computers": An activity theory analysis of differences in the cultures of two engineering firms. *Journal of Business and Technical Communication*, 15(2), pp. 164–194.
Avis, J. (2009). Transformation or transformism: Engestrom's version of activity theory? *Educational Review*, 61(2), pp. 151–165. https://doi.org/10.1080/00131910902844754.
Bakhtin, M. M. (1981). *The dialogic imagination: Four essays*. Austin, TX: University of Texas Press.

Bakhtin, M. M. (1986). *Speech genres and other late essays*. Austin, TX: University of Texas Press.

Bakhurst, D. (2009). Reflections on activity theory. *Educational Review*, 61(2), pp. 197–210. https://doi.org/10.1080/00131910902846916.

Bannon, L. J., & Bødker, S. (1991). Beyond the interface: Encountering artifacts in use. In J. M. Carrol. *Designing interaction: Psychology at the human-computer interface* (pp. 227–253). New York: Cambridge University Press.

Bauer, R. (1952). *The new man in Soviet psychology*. Cambridge, MA: Harvard University Press.

Bertelsen, O. W., & Bødker, S. (2000). Information Technology in Human Activity. *Citeseer*, c, pp. 3–14. http://citeseerx.ist.psu.edu/viewdoc/summary?doi=10.1.1.17.6658.

Blunden, A. (2010). *An Interdisciplinary Theory of Activity*. Boston, MA: Brill.

Bødker, S. (1987). *Through the Interface: A Human Activity Approach to user Interface Design*. Aarhus Universitet. http://pure.au.dk/portal/files/20861897/Full_text.

Bødker, S. (1991). *Through the interface: A human activity approach to user interface design*. Hillsdale, NJ: L. Erlbaum.

Bødker, S. (2009). Past experiences and recent challenges in participatory design research. In A. Sannino, H. Daniels, & K. D. Gutierrez (Eds.). *Learning and expanding with activity theory* (pp. 274–285). New York: Cambridge University Press.

Bødker, S., & Andersen, P. B. (2005). Complex mediation. *Human-Computer Interaction*, 20, pp. 353–402.

Bødker, S., Ehn, P., Kammersgaard, J., Kyng, M., & Sundblad, Y. (1987). A UTOPIAn experience: On design of powerful computer-based tools for skilled graphical workers. In G. Bjerknes, P. Ehn, & M. Kyng (Eds.). *Computers and democracy – A Scandinavian challenge* (pp. 251–278). Aldershot: Avebury.

Bødker, S., & Klokmose, C. N. (2011). The Human-Artifact Model: An Activity Theoretical Approach to Artifact Ecologies. *Human–Computer Interaction*, 26(4), pp. 315–371. https://doi.org/10.1080/07370024.2011.626709.

Bødker, S., & Klokmose, C. N. (2012). Dynamics in artifact ecologies. Proceedings of the 7th Nordic Conference on Human-Computer Interaction: Making Sense Through Design, pp. 448–457. https://doi.org/10.1145/2399016.2399085.

Bødker, S., & Petersen, M. G. (2000). Design for learning in use. *Scandinavian Journal of Information Systems*, 12, 6180. http://citeseerx.ist.psu.edu/viewdoc/download?doi=10.1.1.90.8569&rep=rep1&type=pdf.

Cole, M., & Engeström, Y. (1993). A cultural-historical approach to distributed cognition. In G. Salomon (Ed.). *Distributed Cognitions: Psychological and Educational Considerations* (pp. 1–46). New York: Cambridge University Press.

Engels, F. (1971). *Dialectics of nature*. New York: International Publishers.

Engeström, Y. (1987). *Learning by expanding: An activity-theoretical approach to developmental research*. Helsinki: Orienta-Konsultit Oy. http://lchc.ucsd.edu/mca/Paper/Engestrom/expanding/toc.htm.

Engeström, Y. (1992). *Interactive expertise: Studies in distributed working intelligence*. Helsinki: University of Helsinki.

Engeström, Y. (1996). Developmental work research as educational research: Looking ten years back and into the zone of proximal development. *Nordisk Pedagogik*, 16, pp. 131–143.

Engeström, Y. (1999). Expansive visibilization of work: An activity-theoretical perspective. *Computer Supported Cooperative Work*, 8, pp. 63–93.

Engeström, Y. (2001). Expansive Learning at Work: toward an activity theoretical reconceptualization. *Journal of Education and Work*, 14(1), pp. 133–156. https://doi.org/10.1080/13639080020028747.

Engeström, Y. (2008). *From Teams to Knots: Studies of Collaboration and Learning at Work*. New York: Cambridge University Press.

Engeström, Y. (2009). The future of activity theory: A rough draft. In A. Sannino, H. Daniels, & K. Gutierrez (Eds.). *Learning and expanding with activity theory* (pp. 303–328). New York: Cambridge University Press.

Engeström, Y. (2014). *Learning by Expanding*. New York: Cambridge University Press.

Engeström, Y. (2018). *Expertise in Transition: Expansive Learning in Medical Work*. New York: Cambridge University Press.

Ewing, E. T. (2001). Restoring teachers to their rights: Soviet education and the 1936 denunciation of pedology. *History of Education Quarterly*, 41(4), pp. 471–493.

Freedman, A., & Smart, G. (1997). Navigating the current of economic policy: Written genres and the distribution of cognitive work at a financial institution. *Mind, Culture, and Activity*, 4(4), pp. 238–255.

Haenen, J. (1996). *Piotr Gal'perin: Psychologist in Vygotsky's Footsteps*. Commack, NY: Nova Science Publishers.

Ilyenkov, E. V. (1982). *The dialectics of the abstract and the concrete in Marx's Capital*. Moscow: Progress.

Joravsky, D. (1989). *Russian Psychology: A Critical History*. New York: Blackwell.

Kaptelinin, V., & Nardi, B. A. (2006). *Acting with technology: Activity theory and interaction design*. Cambridge, MA: MIT Press.

Kozulin, A. (1984). *Psychology in Utopia: Toward a social history of Soviet psychology*. Cambridge, MA: MIT Press.

Kozulin, A. (1999). *Vygotsky's Psychology: A Biography of Ideas*. Cambridge, MA: Harvard University Press.

Krementsov, N. (1996). *Stalinist science*. Princeton, NJ: Princeton University Press.

Lamdan, E., & Yasnitsky, A. (2016). Did Uzbeks have illusions? The Luria-Koffka controversy of 1932. In A. Yasnitsky & R. van Der Veer (Eds.). *Revisionist revolution in Vygotsky studies* (pp. 175–200). New York: Routledge.

Latour, B. (1996). *Aramis, or the Love of Technology*. Cambridge, MA: Harvard University Press.

Lenin, V. I. (1987). *Essential Works of Lenin*. (H. M. Christman, Ed.). New York: Dover.

Leont'ev, A. N. (1969). On the biological and social aspects of human development: The training of auditory ability. In M. Cole & I. Maltzman (Eds.). *A handbook of contemporary Soviet psychology* (pp. 423–440). New York: Basic Books.

Leont'ev, A. N., & Zaporozhets, A. V. (1945/1960). *Rehabilitation of hand function*. New York: Pergamon.

Leontiev, A. A. (2005). The life and creative path of A.N. Leontiev. *Journal of Russian and East European Psychology*, 43(3), pp. 8–69. https://doi.org/10.1080/10610405.2005.11059249.

Leontiev, A. N. (1954/1957). The nature and formation of human psychic properties. In B. Simon (Ed.). *Psychology in the Soviet Union* (pp. 226–232). London: Routlege & Kegan.

Leontiev, A. N. (1949/1961). The present tasks of Soviet psychology. In *Soviet psychology: A symposium* (pp. 31–48). New York: Philosophical Library Inc.

Leontiev, A. N. (1967/1972). Some prospective problems of Soviet psychology. In J. M. Brozek (Ed.). *Psychology in the USSR: An historical perspective* (pp. 144–157). Oxford: International Arts and Sciences Press.

Leontiev, A. N. (1940/2005a). The fundamental processes of mental life. *Journal of Russian and East European Psychology*, 43(4), pp. 72–75.

Leontiev, A. N. (1940/2005b). The genesis of activity. *Journal of Russian and East European Psychology*, 43(4), pp. 58–71. https://doi.org/10.1016/j.cell.2005.10.016.

Leontiev, A. N. (1937/2005c). Study of the environment in the pedological works of LS Vygotsky: a critical study. *Journal of Russian and East European Psychology*, 43(4), pp. 8–28. https://doi.org/10.1080/10610405.2005.11059254.

Leontiev, A. N., & Luria, A. R. (1937/2005). The Problem of the Development of the Intellect and Learning in Human Psychology. *Journal of Russian and East European Psychology*, 43(4), pp. 34–47.

Leontyev, A. N. (1978/2005). Will. *Journal of Russian and East European Psychology*, 43(4), pp. 76–92.

Leontyev, A. N. (1978/2009a). *Activity and Consciousness*. Pacifica, CA: Marxists Internet Archive.

Leontyev, A. N. (1959/2009b). *The development of mind*. Pacifica, CA: Marxists Internet Archive.

Levitin, K. (1982). *One is Not Born a Personality: Profiles of Soviet Educational Psychologists*. Moscow: Progress.

Luria, A. R. (1937/1960). *The nature of human conflicts*. New York: Grove Press.

Luria, A. R. (1962/1966a). *Higher cortical functions in man*. New York: Basic Books.

Luria, A. R. (1963/1966b). *Human brain and psychological processes*. New York: Harper & Row.

Luria, A. R. (1968). *Mind of a mnemonist: A little book about a vast memory*. New York: Basic Books.

Luria, A. R. (1972). *The man with a shattered world: The history of a brain wound*. New York: Basic Books.

Luria, A. R. (1976). *Cognitive development, its cultural and social foundations*. Cambridge, MA: Harvard University Press.

Luria, A. R., & I Yudovich, F. Ia. (1959). *Speech and the development of mental processes in the child; an experimental investigation*. London: Staples Press.

Marx, K. (1922). *The Gotha Program*. New York: Socialist Labor Party.

Miller, R. (2011). *Vygotsky in perspective*. New York: Cambridge University Press.

Nardi, B. (Ed.) (1996). *Context and consciousness: Activity theory and human-computer interaction*. Cambridge, MA: MIT Press.

Nummijoki, J., & Engeström, Y. (2010). Toward Co-configuration in Home Care of the Elderly: Cultivating Agency by Designing and Implementing the Mobility Agreement. In H. Daniels, A. Edwards, Y. Engeström, & S. R. Ludvigsen (Eds.). *Activity Theory in Practice: Promoting Learning across Boundaries and Agencies* (pp. 49–71). New York: Routledge.

Osipov, G. V. (2009). The Rebirth of Sociology in Russia. *Russian Social Science Review*, 50 (6), pp. 80–108. https://doi.org/10.1080/10611428.2009.11065377.

Peim, N. (2009). Activity theory and ontology. *Educational Review*, 61(2), pp. 167–180. https://doi.org/10.1080/00131910902846874.

Petrovsky, A. (1990). *Psychology in the Soviet Union: A Historical Outline*. Moscow: Progress.

Rahmani, L. (1973). *Soviet Psychology: Philosophical, Theoretical, and Experimental Issues*. New York: International Universities Press.

Razmyslov, P. (1934/2000). On Vygotsky's and Luria's "Cultural-historical theory of psychology." *Journal of Russian and East European Psychology*, 38(6), pp. 45–58.

Rosenthal, B. G. (2002). *New Myth, New World: From Nietzsche to Stalinism*. University Park, PA: Penn State University Press.

Rudneva, E. I. (1937/2000). Vygotsky's Pedological Distortions. *Journal of Russian and East European Psychology*, 38(6), pp. 75–94.

Russell, D. R. (1997a). Writing and genre in higher education and workplaces: A review of studies that use cultural-historical activity theory. *Mind, Culture, and Activity*, 4(4), pp. 224–237.

Russell, D. R. (1997b). Rethinking genre in school and society: An activity theory analysis. *Written Communication*, 14(4), pp. 504–554.

Schryer, C. F. (1993). Records as genre. *Written Communication*, 10(2), pp. 200–234.

Spasser, M. A. (2000). Articulating Design-in-use of Collaborative Publishing Services in the Flora of North America. *Scandinavian Journal of Information Systems*, 12, pp. 149–172.

Spinuzzi, C. (2002). A Scandinavian challenge, a US response: Methodological assumptions in Scandinavian and US prototyping approaches. In Proceedings of the 20th annual international conference on Computer documentation (pp. 208–215). ACM Press. https://doi.org/http://doi.acm.org/10.1145/584955.584986.

Spinuzzi, C. (2003). *Tracing genres through organizations: A sociocultural approach to information design*. Cambridge, MA: MIT Press.

Spinuzzi, C. (2005). Lost in the translation: Shifting claims in the migration of a research technique. *Technical Communication Quarterly*, 14(4), pp. 411–446.

Spinuzzi, C. (2008). *Network: Theorizing knowledge work in telecommunications*. New York: Cambridge University Press.

Spinuzzi, C. (2011). Losing by Expanding: Corralling the Runaway Object. *Journal of Business and Technical Communication*, 25(4), pp. 449–486.

Spinuzzi, C. (2015). *All edge: Inside the new workplace networks*. Chicago, IL: University of Chicago Press.

Spinuzzi, C. (2017). "I Think You Should Explore the Kinky Market": How Entrepreneurs Develop Value Propositions as Emergent Objects of Activity Networks. *Mind, Culture, and Activity*, 24(3), pp. 258–272. https://doi.org/10.1080/10749039.2017.1294606.

Stalin, J. (1924/1939). *Foundations of Leninism*. New York: International Publishers.

Trotsky, L. (1923/2005). *Literature and Revolution*. Chicago, IL: Haymarket Books.

Valsiner, J. (1991). *Developmental psychology in the Soviet Union*. Bloomington, IN: Indiana University Press.

Van der Veer, R., & Valsiner, J. (1991). *Understanding Vygotsky: A Quest for Synthesis*. Cambridge, MA: Blackwell Publishers.

Vygotski, L. S. (1930/1994). The Socialist alteration of man. In R. van der Veer & J. Valsiner (Eds.). *The Vygotsky Reader* (pp. 175–184). Cambridge, MA: Blackwell.

Vygotsky, L. S. (1927). *The Historical Meaning of the Crisis in Psychology: A Methodological Investigation*. https://www.marxists.org/archive/vygotsky/works/crisis.

Vygotsky, L. S. (1974). *The psychology of art*. Cambridge, MA: MIT Press.

Vygotsky, L. S. (1978). *Mind in society: The development of higher psychological processes*. Cambridge, MA: Harvard University Press.

Vygotsky, L. S. (1934/2012). *Thought and Language* (3rd edn.). Cambridge, MA: MIT Press.

Vygotsky, L. S. (1929/1994). The problem of the cultural development of the child. In R. van der Veer & J. Valsiner (Eds.). *The Vygotsky Reader* (pp. 57–72). Cambridge, MA: Blackwell.

Vygotsky, L. S. (1934/1997a). On psychological systems. In R. W. Rieber & J. Wollock (Eds.). *The Collected Works of L.S. Vygotsky: Volume 3: Problems of the Theory and History of Psychology* (pp. 91–107). New York: Springer.

Vygotsky, L. S. (1931/1997b). *The collected works of L.S. Vygotsky Volume 4: The history of the development of higher mental functions*. New York: Plenum.

Vygotsky, L. S. (1930/1997c). The Instrumental Method in Psychology. In R. W. Rieber & J. Wollock (Eds.). *The Collected Works of L.S. Vygotsky: Volume 3: Problems of the Theory and History of Psychology* (pp. 85–89). New York: Springer.

Vygotsky, L. S. (1934/1997d). Psychology and the theory of the localization of mental functions. In R. W. Rieber & J. Wollock (Eds.). *The Collected Works of L.S. Vygotsky:*

Volume 3: Problems of the Theory and History of Psychology (pp. 139–144). New York: Springer.

Vygotsky, L. S., & Luria, A. R. (1930/1993). *Studies on the history of behavior: Ape, primitive, and child.* Hillsdale, NJ: Erlbaum.

Vygotsky, L. S., & Luria, A. R. (1930/1994). Tool and symbol in child development. In R. van der Veer & J. Valsiner (Eds.). *The Vygotsky Reader* (pp. 99–174). Cambridge, MA: Blackwell.

Yamazumi, K. (2007). Human Agency and Educational Research: A New Problem in Activity Theory. *Actio: An International Journal of Human Activity Theory*, 1(1), pp. 19–39.

Yasnitsky, A. (2018). *Vygotsky: An Intellectual Biography.* London & New York: Routledge.

Zaporozhets, A. V., Gal'prin, P. I., & El'konin, D. B. (1969/1995). Problems in the Psychology of Activity. *Journal of Russian and East European Psychology*, 33(4), pp. 12–34.

Zavershneva, E. (2016). "The way to freedom": Vygotsky in 1932. In A. Yasnitsky & R. van der Veer (Eds.). *Revisionist revolution in Vygotsky studies* (pp. 127–140). New York: Routledge.

7

ON VYGOTSKY'S INTERNATIONAL CELEBRATION, OR HOW TO CRITICALLY APPROPRIATE AUTHORS FROM THE PAST

Luciano Nicolás García

> Chi narra una storia, racconta il mondo, che contiene pure lui stesso
> *Claudio Magris,* Danubio

Introduction

The image of the "genius" seems to be closely associated with L. S. Vygotsky's name in the current representation of his work and persona. This follows a well-established notion of geniality as a group of individual traits – unmatched intelligence, sheer creativity, extensive foresight, unique skills – all of which Vygotsky has been said to have, and which grant him a place in the international canon of psychology. Yet, this individual outlook usually outshines its counterpart, that is, the geniality of an individual is also dependent on who recognizes it. For someone to become a "genius" in a discipline, there must be a community within that field, which sets the criteria for judging that person as such. This chapter will deal with the latter part, the process of recognizing Vygotsky as an outstanding scholar. Whether Vygotsky actually had those traits is not the main issue, but rather the histories we make when we assume them to be present in an author. In other words, this chapter uncovers how we relate to past authors and knowledge, and why we consider them relevant and productive to the present day.

However, the image of the "genius" as an extraordinary individual acts as a hindrance to such historical and epistemological reflexivity. The primacy of the individual in the history of science still adheres to the ahistorical assumption of a "disembodied rationality," the idea that good science is, or should be in a high degree, autonomous from the context of its production and readily available for anyone. Thus, scientific "geniuses" are usually regarded as misunderstood by their contemporaries because they tell truths that are displaced of their own time. Once the discipline has moved forward, the disregarded scholars become truly appreciated by a consensual recognition of an international community of peers. As such, the image and narrative of the "genius" neglect two aspects of any historical process in science. Firstly, no author works alone, but is indebted with collective labour and tied to the possibilities and limits of his/her own milieu. Secondly, science is not merely or automatically a cognitive activity and a universal value. Rather, it depends on material circuits of knowledge with specific directions, the limits and possibilities of other contexts of production when receiving knowledge from other spheres and times, and institutional mechanisms of interactions, which define legitimacy criteria and are entangled with social and political issues.

Following the work done on other psychological traditions in Russia and the USSR (e.g. Joravsky, 1989; Etkind, 1997; Todes, 2014), recent publications have deepened our understanding of both Vygotsky's *oeuvre* and his conjuncture (e.g. Veresov, 1999; van der Veer, 2007; Yasnitsky, van der Veer & Ferrari, 2014; Yasnitsky & van der Veer, 2016; van der Veer & Zavershneva, 2018; Yasnitsky, 2011; Yasnitsky, 2018). This new view on Vygotsky's biography, intellectual endeavour and context of production, is neither the "finally true" history, nor another version among others; it has enough material and insights to reconsider the way we approach authors as sources of knowledge, and the way we use them as legitimacy artifacts, epistemic standards, identity kernels, and agendas of research. A serious and productive stance on Vygotsky informs us about him and his conditions, and also, by contrast, about us and our conditions. To trace the way an author was appropriated is to illuminate the possibilities and limits of each context, his/hers and ours.

Considering the above, along with a critical history of Vygotsky, a history of *Vygotskianism* is also needed – an account of the network of scholars who actively appropriated his ideas, disseminated his work, and tried to align their research with Vygotsky's. We still lack a history of the organization of that transnational Vygotskianism, without which Vygotsky would not be as we know him. However, studies on Vygotsky appropriations in other contexts do not keep pace with the large-scale and systematic studies about Vygotsky himself, as they are quite an unbalanced and unsystematic collection (Prestes, 2010; van Oers, 2012; Dafermos, Kontopodis & Chronaki, 2012; Mecacci, 2015; Aguilar, 2016; García, 2016b). We still barely know how and why Vygotsky became part of an international psychological canon, and thus, we keep repeating the simplified narration of the exceptional figure who obtained universal recognition merely by the power of his ideas.

From a historical standpoint which focuses on the transnational circulation of scientific knowledge and how it embeds in new contexts (cf. Secord, 2004; Saunier, 2013; García, 2018), we see the different ways Vygotsky's published work was appropriated in the West, particularly in the USA, France, Spain and Argentina, in their respective languages. This was made through a network which combined psychologists, psychiatrists and philosophers, whose political positions ranged from sympathies with leftist ideas to full members of communist parties. This network, especially from the late 1970s onwards, constructed the public image of Vygotsky, typically as a major representative of Soviet psychology. The reference to the USSR is important, not only because of the bipolar organization of the world at that time, something no Vygotskian overlooked before 1991, but also because the communist culture was the setting within which such a network of scholars played their role in the circulation of the ideas, publications and construction of the image of Vygotsky. After revisiting this historical context, I will briefly discuss the epistemological implications of rediscovering authors form the past, putting them into renewed circulation, and the status of canonical figures for research. However, no normative models or readymade epistemic criteria are given; instead, this chapter seeks to show the possibilities of a proper historical thinking for a more sophisticated reflexivity on why and how we use past authors to tackle present issues.

Vygotsky's ascension to international canon.

The emergence of a celebratory narrative of Vygotsky was a result of the intertwining – even muddling– of several academics and professionals from different places, more or less during the same period, from the late 1970s to the early 1990s, with some noteworthy precedents. As shown by Yasnitsky (2018), immediately after Vygotsky's death his Soviet colleagues initiated the construction of a canonical Vygotsky with obituaries, texts about his ideas, a plan for a volume dedicated to his memory, and by editing his work and commenting on it to international scholars, such as Kurt Koffka, Arnold Gessel, Frederic Buytendijk, and Henri Wallon, among others (Yasnitsky, 2016).

On the one hand, it seems clear that his colleagues were enthralled with Vygotsky's charisma; for example, in 1944 Leontiev wrote:

> Ten years have now passed since Vygotsky is no more; but the image of L.S., precious and beloved, has already begun to be covered by the haze of time. The details have begun to evaporate from memory. I think I have even begun to idealize him. Sometimes it seems to me that he is great and powerful. I catch myself ascribing to him features he never had, views and actions he never said or never did.
>
> *quoted in Vygodskaia & Lifanova, 1999b, p. 45*

Forty-four years later, Natalia G. Morozova stated that: "He was our authentic intellectual father. Our trust in him was unbounded. We related to him as the disciples related to Christ" (quoted in Vygodskaia & Lifanova, 1999a, p. 39).

On the other hand, perhaps more importantly, he was placed as a leading figure who provided a research programme and set future work. It is known that Luria openly and frequently stated that he considered Vygotsky a genius and that his own labour was a continuation of the ideas of his mentor (e.g. Luria 1966; Luria 1979). In the early 1980s Piotr I. Galperin stated that: "All my generation, Elkonin, Leóntiev, Zeigarnik, Luria and others, I do not doubt we have played an extensive role, important or not, I do not know, but I can assure that we continued Vygotsky's idea, who truly revolutionized psychology". Bluma V. Zeigarnik followed suit: "I confess that the most important thing for me, and I want to be crystal clear about it, is that my humble contribution is nothing more than the logical continuation and coherent development of Vygotsky's train of thought" (Golder, 1986, p. 31, p. 96; all translations are mine).

The commitment of Vygotsky's associates to the dissemination of his work was remarkably sustained for decades – a hint that his name retained symbolic capital in their field. Many of them participated in the publication of the *Collected works*, from 1982 to 1984, a landmark in the development of an international Vygotskianism, as it provided a considerable body of work to organize readings and discussions – but also with enough editing problems so as to provide a quite baffling picture of his work, persona and times. These volumes also have a series of texts and annexes which praised Vygotsky and promoted him to the short list of renowned names in the psychological world. Just as an example, Leontiev, in the prologue of the first volume – written no less than three or four years before its publication in 1982 – made this assertion: "Being one of the greatest theoretical psychologists of the 20th century, he was truly decades ahead of his time." (Leontiev, 1982/1997, p. 9).

The appearance of the *Collected Works* was accompanied by the book *One is Not Born a Personality* (Levitin, 1982), published both in Russian and English, which compiled letters, recollections, interviews and articles about Vygotsky from his colleagues and some scholars, all of whom offered praise of the Soviet psychologist. Of the many attributions given to Vygotsky, two are the most relevant here. Firstly, his intellect was well forward in relation to his context.

> Vygotsky was far ahead of his time, and some of his basic ideas can only now be clearly formulated with the help of the terminology developed in the 1960s and 1970s. But perhaps only future developments in philosophy and methodology will enable all his main ideas to be adequately stated.
>
> *Levitin, 1982, p. 10*

Secondly, important in the Soviet context, he was the first to offer a true and productive articulation between psychology and Marxism:

> It is not a matter of Vygotsky "poaching" on Marx's method and applying it to his own particular field. He accomplished something incomparably greater: he became imbued with Marx's thoughts and ideas.
>
> *Levitin, 1982, p. 10*

During the 1980s, political mood changed drastically in the USSR due to the process of general revision and criticism opened by the *Perestroika* and *Glasnost*, which led to pessimism and discontent among Soviet intellectuals (Kagarlitsky, 1989). Scientific disciplines and the figure of Vygotsky were not beyond those discussions, yet his image was not necessarily harmed. In this respect of particular interest are the statements of Leonid Radzijovski, one of the editors of the *Collected Works*. In January 1988 he stated that the renovation of Soviet psychology would come from a somewhat distant and exceptional past, a kind of "golden century" – though he clarified that there were only "five or six years", that is, between Lenin's death and Stalin's seizure of power, the moment when Vygotsky organized his research groups. Radzijovski said there existed:

> ... a creative atmosphere, there were beliefs, there was science, there was something that was rapidly carried on or achieved, there was real work beyond the disputes. And now, in the present, seventy years later, we remember that era. Evidently, we did not have that moment. That situation in the social biography of psychology did not repeat.
>
> *quoted in Golder 2002, p. 34, all translations are mine*

Nine months later, he claimed that in Soviet psychology "there are several myths. The first being that a Marxist psychology exists, when it does not"; Vygotsky merely "tried to build a Marxist psychology" (quoted in Shuare, 1990, pp. 269–270).

This account seems to contradict that of the idealized version of Vygotsky, yet in fact shows the way the celebratory image of Vygotsky was widened as it received feedback from two positions, those who highlighted as necessary the bond between Marxism and Vygotsky's psychological ideas, and those who considered that Marxism did not play a central role in his thinking. That double reading is part of an ongoing discussion about the status of Marxism in Vygotsky's thinking, which in fact contributed to reaffirming his exceptionality, questioning whether he understood better than anyone else the articulations between Marxism and psychology, or could he be a heterodox leftist in an increasingly orthodox Soviet milieu.[1] That, articulated with the idea that he was limited or censored by the rise of Stalinism and his work was directly productive seventy years later, allowed for the combined and incremental removal of him and his theories from his own context. He was historically "displaced" when it was considered both that he was ahead of his time, and that he genuinely understood Marx's ideas produced in mid-19th Century. He was made a "man for all seasons" from that conjunction of past and future, and the ambiguous role of his context in the celebratory account appears to have been no more than a trigger for his thinking. This displacement also served the internal disputes in the USSR. To claim that Vygotsky had the only "true" interpretation of Marxist psychology, meant that other renowned figures of Soviet psychology – in particular Sergei Rubinstein and Boris Lomov – had not. Only those who recognized themselves within the genealogy of Vygotsky's collaborators could settle that matter. The authorization of the image of Vygotsky meant the disavowal of competitors. Quarrels over the genuine interpretation of Marxism were almost ritual in the Soviet context, yet their outcome had serious consequences, both politically and scientifically.

But the construction of that universal Vygotsky was not only, nor even predominantly, a Russian endeavour; it was carried out together with a network of western scholars who also became promoters of Vygotsky's work and, in many different ways, had links to Soviet Vygotskianism. The fact that it was in the USA, during the years of global dispute between the two major powers, where he also received laudatory remarks definitely contributed to his universal image.

Luria was crucial to the reception of Vygotsky in the USA. He had contact with the North American scene early on, resulting in the publication of his book *The Nature of Human Conflicts* in 1932, and he maintained that connection throughout his life. During the 1930s, Vygotsky also gained attention from the psychologist Eugenia Hanfmann and the psychiatrist Jakob Kasanin, whose adaptation of the Vygotsky-Sakharov test for schizophrenia proved very important as it showed the possibility of actually applying Vygotsky's theories, particularly in a North American context (van der Veer & Yasnitsky, 2016). Luria was also instrumental in the publication of two books which obtained wide circulation.

First, *Thought and Language*, which was published in 1962 thanks to Luria's connections with MIT-based Russian linguist Roman Jakobson. Jerome Bruner, also at MIT then, in the prologue of the volume introduced the idea that Vygotsky's book was "officially suppressed" by "doctrine guardians" during Stalinism (Vygotsky, 1962, p. v–vi). For him, "Vygotsky is an original", not to be reduced to "the usual functionalism of the James-Dewey variety or the conventional historical materialism of Marxist ideology"; furthermore, "[his] developmental theory is also a description to the many roads to individuality and freedom", and because of that he "transcends, as a theorist of the nature of man, the ideological rifts that divide our world so deeply today" (Vygotsky, 1962, p. vi, p. x). Bruner also showed his own agenda in the local psychological field, as "Vygotsky also represents still another step forward in the growing effort to understand cognitive processes" (Vygotsky, 1962, p. ix). Vygotsky was placed above and beyond his context, in a way that made him more accessible to the North American public – and therefore, by the traditional assumption, to the mythical "West" as an indiscriminate whole. In that way, his circulation and decontextualization was one and the same operation.

Vygotsky was again published in English in 1971 – *Psychology of Art* – but the book that propelled him to international recognition was *Mind in Society*, published 1978, again with the intervention of Luria, who knew Arthur Rosenthal, then in charge of Harvard University Press, and Michael Cole, who had studied closely with Luria in Moscow during the 1960s and was later the main editor of the journal of translations *Soviet Psychology*. The editors of the book – Cole, Sylvia Scribner, Vera John-Steiner and Ellen Souberman – considered that the more than 40-year-old theories and methods "are not historical relics. Rather, we offered them as a contribution to quandaries and discussions in contemporary psychology". Reproducing Bruner's gesture, Vygotsky's work was not only valuable to the discipline, but also had political significance. In the afterword, it was stated that: "His legacy in an increasingly destructive and alienating world is to offer through his theoretical formulations a powerful tool for restructuring human life with an aim toward survival" (Vygotsky, 1978, p. 1, p. 133).

Mind in Society had wide repercussions and, with *Thought and Language*, it became the most read text under the name of Vygotsky for many years. A review of this book also became widely known among Vygotskians of that time, that of philosopher of science Stephen Toulmin, who did not hesitate to compare Vygotsky with Mozart – one of the western icons of young genius who died too soon, Wittgenstein – the prophet-like major philosopher in the analytic tradition, and Galileo – who embodied the prototype of the "founding fathers" of science. Toulmin had a quite negative opinion of North American psychology at that time, due to its general tendency towards reductionism and the rift between behavioural and cognitive trends. He found in Vygotsky and Luria a psychology with a strong and wide-ranging holistic approach due to their Marxist inspiration (Toulmin, 1978).

Interestingly, this optimistic review of Vygotsky's approach was reproduced in Levitin's *One is Not Born a Personality*, in which North American Vygotskians were also included, such as James Wertsch and Michael Cole. Soviet Vygotskians were aware of the up-and-coming status of Vygotsky in the USA and supported it. For example, Galperin considered that "Cole, I can affirm that he is, how to put it? One of ours", while Zeigarnik remarked that "there is a renewed interest in the world for getting to know Vygotsky's work, especially in the USA...; the work received is very interesting, you can discuss some aspects, but in general it shows a profound respect for his work" (quoted in Golder, 1986, p. 29, 110).

This feedback loop between Soviet and North American scholars allows us to consider two aspects of the narrative being analysed here. First, the praising of Vygotsky, though it cannot be said that it was "orchestrated," was nevertheless an effort made in collaboration between both the context of production and the contexts of reception. Second, that this effort was also politically laden, as it was a scientific collaboration between scholars of the two opposing global powers, a gesture to show real bonds and productive dialogues contrary to the ideologues that fuelled the geopolitical struggles.

In the following years, the picture of a Vygotsky who was at the same time truly Marxist but not Soviet was firmly established. For example, Russian psychologist Alex Kozulin, who immigrated to the USA in 1979, stated that: "Vygotsky remains the most thoughtful Soviet interpreter of Marx's method in its relation to the problems of behavioural science" (Kozulin, 1984, p. 102), yet at the same time, he concluded that Marxism was no more than a theoretical resource among others, "he gave no sign of submission to Marxism as an ideology. He took the most sober and, at least under Soviet circumstances, the most difficult position: He treated Marx as *a* theoretician, without prejudice, on par with his treatment of Hegel, Freud and, Durkheim" (Kozulin, 1984, p. 166, italics from author).

Three years later the North American edition of the *Collected Works* started to be published. Bruner was again in charge of the introduction; there he regarded Vygotsky as a "visitor form the future," whose ideas were compatible with those of authors like philosophers John Austin and John Searle and anthropologist Clifford Geertz. Precisely, as a genial voice from the yet to come, his writings "are timeless masterpieces: elegantly and powerfully argued, full of surprises, swift" (Vygotsky, 1987, pp. 5–7). The timelessness of his scientific foresight made his situatedness a secondary factor, as if the mere intellectual skills of his ideas raised him to international canon:

Vygotsky was one of the great theory makers of the first half of this century – along with Freud, McDougall, Piaget, and a very few others. Like them, his ideas are situated in his times. But like the best of them, those ideas still point the way to the future of our discipline.

quoted in Vygotsky, 1987, p. 16

Later, psychologists René van der Veer and Jaan Valsiner published *Understanding Vygotsky* (1991), by then the most comprehensive account of Vygotsky's history and ideas, and still being cited as a reference text. Despite the erudition of the book, it retained the perspective that if Vygotsky was a valuable author, it was because he had vague connections with the Soviet scenery: "Vygotsky was a member of the international psychological community of his time (even if he only left the USSR once), rather than a Soviet psychologist" (van der Veer & Valsiner, 1991, pp. 396–397). His universal outlook depended more on his efforts to deal with foreign scholars' ideas rather than with the problems and political-philoso-phical discussions in the USSR: "Vygotsky's indifference to the general ideological climate may again reflect one of the basic dialectics of his personal life: a relative ideological independence based on a generally hopeless physical condition" (van der Veer & Valsiner, 1991, p. 111). While not rejecting the fact that Marxism is clearly present in Vygotsky's thought, it was circumscribed to some methodological issues and a general notion of the social origin of consciousness, and that was interpreted as a sign of independence from the specific Soviet context and its tra-dition of Marxist-Leninist thought and "party-ness" (*partiinost'*).

This does not mean that there were no political readings of Vygotsky in the West. For example, North American psychologist Lois Holzman published a series of interviews with that perspective:

As a Marxist activist and developmental psychologist, who has been a "Vygotskian" for the past fifteen years (roughly form the beginning of Vygotskian research in the US), I believe we are in the midst of a develop-ment of a significant international scientific/political movement; that there is now something that can legitimately be called "the Vygotsky movement."

Holzman, 1990, p. 11

She interviewed Guillermo Blanck, Christine Lacerva, Luis Moll, David Bakhurst, Mariane Hadegaard, David Joravsky, Siebren Miedema, and James Wertsch. All of them, especially the first three, underlined the political aspects of Vygotsky's ideas. Nonetheless, while some emphasized Vygotsky's Marxism and others diminished it, that difference did not impede Vygotsky's celebration; all of them, with the exception of Joravsky, maintained the interpretation of a Vygotsky almost com-pletely incompatible with his context, as if he did not owe his intellectual maturity and practical aims to the Soviet circumstances and institutional politics of 1924–1934.[2] There is also a subsequent consequence of this narrative; if Vygotsky's genius allowed him not to be entangled in Stalinist dynamics, that means that no other Soviet psychologist was able to do that, even his colleagues. The shadow of Stalinism is removed from Vygotsky to be cast over the rest of the Soviet psychologists, so that they become secondary characters, at best, in Vygotsky's biography. This enforces the idea of his exceptionality, and allows for continuing his work overlooking the research done in the USSR. The celebration came at a price: the indifference and ignorance of how much Vygotsky depended on and borrowed from the work of his colleagues. The rescue of such a bright figure involved a general disdain of an entire Soviet tradition of psychology. As a result, the work of not only Vygotsky's direct associates – who, with the exception of Luria and to some degree Leontiev, remain practically unknown – but also his critics and other groups of Soviet psychologists has remained obscure in the West.

This narrative of Vygotsky might be considered a version of Sigmund Freud's "splendid isolation" from a so-called "Victorian" Europe (Sulloway, 1992, p. 449ff). There are however, two important differences. First, *Robinsonade* was proposed by Freud himself in a deliberate retrospective construction of his own image, and was later promoted by his most loyal followers. Second, the context of Imperial Vienna is radically different from the one in the USSR, especially when it comes to the engagement of scientists and intellectuals to political matters and the institutions of research. Vygotsky's "isolation" was a result of how he was edited and read both in the USSR and the West. This conception of a non-situated and outstanding Vygotsky had a long-lasting effect in Anglo-Saxon scholarship, so that even a refined historian of psychology like Kurt Danziger could endorse it when criticizing the individualistic assumptions of western psychology: "Vygotsky and Luria's rejection of the metaphysics of individualism came at the wrong time and in the wrong place" (Danziger, 2008, p. 265).

By the early 1980s western celebration of Vygotsky was already launched with only a handful and seldom-known articles, and three books heavily modified by Soviet and North American scholars.[3] Yet the USSR and the USA were not alone in an international feedback loop, which included other agents in the circuit of the "canonization" of Vygotsky that was paralleled by the emergence of an international Vygotskianism.

The celebration of Vygotsky in the Spanish speaking world also started with the publication of his books. The 1964 Argentinian translation of *Thought and Language* did not include Bruner's prologue. A new introduction was published instead, written by Pavlovian psychiatrist and member of the Argentinian Communist Party, José Itzigsohn. This edition is quite curious: published by a communist publishing house, it claimed the book was translated directly from Russian. However, in fact it was retranslated from the USA edition, though Itzigsohn read Russian and knew the Soviet version of 1956. Yet times had changed quickly during the 1960s in South America, and after the victory of the Cuban revolution (1959) local communist parties across the continent became increasingly criticized domestically and abroad. Itzigsohn's prologue reflects this crisis when he denounces the "negative tendencies" in the USSR, such as the cult of personality, which interfered with the scientific development. In fact, his prologue was one of the most clear and extended critiques of Stalinist intervention in science written by a communist. This introduces and changes the use of the narrative of the "censored" Vygotsky, as his publication was in itself a political intervention. It also shows a transnational circuit composed of communist scholars and professionals that disseminated Soviet scholarship as part of their political activities. Later publications of Vygotsky materialized in Spain, as we shall see, yet Itzigsohn's prologue became the first contact with the biography of Vygotsky for generations of Spanish-speaking psychologists, as it was reprinted no less than a dozen times in several countries into the 21st century.

Both *Psychology of Art* and *Mind in Society* were published in Spain, in 1970 and 1979, respectively. One of the main promoters of Vygotsky in Spain was *grupo Aprendizaje*, led by Pablo del Río Pereda and Amelia Álvarez. This group, formed in the late 1970s by some of the most notable psychologists of the later decades in Spain, was very committed to the development of psychology and academic institutions after the end of Francoism (1975), and most of them were associated with socialism and communism (Travieso, Rosa & Duro, 2001). This group published the journal *Infancia y Aprendizaje*, which offered many articles of Soviet and North American Vygotskians. In 1984 the journal published a special issue to mark the 50th anniversary of Vygotsky's passing. Ángel Rivière wrote a lengthy essay on his ideas, mainly on the basis of the bibliography his colleague Alberto Rosa obtained from his studies in the Laboratory of Comparative Human Cognition, directed by Michael Cole in the USA. In that essay, later published as a book and reprinted several times, the author yet again endorsed the idea of a Vygotsky who spoke from the future:

> Vygotsky is still, in many aspects, a strictly contemporary psychologist, and in others, apparently ahead of our own time. It seems it only took him ten years to see the perspective for a century. Ten years of fury, twenty of oblivion, and then the recovery, more and more evident, of a perspective that, for many of us, still has some of the most promising proposals and insightful analysis of our current psychology.
>
> *Rivière, 1984, p. 8*

In 1985 Miguel Siguán, who participated in the homage in *Infancia & Aprendizaje*, organized a commemoration of Vygotsky in the Spanish Society of Psychology, and then another one in the I Congress of the International Society of Psycholinguistics, held in Barcelona. The articles of the latter were published that same year in the *Anuario de Psicología* of the Autonomous University of Barcelona, a journal Siguán created and directed, along with a lesser-known text of Vygotsky, "Le problème des fonctions intellectuelles supérieures dans le systeme des recherches psychotechniques". This text was sent to the IV International Conference of Psychotechnics held in Barcelona in 1930, which Vygotsky ultimately did not attend.

In Argentina there was a similar celebration. A few months after the return of democracy in December 1983, a symposium on Vygotsky was organized by the

Argentinian Society of Cultural Relationships with the Soviet Union, which was dependent on the Soviet Embassy and was organized mainly by communist activists. The speakers, all communists, were the neurologist Juan Azcoaga, the psychiatrists César Cabral and Guillermo Blanck, and the psychologist Mario Golder. The first two used to be Pavlovian comrades of Itzigsohn – by then an ex-communist exiled in Israel. The latter two, who belonged to a younger generation, had not been trained during the years of Stalinism; Golder was the first of two Argentinian psychologists who obtained a doctorate in the USSR, and Blanck became one of the main promoters of Vygotsky's works in Spanish. Golder, as it was already mentioned, published through a communist publishing house a series of interviews to Soviet Vygotskians and during the first half of the 1970s he taught Soviet authors at the National University of La Plata, before losing his position because of the establishment of the fierce dictatorship of 1976. Blanck in 1984 published an independent book in which he compiled materials he obtained from Soviet Vygotskians, passages of Vygotsky's Russian publications, interviews, Toulmin's review, and an extended biography, with contributions he collected by mail form various authors. That biography, while quite informed for its time, again exalted Vygotsky, yet in a more communist fashion: "There cannot be a scientific theory of the psyche without a scientific theory of man; and there cannot be an accurate conception of man that does without Marx: That was the key element inspired by Vygotsky's genius" (Blanck, 1984, p. 31).

Soon thereafter Argentinian and Spanish Vygotskians commenced establishing bonds. The members of the Argentinian symposium gathered with Siguán at the XXIII International Congress of Psychology at the Acapulco Convention Center in Acapulco, Mexico (Golder, 1985a), and the following year Golder participated in the commemoration of the I Congress of the International Society of Psycholinguistics (Golder, 1985b). Luis Moll and Alberto Rosa published a laudatory review of Blanck's book (Moll & Rosa, 1985), who also published in the book which compiled the commemoration of the Spanish Society of Psychology, along with added texts of van der Veer, Rivière and Siguán (Siguán, 1987). Blanck, who kept a copious amount of letter exchange with Vygotskians in the USA, Europe and the USSR, was also present at the public presentation of the North American release of the first book of Vygotsky's six-volume *Collected Works* (1987) and was able to visit Vygotsky's daughter, Gita Vygodskaya, to whom many documents refer. He then prepared a new biography, this time published in an edited volume by Moll (1990), which granted him some international recognition, as seen in Holzman's article (above). In 1990 the psychologist Marta Shuare, a colleague of Golder and Azcoaga who also was the second and last Argentinian to obtain a doctorate in the USSR, was asked by the Soviet Union's international Progress publishers to write a book in Spanish about Soviet Psychology. In her account, Vygotsky, the only author who was worthy of a whole chapter to himself, had "the invaluable merit of creatively applying dialectical and historical materialism to psychological science and because of that had placed it 'on its feet', causing a truly Copernican revolution," in almost direct opposition with what Radzijovski told her in the interview also published in the book (Shuare, 1990, p. 57). Though she commented on the works of other Soviet psychologists such as Sergei Rubinstein, Boris Teplov, Dimitri Uznadze and Vladimir Miasischev, among other non-Vygotskian Soviet authors, she nonetheless stated that Vygotskian tradition was "the most fruitful direction of Soviet psychology's development" (Shuare, 1990, p. 58).

In 1991 the first volume of the Spanish version of the *Collected works* was published in Spain. Pablo del Río, who had run his own publishing house since the late 1970s, obtained its rights for publication in the early 1980s directly from *Pedagogika* publishing house, but it was not until years later that he could publish it with the collaboration of a bigger publishing house, Visor, and the support of the Spanish Ministry of Education and Science. Again, the introduction of Álvarez and del Río insisted on the relevance of Vygotsky's work for current and future psychology:

> Vygotsky's work is contemporary, because its historical role in psychology was only partially fulfilled and has been kept in suspense, so that until this scientific discipline makes good use of Vygotsky's ideas, with more or less benefit, we can not determine what is the actual meaning of his thinking in the history of psychology.
>
> *Álvarez and del Río in Vygotski, 1991, p. xvi*

Thus, the "historical meaning" does not relate to the circumstances in which that work was produced, but it is displaced towards a future beyond and outside the USSR, a future of a discipline understood as an international community. Again, this account aims to demarcate Vygotsky from the Bolshevik and Stalinist science, which after the "Lysenko affaire" has usually been seen in the West as synonymous with dubious science, more driven by political interests than by rigorous research. However, political agendas always define science; while in the USA the image of Vygotsky could be interpreted as a symbolic promise of a peaceful and productive approach between the two competing and belligerent global powers, in the Spanish-speaking world Vygotsky was part of the restoration of a leftist agenda. This is particularly true of Argentina and Spain where new democratic periods emerged in the 1980s after strongly anti-Marxist dictatorships, when any intellectual exchange with the communist countries could be censored or even pose a personal danger. In this sense, communism as a cultural and political organization had different meanings in the West, depending on local histories.[4]

Interestingly, France, which had one of the most powerful communist parties in the West, was a somewhat latecomer in this Vygotskian circuit. The *Collected works* as such were never published in French, and most of Vygotsky's texts appeared late in the 1980s and 1990s. One could speculate that Henri Wallon and René Zazzo, both communist psychologists, already occupied the place of a leftist developmental psychology – maybe even Piaget, whose ideas had been considered compatible with Marxism by several authors (cf. Goldmann, 1959; Piaget et al., 1971).

However, there were early contacts between Soviet psychologists and their French communist counterparts: Wallon went to the Moscow International Conference of Psychotechnics in 1931, and later exchanged letters with Luria (Luria, 1936; Gouarné, 2007), and Zazzo met with Leontiev in Paris in 1954 and, according to Zazzo's account, the former asked for the latter's help in promoting Vygotsky in the West (van der Veer & Yasnitsky, 2016, p. 146ff). Lucien Sève, one of the most prestigious philosophers of French communism, included some ideas of Vygotsky in his 1969 book *Marxisme et théorie de la personnalité*, read through Luria's and Leontiev's Francophone texts, which in fact had some circulation among French communists (e.g. Leontiev, 1957; Luria, 1965; Leontiev, 1965; Leontiev, Luria & Smirnov, 1966). However, it was not until 1985, when Vygotsky's *Thinking and Speech* was translated into French, that Vygotsky was read directly. The publication was made by Les Éditions sociales, along with many other communist publications, and translated by Françoise Sève, who had started the translation in the 1970s from the 1956 Soviet edition that Leontiev had given to her. The prologue, written by her husband Lucien Sève, essentially repeated the narrative of Leontiev's prologue of the *Collected Works* and Blanck's book of 1984. It is no surprise then that the prologue reiterated some of the conceptions already mentioned in those texts: the Stalinist "complete censorship" and the perennial relevance of his work, "an oeuvre always alive and highly revealing of the endless contributions of a Marxist approach" (L. Sève in Vygotski, 1985, p. 16). Sève saw this late diffusion of Vygotsky as an "inconceivable bibliographical omission" (L. Sève in Vygotski, 1985, p. 7), yet, from the point of view of this chapter, that omission was not acceptable due to the already canonical status of Vygotsky in the West. In short, Vygotsky's image was introduced in France in the same fashion as in the English- and Spanish-speaking world, albeit notably boosted by the actual international fame of Vygotsky. Such transnational canonization of Vygotsky was possible by figures who formed a dynamic interpersonal network and were related in different ways to a communist culture, ranging from relatively moderate *philosovietism* to extensive formal training and propagandist brainwashing in the USSR and Communist Party activism.

The transnational circulation of Vygotsky was a curious case where a narrative of the person preceded the knowledge of his actual work. Is such a narrative on Vygotsky just a case of historical ignorance? Or is it just another typical strategy for legitimizing a new understanding to dispute the mainstream of a discipline? Both can be answered positively. Yet, we still do not fully understand the process of transnational diffusion in science, and it won't be solved only by having a "true" account of Vygotsky's life and context, nor by viewing his reception as a mere instrument of academic power. His celebration is not about his alleged exceptional thinking in his social and historical context, but more about how Vygotskians were proposing the epistemic norms for the future development of the discipline. Vygotsky's displacement from the original context if his life and work and, thus, ahistorical and universal positioning, has been instrumental in discussing the present and future agenda of psychology as a whole. Thus, Vygotsky's advocates created an epistemological account of the possibilities and requirements for a science of mind, emotions and behaviour, and with that, a notion of the human, the political and the historical. This is particularly notable in the field of educational and psychological studies that promote the idea that society and culture are constitutive of the psyche. However, even if that aim is desirable and justifiable, the "canonization" of Vygotsky hampers that intention. Circulation of knowledge through time and geographies involves a process which is both historical and epistemological, which needs the exercise of *reflexivity* (i.e. unbiased self-observation and critical collective self-examination) to reconsider what we have done and what could be done with Vygotsky's "heritage." The following section will tackle that issue.

Vygotsky and the past as a source for present research.

It might seem paradoxical that Vygotskian scholars, whose aim is to provide psychology with historical, social cultural views and tools, adhere to an ahistorical conception of scientific production when it comes to Vygotsky, but this has been the case. This depended on multiple problems in the translations and edition of his work, and the adherence to the standard historical account for noted authors – celebratory accounts are not exclusive to Vygotskians, but are common in science in general.

Actually, Vygotskians themselves noticed this "paradoxical" reading of Vygotsky, and from the 2000s onwards they have generally started to consider Marxism and his involvement with Soviet institutions as an inextricable component of his thought and social aims, though this issue is far from being settled (cf. Valsiner & van der Veer, 2000, p. 332ff; Veresov, 2005; Castorina, 2009). Part of the problem in arriving at a consensus on the assessment of Marxism and the Soviet origin of Vygotsky's ideas is that the presuppositions of the celebratory narrative are still active. On the one hand, it is assumed that the Soviet version of Marxism is by no means acceptable, which in itself is a retrospective assessment that Vygotsky did not, and could not, hold. It seems hard for Vygotskians to consider that in the 1920s and 1930s, in the USSR and for many western intellectuals and scientists, Soviet Marxism was both a productive intellectual novelty and a more than worthy account of socialism, as it was the outlook of those who actually made the first revolution in its name and were in a position to build a state and a society following it (e.g. Gouarné, 2013; García, 2016a). On the other hand, the reference to "real socialism" becomes controversial when issues such as cultural diversity and social inequality are at stake, problems that are intrinsically political, but nevertheless have direct epistemic implications in the building of scientific theories and practices (cf. Elhammoumi, 2001; Matusov, 2008; Lamdan & Yasnitsky, 2016). "Real socialism" has barely existed since 1991, yet it still retains considerable significance, as if its dangers could be recreated anywhere, and thus Marxist and non-Marxist scholars are reluctant to address it in constructive terms. This is perfectly understandable, yet the situation is a result of a series of highly problematic historiographical assumptions.

Historians of psychology have sufficiently shown that psychological knowledge is inseparable from the cultural and institutional circumstances in which scholarly knowledge is produced (e.g. Brock, 2006; Ash & Sturm, 2007; Pickren & Rutherford, 2010; Valsiner, 2012; Talak, 2014). The acknowledgement of the embeddedness of psychological knowledge implies that its wider circulation and reception, geographically and/or historically, is not a self-evident process, but raises questions about the precise means of diffusion, how it was "adapted" to each context, and which and why certain knowledge or authors became relevant in a particular place and not in others.

This does not mean that epistemic norms and procedural criteria become superfluous, only that they cannot be considered as existing beyond their specific circulation, reconstruction and use. Psychology has permanently proposed such means to produce scientific knowledge. This issue has been tackled by recent scholarship which renews the efforts to intersect philosophy and history of science (e.g. Renn, 1996; Daston & Galison, 2007; Rheinberger 2010; Sturm, 2011).

Actual practitioners of psychology have usually preferred to adopt strongly normative standpoints, to which celebratory accounts of the history of their discipline become useful as they point out a canon of authors that clearly distinguish adequate problems, objects and methods from those inadequate. While this need for a normative framework is understandable, especially given the immense proliferation of psychological knowledge and the always dubious scientific status of psychology, celebratory accounts are a poor conception of the past and the present of the discipline, as they reduce history to a hierarchical list of names based only in quasi-platonic epistemology and obscures the actual formation of disciplines and epistemologies in a global scene. History of psychology is then not just a reconstruction of "backgrounds" but of the very essence of knowledge production and social consensus formation. A historical view of how theories, methods and problems have been considered relevant and how they were reconfigured for scientific research is crucial to assess what to do with "heritages" from other times and locales, as they most likely have important differences from our present criteria. Moreover, if all knowledge is embedded in the factors and conditions of possibilities available in a certain moment and place, its historicity is of value in itself.[5] And if scientific knowledge, as a premise, does not conceive itself as limited to remaining in a specific time and space, then circulation between contexts is also part of its making. Thus, history is a part of precise knowledge and the norms used or assumed to produce and receive it. There are no epistemic criteria beyond historical processes, nor proper histories of knowledge and disciplines that do not consider them. More sophisticated accounts of history not only provide a better conception of the past, but also allow contrast and comparisons with other contexts and with the present situation itself, which result in more awareness on the possibilities and limits of epistemic norms in concrete situations.

The standpoint of reception and transnational studies allow us to pose certain useful questions to counter historical *naïveté*: How can the past of a discipline be a relevant or useful resource to produce new knowledge and practices? What are the aims and means involved in the circulation and appropriation of knowledge? How and why does knowledge or a certain figure become important in specific places? Do conditions of possibilities, criteria of legitimacy and epistemic values travel with knowledges? If they do, how? Reception studies highlight the specific activity and means of the agents who appropriate ideas and practices. The different local actors, mediations, material conditions and knowledge already available in each context introduce modifications in a received author or oeuvre; they change the network of ideas and practices that knowledge originally had, and this happens every time it is received or rediscovered from the past, introducing systematic differences in the assessment and productivity of what is received. For example, Vygotsky read and discussed ideas of Piaget, Freud and Thorndike, and was well familiar with "behaviourism" in the 1920s and 1930s. Yet for Bruner's USA in the 1960s "behaviourism" was a very different thing. Rivière's possible readings of Piaget in Spain was not Vygotsky's, and psychoanalysis in post-war Argentina became radically different to what it was in the USSR from the 1930s onwards. Moreover, Vygotsky was in dialogue with other knowledge and authors unavailable to him. The decontextualization that was part of Vygotsky's celebration then was in itself a displacement that affected the reception of the value of his work. Every reception involves displacements, variations, omissions, additions and substitutions given the different reading operations and the dissimilar aims and references of each conjuncture, yet the productivity of those conceptual and material translations has to be reconstructed and assessed. That means that a solid historical account of Vygotsky's productivity requires not only a study of his context, but also a study of the Vygotskianism that formed local traditions and generated different results with his work.

This does not involve plain relativism that abolishes any normativity and possible translation. On the contrary, a historical *reflexivity* helps assess the validity and productivity of knowledge from the fact that both producer and receiver are situated, and that differences between the context of production and reception exist. Circulation also requires critical self-assessment, as it can lead to the unjustified enthronement or imposition of an author or theory lacking support or proving unproductive beyond particular contexts.

The reconsideration of knowledge of the past has to be aware of two historiographical flaws. First, the search for anticipations in the past of knowledge from the present, an operation known as *prolepsis*. Second, the assumption that ideas, theories, concepts and vocabulary of the past could simply be reused now even though the assumptions and conditions that served as their basis have disappeared or are not available in the context of reception; that is the operation of *retrolepsis* (Palti 2007, pp. 53–54). The celebratory account of Vygotsky has both flaws, as it assumes his work is considered ahead of its time and that it could be equally productive in any context of production. Reconsidering the past is a complex historiographical operation that requires certain tools and caution to avoid dislocating the historical figures and ideas from their original environment and producing a narrative of the past that is inherently ahistorical. Vygotskians are supposed to be very aware of the perils of cultural extrapolation, yet they don't seem to be aware and cautious enough when it comes to Vygotsky. *Retrolepsis* is particularly problematic regarding the USSR as, from the standpoint of circulation of knowledge, it is not enough to reconstruct how Vygotsky read Marx, Engels, Plekhanov, Lenin, Trotsky, and other Marxist figures. What is needed is to consider the current relationship of Marxism with psychology, philosophy of sciences, and political local scenarios. Vygotsky's work requires a reading according to a triple parameter: historical, epistemological and political. The answer to the question "Is Vygotsky's effort to propose a Marxist psychology oriented towards the building of socialism in the current situation of Europe and the Americas viable?" accepts the most diverse approaches which define how Vygotsky's work would be read and applied. Thus, it becomes evident that only an intellectual normativity sensitive to the changing relationship of epistemic, cultural and political values is suitable for such endeavour.

A historical outlook that acknowledges this issue will recognize that the inherent diversity of circulation process is antithetical with dogmatisms and orthodoxies, which are progressively reified, ahistorical, provincial and unproductive accounts. It could be said that the celebration of Vygotsky was instrumental, even necessary, in rediscovering a quality author and questioning psychology's *status quo*; even if that proves to be true, that operation no longer seems instrumental to those aims. Without a *reflexive* stance, that celebration becomes unsatisfactory in many aspects, whether it establishes new authorities that police "correct" production, or because the aims and means of research proposed are not well suited to its milieu as it omits the conditions necessary to make it operative both in the original and the local contexts. In general terms, celebratory accounts and orthodoxies go hand in hand as they are both the result of a perspective of knowledge that assumes it has universal and ahistorical truths. What is needed is the development of an historical *reflexivity* that shows that productivity does not lie merely within authors' ideas, but in the informed comprehension of the situation of reception, their insertion in different weaves of references that provides new readings and critical efforts to test them in diverse settings. This way, instead of trying to "accurately" reproduce past knowledge, it is possible to produce new perspectives..

The current revision of Vygotsky's history and ideas, followed by the publication of new writings and revised translations (e.g. del Río & Álvarez, 2007; Vigotski, 2007; Yasnitsky, 2018; van der Veer & Zavershneva, 2018) is, without doubt, an important and promising task. Yet without a critical stance it can lead to the formation of orthodoxies that claim the "true" readings of Vygotsky. The perspective of the transnational circulation of knowledge is not about "loyalty" or "faithfulness" to an author, nor the ambition to claim that a single person can be the pivotal point for the formation of a research tradition. The point is to develop a *historical* viewpoint of the conditions of production of certain ideas and practices to contrast them to the current conditions. This way we might be able to better understand how productive they actually were, and consider their potential productivity in a new setting. Obviously, this does not mean that the work of the Vygotskians here mentioned can be reduced or dismissed as mere gestures of exaltation or unproductive misunderstandings; most of them have certainly achieved worthy results, from their respective vantage points, at least. It only means that even recognized researchers can share blind spots in the understanding of an author and that a "return to Vygotsky" will not necessarily imply better results or boost Vygotsky-inspired scholarship.

Vygotsky's rediscovery from the past is also an interesting case for other authors, Soviet or not. As no research is done single-handedly, psychologists such as Piotr Galperin, Filipp Bassin, Daniil Elkonin, Aleksandr Zaporozhets, and many others still remain virtually unknown in the West. A proper reconstruction of Vygotsky's milieu might also offer a critical and fair assessment of the collective work of which he was a part. In any case, it is not acceptable to assume *a priori* that Vygotsky was unsurpassed among his peers and that his work owes nothing to them. Besides, later years have seen the rediscovery of many other authors, among Vygotskians and in other traditions, with the idea that past ideas are still relevant for current research and discussions.[6] In that perspective, a sophisticated account of Vygotsky's history and circulation could also be a model for the rediscovery of other researchers and groups of research.

Conclusions

Vygotsky was celebrated and situated in the canon of psychology, even though his work was only known very selectively and in fragments. One might say that Vygotsky was invented as a figure, and his legacy was socially constructed and rearranged according to the reception needs. Yet this invention, with all the problems mentioned, offers an important lesson: the past, far from being superfluous, could still be useful for the discipline, its potential may not have been exhausted, and it may even provide authors and knowledge that can challenge the *status quo* of the discipline. But this operation may also lead to dogmatisms or constrain research if it is carried out without proper intellectual tools.

Whether Vygotsky was actually a "genius" or not becomes irrelevant to the perspective outlined here, it is the context of appropriation – meaning ourselves as researchers and practitioners – that defines a "heritage", which is not any given to us to follow or develop. Instead, we construct it in unprecedented ways. A better knowledge of Vygotsky's contexts of both production and reception also illuminates the differences with ours, and that allows us to see how his ideas could actually be relevant and useful, what has to be changed in order to attend to the peculiarities of each conjecture, and what knowledge available now might endorse, renovate or refute Vygotsky's work. His productivity lies more in the *problems* stated and his attempts to solve them, rather in his actual *answers*, as those problems may well have changed and surely new ones have emerged in the years and kilometres that set him apart from us. In that way, our own work could be productive, instead of waiting for a brilliant mind to emerge and solve presumably universal problems for us in any context.

Nevertheless, canonical figures may still have a role as a guide for research and professional practice. Instead of being considered unreachable geniuses beyond criticism who have settled in advance the core topics and procedures to produce certain knowledge, they can be thought, following Araujo's (2009) suggestion about Wundt, as parameters of *reflexivity* and standards for our own work. In other words, transform the "founding fathers" into talented colleagues with whom we can discuss issues, so as to avoid reproducing outdated ideas and previous errors, and thus propose more solid and innovative theories and methodologies, more relevant to present state of the art, in dialogue with different interlocutors, and to tackle present issues. Vygotsky might be regarded then as a challenge to the current state of psychology, even to Vygotskianism itself, if we leave aside the "genius" narrative and see him as a perfectible model for a broad and inquisitive theorization, a continuous search for novel methodologies, and a wide-raging culture as supply for refined understanding of psychology.

Notes

1 For the issue of Marxism in Vygotsky's work, see Peter Jones' chapter in this volume.
2 In his historical reconstruction of Soviet psychology, Joravsky proposed an interpretation of the changes of Vygotsky's ideas and research in relation with the establishment of Stalinism (Joravsky, 1989, pp. 262–268). Accordingly, he did not foster any celebratory account of Vygotsky.
3 For a bibliometric view on the available publications of Vygotsky in English at that time, see Valsiner (1988, pp. 156–162); for a more detailed commentary on the modifications of original texts see van der Veer & Yasnitsky (2016).
4 The reader might wonder what happened with Vygotsky's reception in Cuba, as they had many psychologists trained in the USSR from the 1960s until its dissolution. Though there are hints in some publications, like *Revista Cubana de Psicología*, they are not enough to reconstruct a proper case yet. As far as I know, we lack a serious study of the Cuban psychological community environment and the entanglement of science and politics in the reception of Vygotsky in communist Cuba.
5 There is a duality in the idea of historicity worth mentioning in the case of psychology. On the one hand, the historicity of human beings as study matter, that means, a historical ontology of the psyche. On the other hand, the historicity of disciplinary development as a collective effort to produce knowledge and organize institutions and practices. Here only the latter is considered, yet Vygotsky actually tried to articulate both meanings (see Shotter, 2000 and Jovanović, 2015).
6 See, for example, the discussion of William Stern (Lamiell & Deutsch, 2000), Heinz Werner (Valsiner, 2005), Husserl and Merleau-Ponty (Gallagher & Schmicking, 2010), psychology produced by women (e.g. Rutherford & Granek, 2010; Johnston & Johnson, 2017), or even whole schools of psychology like the one from Tblisi (Imedadze, 2009) or Lvov-Warsaw (Citlak, 2016).

References

Aguilar, E. (2016). Vygotski en México: Una travesía bibliográfica y otros temas breves. In A. Yasnitsky, R. van der Veer, E. Aguilar, & L. N. García (Eds.) *Vygotski revisitado: una historia crítica de su contexto y legado* (pp. 361–373). Buenos Aires: Miño y Dávila.

Araujo, S. (2009). Uma visão panorâmica da psicologia científica de Wilhelm Wundt. *Scientiae Studia*, 7(2), pp. 209–220.

Ash, M. & Sturm, T. (Eds.) (2007). *Psychology's Territories. Historical and Contemporary Perspectives from Different Disciplines*. London: Lawrence Erlbaum.

Blanck, G. (Ed.) (1984). *Vigotski. Memoria y Vigencia*. Buenos Aires: C & C.

Brock, A. (2006). *Internationalizing the History of Psychology*. New York: New York University Press.

Castorina, J. (2009). El significado de la dialéctica en la tradición vigotskyana de investigación y su carácter irrenunciable. *Revista Psyberia*, 1(2), pp. 23–36.

Citlak, A. (2016). The Lvov-Warsaw School: The forgotten tradition of historical psychology. *History of Psychology*, 19(2), pp. 105–124.

Dafermos, M., Kontopodis, M., & Chronaki, A. (2012). How do socio-cultural-historical approaches to psychology and education travel? Translations and implementations in Greece and epistemological implications. Retrieved from https://mkontopodis.files. wordpress.com/2010/04/dafermkontopchronaki2012schpsychologytravel.pdf

Danziger, K. (2008). *The Making of the mind. A history of memory*. Cambridge, MA: Cambridge University Press.

del Río, P. & Álvarez, A. (Eds.) (2007). *Escritos sobre arte y educación creativa de Lev S. Vygotski*. Madrid: Fundación Infancia y Aprendizaje.

Daston, L. & Galison, P. (2007). *Objectivity*. New York: Zone Books.

Elhammoumi, M. (2001). Lost or Merely Domesticated? The Boom in Socio-Historic Cultural Theory Emphasizes Some Concepts, Overlooks Others. In S. Chaiklin (Ed.). *The Theory and Practice of Cultural-Historical Psychology* (pp. 200–217). Aarhus: Aarhus University Press.

Etkind, A. (1997). *Eros of the impossible. The history of psychoanalysis in Russia*. Boulder, CO: Westview Press.

Gallagher, S. & Schmicking, D. (Eds.) (2010). *Handbook of Phenomenology and Cognitive Science*. Dordrecht: Springer.

García, L. N. (2016a). *La psicología por asalto. Psiquiatría y cultura científica en el comunismo argentino (1935–1991)*. Buenos Aires: Edhasa.

García, L. N. (2016b). Before the "boom": Readings and uses of Vygotsky in Argentina (1935–1974). *History of Psychology*, 19(4), pp. 298–313.

García, L. N. (2018). On Scientific Knowledge and its Circulation: Reception Aesthetics and Standpoint Theory as resources for a Historical Epistemology. *Pulse: A History, Sociology, & Philosophy of Science Journal*, 5, pp. 27–45.

Golder, M. (1985a). Intento de análisis crítico del XXIII Congreso Internacional de Psicología. Acapulco, México, 2 al 7 de Septiembre de 1984. *Revista Cubana de Psicología*, 2(1), pp. 65–74.

Golder, M. (1985b). Dos experiencias científicas en España. *Cuadernos de Cultura*, 3, pp. 120–124.

Golder, M. (1986). *Reportajes contemporáneos a la psicología soviética*. Buenos Aires: Cartago.

Golder, M. (2002) *Angustia por la utopía*. Buenos Aires: Ateneo Vigotskiano de la Argentina.

Goldmann, L. (1959). *Recherches dialectiques*. Paris: Gallimard.

Gouarné, I. (2007). La VIIe Conférence de psychotechnique (Moscou, septembre 1931). *Cahiers d'histoire. Revue d'histoire critique*, 102, pp. 65–87.

Gouarné, I. (2013). *L'Introduction du marxisme en France. Philosoviétisme et sciences humaines 1920–1939*. Rennes: Presses Universitaires de Rennes.

Holzman, L. (1990). Lev and let Lev: a dialogue on Vygotsky. *Practice: The Magazine of Psychology and Political Economy*, 7(3), pp. 11–23.

Imedadze, I. (2009). Uznadze's Scientific Body of Work and Problems of General Psychology. *Journal of Russian and East European Psychology*, 47(3), pp. 3–30.

Johnston, E. & Johnson, A. (2017). Balancing life and work by unbending gender: Early American women psychologists' struggles and contributions. *Journal of the History of the Behavioral Sciences*, 53(3), pp. 246–264.

Joravsky, D. (1989). *Russian Psychology. A critical history*. Oxford: Blackwell.

Jovanović, G. (2015). Vicissitudes of history in Vygotsky's cultural-historical theory. *History of the Human Sciences*, 28(2), pp. 10–33.

Kagarlitsky, B. (1989). *The Thinking Reed: Intellectuals and the Soviet State from 1917 to the Present*. London: Verso.

Kozulin, A. (1984). *Psychology in Utopia: Toward a Social History of Soviet Psychology*. Cambridge, MA: MIT Press.

Lamdan, E. & Yasnitsky, A. (2016). Did Uzbeks have illusions? The Luria–Koffka controversy of 1932. In A. Yasnitsky & R. van der Veer (Eds.). *Revisionist revolution in Vygotsky studies* (pp. 175–200). London: Routledge.

Lamiell, J. & Deutsch, W. (2000). In the Light of a Star: An Introduction to William Stern's Critical Personalism. *Theory & Psychology*, 10(6), pp. 715–730.

Leontiev, A. N. (1957). Problèmes théoriques du développement psychique de l'enfant. *La Raison*, 19, pp. 85–95.

Leontiev, A. N. (1965). L'homme et la culture. *Recherches internationales à la lumière de Marxisme*, 46, pp. 47–67.

Leontiev, A. N. (1982/1997). On Vygotsky's Creative Development. In R. Rieber & J. Wollok (Eds.). *The Collected Works of L. S. Vygotsky, Volume 3: Problems of the Theory and History of Psychology* (pp. 9–32). New York: Springer.

Leontiev, A. N., Luria, A. R. & Smirnov, A. A. (Dirs.) (1966). *Recherches Psychologiques en U.R.S.S.* Moscow: Editions du Progrès.

Levitin, K. (1982) *One is not Born a Personality. Profiles of Soviet Educational Psychologists*. Moscow: Progress.

Luria, A. R. (1936). Alexander Luria to Henri Wallon, September, 27, 1936. *Letter*. Fonds Wallon, Cote 360AP/28/A, Archives Nationales, site de Pierrefitte-sur-Seine, Paris, France.

Luria, A. R. (1965). Le cerveau et le psychisme. *Recherches Internationales à la Lumière du Marxisme*, 46, pp. 26–46.

Luria, A. R. (1966). Vygotski et l'etude des functions psychiques superieures. *Recherches Internationales à la Lumière du Marxisme*, 51, pp. 93–103.

Luria, A. R. (1979). *The Making of Mind: A Personal Account of Soviet Psychology*. Cambridge, MA: Harvard University Press.

Matusov, E. (2008). Applying a Sociocultural Approach to Vygotskian Academia: "Our Tsar Isn't Like Yours, and Yours Isn't Like Ours". *Culture & Psychology*, 14(1), pp. 5–35.

Mecacci, L. (2015). Vygotsky's reception in the West. The Italian case between Marxism and communism. *History of the Human Sciences*, 28(2), pp. 173–184.

Moll, L. (Comp.) (1990). *Vygotsky and Education. Instructional implications and applications of sociohistorical psychology*. Cambridge, MA: Cambridge University Press.

Moll, L. & Rosa, A. (1985). Vygotsky. Alive and Well in Argentina. *Contemporary Psychology*, 30(12), p. 968.

Palti, E. (2007) *El tiempo de la política. El siglo XIX reconsiderado*. Buenos Aires: Siglo XXI.

Piaget, J., Fraisse, P., Zazzo, R., Galifret, Y., Ricoeur, P. & Jeanson, F. (1971). *Psychologie et marxisme*. Paris: Unions générale d'Editions.

Pickren, W. & Rutherford, A. (2010). *A History of Modern Psychology in Context*. Hoboken, NJ: John Wiley & Sons.

Prestes, Z. R. (2010). *Quando não é mais a mesma coisa. Análise de traduções de Lev Semionovitch Vigotski no Brasil. Repercussões no campo educacional*. (Doctoral dissertation). Brasília: Universidade de Brasília.

Renn, J. (1996). *Historical epistemology and the advancement of science*. Berlin: Max-Planck-Institut für Wissenschaftsgeschichte. http://www.mpiwg-berlin.mpg.de/Preprints/P36. PDF.

Rheinberger, H. (2010). *On historicizing epistemology: an essay*. Standford, CA: Stanford University Press.

Rivière, Á. (1984). La psicología de Vygotski: sobre la larga proyección de una corta biografía. *Infancia y Aprendizaje*, 27/28, pp. 7–86.

Rutherford, A. & Granek, L. (2010). Emergence and Development of the Psychology of Women. In J. C. Chrisler, D. R. McCreary (Eds.), *Handbook of Gender Research in Psychology, Vol. 1: Gender Research in General and Experimental Psychology* (pp. 19–41). New York: Springer.

Saunier, P. (2013). *Transnational History*. New York: Palgrave Macmillan.

Secord, J. (2004). Knowledge in transit. *Isis*, 95(4), pp. 654–672.

Shotter, J. (2000). Seeing Historically: Goethe and Vygotsky's "Enabling Theory-Method". *Culture & Psychology*, 6(2), pp. 233–252.

Shuare, M. (1990). *La psicología soviética tal como yo la veo*. Moscú: Progreso.

Siguán, M. (Coord.) (1987). *Actualidad de Lev Vigotski*. Barcelona: Anthropos.

Sturm, T. (2011). Historical Epistemology or History of Epistemology? The Case of the Relation between Perception and Judgment. *Erkenntnis*, 75(3), pp. 303–324.

Sulloway, F. (1992). *Freud, Biologist of the Mind: Beyond the Psychoanalytic Legend*. Cambridge, MA: Harvard University Press.

Talak, A. M. (Coord.) (2014). *Las explicaciones en psicología*. Buenos Aires: Prometeo.

Travieso, D., Rosa, A. & Duro, J. C. (2001). Los comienzos de la institucionalización profesional de la psicología en Madrid. *Papeles del Psicólogo*, 80, pp. 14–31.

Todes, D. (2014). *Ivan Pavlov. A Russian Life in Science*. New York: Oxford University Press.

Toulmin, S. (1978). The Mozart of psychology. *Mind in society: The development of higher psychological processes* by L.S. Vygotsky, edited by Michael Cole, Vera John-Steiner, Sylvia Scribner, Ellen Souberman; *The psychology of art* by L.S. Vygotsky, *Soviet developmental psychology: An anthology*, edited by Michael Cole. *New York Review of Books*, 25(14), pp. 51–57.

Valsiner, J. (1988). *Developmental Psychology in the Soviet Union*. Bloomington, IN: Indiana University Press.

Valsiner, J. (Ed.) (2005). *Heinz Werner and Developmental Science*. New York: Kluwer Academic Publishers.

Valsiner, J. (2012). *A Guided Science. History of Psychology in the Mirror of Its Making*. New Brunswick, NJ: Transaction Publishers.

Valsiner, J. & van der Veer, R. (2000). *The Social Mind. Construction of the Idea*. Cambridge, MA: Cambridge University Press.

van der Veer, R. (2007). Vygotsky in Context: 1900–1935. In H. Daniels, M. Cole, J. V. Wertsch (Eds.). *The Cambridge companion to Vygotsky* (pp. 21–49). New York: Cambridge University Press.

van der Veer, R. & Valsiner, J. (1991). *Understanding Vygotsky. A Quest for Synthesis*. Oxford: Blackwell.

van der Veer, R. & Yasnitsky, A. (2016). Translating Vygotsky: some problems of transnational Vygotskian science. In A. Yasnitsky & R. van der Veer (Eds.). *Revisionist revolution in Vygotsky studies* (pp. 143–174). London: Routledge.

van der Veer, R. & Zavershneva, E. (2018). *Vygotsky's Notebooks. A Selection*. New York: Springer.

van Oers, B. (2012). Developmental education: Reflections on a Chat-research program in the Netherlands. *Learning, Culture and Social Interaction*, 1(1), pp. 57–65.

Veresov, N. (1999). *Undiscovered Vygotsky: etudes on pre-history of cultural-historical psychology*. Frankfurt: Peter Lang.

Veresov, N. (2005). Marxist and non-Marxist aspects of the cultural-historical psychology of L. S. Vygotsky. *Outlines*, 1, pp. 31–49.

Vigotski, L. (2007). *Pensamiento y habla*. Buenos Aires: Colihue.

Vygodskaia, G. L. & Lifanova, T. M. (1999a). Lev Semenovich Vygotsky. *Journal of Russian and East European Psychology*, 37(3), pp. 3–93.

Vygodskaia, G. L. & Lifanova, T. M. (1999b). Lev Semenovich Vygotsky. *Journal of Russian and East European Psychology*, 37(4), pp. 3–78.

Vygotski, L. S. (1985). *Pensée et Langage*. Paris: Editions Sociales.

Vygotski, L. S. (1991). *Obras escogidas, tomo I*. Madrid: Aprendizaje/Visor.

Vygotsky, L. S. (1962). *Thought and language*. Cambridge, MA: MIT Press.

Vygotsky, L. S. (1978). *Mind in society: The development of higher psychological processes*. Cambridge, MA: Harvard University Press.

Vygotsky, L. S. (1987). *The collected works of L. S. Vygotsky*. New York: Plenum.

Yasnitsky, A. (2011). Vygotsky Circle as a personal network of scholars: Restoring connections between people and ideas. *Integrative Psychological and Behavioral Science*, 45(4), pp. 422–457.

Yasnitsky, A. (2012). The Complete Works of L.S. Vygotsky: PsyAnima Complete Vygotsky project. *PsyAnima, Dubna Psychological Journal*, 5(3), pp. 144–148.

Yasnitsky, A. (2016). A transnational history of "the beginning of a beautiful friendship": the birth of the cultural-historical Gestalt psychology of Alexander Luria, Kurt Lewin, Lev Vygotsky, and others. In A. Yasnitsky & R. van der Veer (Eds.). *Revisionist revolution in Vygotsky studies* (pp. 201–225). London: Routledge.

Yasnitsky, A. (2018) *Vygotsky. An intellectual biography*. London: Routledge.

Yasnitsky, A., van der Veer, R. & Ferrari, M. (Eds.) (2014). *The Cambridge Handbook of Cultural-Historical Psychology*. Cambridge, MA: Cambridge University Press.

INDEX

abstraction 24, 29, 43, 46, 48–50, 54, 56–58, 81, 139; *see also* concrete, generalization

action 24, 26–30, 35, 38, 50, 52–53, 56–57, 70, 72–73, 76, 79–80, 98–99, 133–134, 144–145, 148, 152, 163; *see also* activity, interaction, reaction

activity: cognitive (mental) activity 37, 122, 167; higher nervous activity 84, 100; human activity 107, 137, 141, 144; labor activity 40, 131, 141–142, 144–146, 154; mediated activity 141, 152; mediating activity 30, 137; productive activity 26, 34, 109, 141, 144; psychical activity 108, 110; social activity 26–27, 30, 33, 38, 40–41, 144; *see also* activity theory

activity theory (Leontiev's) 17, 23, 40, 113, 132–134, 139–140, 146–150, 154–155; *see also* cultural-historical activity theory (CHAT)

affect (*psychological category*) 45–46, 70–72, 74, 78–79, 87, 89; *see also* emotion

apostles *see* Jesus Christ

association (*psychological category*) 47, 51, 67–68, 71, 77

attention (*psychological category*) 13, 27–28, 30, 47, 60, 73, 96–98, 107, 111, 116, 135

Bakhtin, Mikhail 148

behavio(u)rism 2, 3, 29, 34, 43, 52, 62, 70, 73, 76, 97, 100, 176

Bolshevik 7, 22, 38, 40, 57, 120, 172; *see also* Communists, Marxism, Marxists

Bruner, Jerome 1–2, 166–167, 169, 176

Bukharin, Nikolai 22, 24, 28–29, 37, 40

CHAT *see* cultural-historical activity theory (CHAT)

Christ *see* Jesus Christ

Cole, Michael 4, 38, 95, 122, 147–148, 151, 155, 166–167, 170

Collected Works (Vygotsky) 9–12, 92, 164, 167, 171–173

communication 25–26, 29–31, 33–34, 37–38, 43–44, 49, 51, 55, 60, 62, 99, 133, 137, 139; *see also* dialogue, interaction

Communism 6, 15, 34–36, 62, 143, 170, 172–173

Communists 5, 7, 23–24, 62, 68, 71–72, 84, 100, 105, 108, 111, 120, 141, 162–163, 169–173, 179; *see also* Bolshevik, Marxism, Marxists

concept formation 45, 54, 166; *see also* abstraction, generalization, thinking

concrete, the 6–8, 15–18, 23, 29–30, 37–38, 43, 45–46, 53, 55, 72, 81, 98, 109, 111, 175; *see also* abstraction

conditional reflex *see* reflex

conscious(ness) 13, 26–27, 30, 34, 36–37, 46–48, 52, 57, 62, 67, 83–84, 102, 105–109, 119–120, 125, 131, 134, 141–143, 145–146, 149, 151, 168; conscious awareness 45–47, 51, 53, 55, 62; societal consciousness 118;